Beyond *His Dark Materials*

Susan Redington Bobby
is also the editor of
*Fairy Tales Reimagined: Essays on
New Retellings* (McFarland, 2009)

Beyond *His Dark Materials*

Innocence and Experience in the Fiction of Philip Pullman

SUSAN REDINGTON BOBBY

McFarland & Company, Inc., Publishers
Jefferson, North Carolina, and London

LIBRARY OF CONGRESS CATALOGUING-IN-PUBLICATION DATA

Bobby, Susan Redington, 1969–
    Beyond His dark materials : innocence and experience in the fiction of Philip Pullman / by Susan Redington Bobby.
      p.   cm.
    Includes bibliographical references and index.

    ISBN 978-0-7864-6508-8
    softcover : acid free paper ∞

    1. Pullman, Philip, 1946– — Criticism and interpretation. 2. Fantasy fiction, English — History and criticism. 3. Young adult fiction, English — History and criticism. I. Title.
    PR6066.U44Z56 2012
    823'.914 — dc23   2012032248

BRITISH LIBRARY CATALOGUING DATA ARE AVAILABLE

© 2012 Susan Redington Bobby. All rights reserved

No part of this book may be reproduced or transmitted in any form or by any means, electronic or mechanical, including photocopying or recording, or by any information storage and retrieval system, without permission in writing from the publisher.

Front cover image © 2012 Shutterstock

Manufactured in the United States of America

McFarland & Company, Inc., Publishers
   Box 611, Jefferson, North Carolina 28640
      www.mcfarlandpub.com

For Mom and Dad,
because the first word you taught me was "book."

Table of Contents

Acknowledgments ix

Introduction: Embracing Change, Loss and Growth on the Path from Innocence to Experience 1

Part I: Stories of Innocence: The Quest and the Path to Maturity 7

One. *Mossycoat*, *Puss in Boots* and *Aladdin and the Enchanted Lamp*: Fairy Tale and Folktale Re-visions 9

Two. *The Firework-Maker's Daughter* and *The Scarecrow and His Servant*: Quest-Driven Tales 30

Three. *Count Karlstein, or The Ride of the Demon Huntsman*: The Influence of German Romanticism and the Gothic on an Evolving Text 50

Four. *Spring-Heeled Jack* and *The New Cut Gang: Thunderbolt's Waxwork* and *The Gas-Fitters' Ball*: Narratives of Orphaned, Displaced, and Dispossessed Children 72

Part II: Stories of Experience: Betrayal and the Path to Maturity 93

Five. *The Sally Lockhart Quartet*: Socially-Conscious Penny Dreadfuls 95

Six. *I Was a Rat!* and *How to Be Cool*: The Intersection of Fantasy and Realism Through Social Satire 118

Seven. *The Broken Bridge* and *The White Mercedes*: The Impact of the Sins of the Father (and Mother) in Young Adult Contemporary Novels 143

Table of Contents

Eight. *The Good Man Jesus and the Scoundrel Christ*: A New Path from Innocence to Experience   163

Chapter Notes   181
Bibliography   187
Index   193

Acknowledgments

The idea to write about Philip Pullman's works was brewing in my mind since 2003 when I published my first essay on *His Dark Materials*, dæmons, and dual audience. However, I was not able to find my subject and approach until 2010 when I was dragged kicking and screaming into the most chaotic period of my life. In the midst of the darkness, I viewed Pullman's fiction in a very different light, and I saw something I had never seen before. Just as I argue that Pullman's characters cannot grow and mature if they do not face trials and suffering, I could not have conceived of the following if I had not faced the same.

Through any dark time in our lives, there are lights along the way that show us the path out of the deepest parts of the forest. At first we are only able to see those lights flicker, but the stronger we become, the stronger we perceive those lights to be, and they become beacons, guiding us into the sunlight. I would like to recognize and thank those lights in my life, because this work would not exist without them.

To my family: Mom, Dad, Bobby, Lori, and Kelly, whose love and support never wavers. I want to thank Mom for helping me settle on the organization for the book, for assisting with the concept of Chapter 8, and for helping with editorial tasks. I also want to thank her for taking me to the library and instilling in me a love of reading. My happiest childhood memories include a stack of books nearby, and the love of stories is what drives my career and authorial aspirations. I also want to thank my father for being a natural-born storyteller. Perhaps it is the Irish in him, but when my father gets going, he can spin a good yarn, and I am sure that his influence carries on with me. My brother Bobby's contribution was his willingness to assist with household problems, allowing me more time to focus on my writing. My sister Lori had the voice that grounded me, supported me, and humored me when I was mired in difficulty or forgetting to just breathe. Finally, my sister Kelly, the other literature lover in the

Acknowledgments

family, read much of Pullman's work and was able to reinforce the angle of my approach at various stages of the manuscript.

To my honorary sisters: I want to thank Marlisa Santos, who has assisted me through literary endeavors and personal crises, providing sisterhood in the most troubling of times. Her own first book, penned in the midst of a full-time administrative position, was truly inspirational to me, and she often helped me with learning to budget my time and keep my focus. I want to thank Jenna Kutzor, a friend from another lifetime who magically came back into my midst when I needed her most. She has been an incredibly calming, intuitive, and supporting presence in my life. Lastly, I must acknowledge Katie Kress, my newest sister, whose passion for literature helps inspire my own and whose gifts, both literal and figurative, always seem to arrive at the perfect time.

To the woman who most inspires me intellectually: I want to thank Linda De Roche, who first hired me as an adjunct and shepherded me through all the tests and trials of my career. I might not have ever become a published writer without her support and guidance, and her friendship is the cherry on top of our relationship. Linda has always been and will always be an inspiration, blazing a trail for other women writers and teachers to follow.

To my many dear friends, colleagues, and professional contacts, all of whom have shown me patience, understanding, inspiration, and support: Carol Lin Smith, Jeffrey Gibson, Jeffrey Mask, Victor Greto, Mike Nielsen, Randall Clack, Emily Hall, Angela Zvesper, Matt Gallagher, Angela D'Antonio, Eric M. Santos, and Missy Ann Walker; the members of the DB message board and friends online; Dr. Lillian Kramen-Roach and Dr. Kim Furtado for their wisdom; Martha Boyd for the innumerable library requests; Victoria Faught-Hodgson, Shanna Bryant, and Jeremy Harper for research assistance; Dr. Patricia Dwyer, Dr. Bill Johnston, and the members of the Board of Trustees of Wesley College who supported me with a sabbatical.

To the Redington Bobby cats, my muses in fur. In particular, I want to commemorate Dobbsie, my dæmon, and his mother Mommie, both of whom passed during the writing of this book.

To my students: I hope I have taught you the importance of stories and encouraged you to tell many tales to others.

And lastly, to Philip Pullman, whose work has inspired me, soothed me, and excited me for more than ten years. Your words have had a greater impact on my life than you will ever know. May this illuminate your stories for others as your work has been my beacon in the darkness.

Introduction: Embracing Change, Loss and Growth on the Path from Innocence to Experience

> "You can't gain wisdom until you lose, that's the way it works."
> — Philip Pullman, "In Conversation with Marie Bridge"[1]

Philip Pullman's stunning trilogy *His Dark Materials*, influenced and inspired by John Milton's *Paradise Lost*, William Blake's *Songs of Innocence and Experience*, and Heinrich von Kleists's "On the Marionette Theater," has an ambitious goal. Pullman wants his readers to question the nature of a single word: betrayal. The sum of Christian faith and belief is informed by the fall of man, and the blame for original sin is placed squarely at Eve's feet. Eve is the great betrayer of mankind, for it was her act of disobedience that set tragedy into motion:

> So saying, her rash hand in evil hour
> Forth reaching to the Fruit, she pluck'd, she eat:
> Earth felt the wound, and Nature from her seat
> Sighing through all her Works gave signs of woe,
> That all was lost [Milton, *Paradise Lost* 780–84].

There are many different meanings of the word betrayal, but one common characteristic is the assumption of intention. We think of a great betrayer as one who acts with deliberation to hurt another. We think of betrayal as inherent in the darker part of human nature, emanating from a place of evil or ill will. Such an assumption makes it easier, perhaps, for us to label the betrayer a sinner, and in Eve's case, she was considered perfect and holy until that single act of betrayal, which condemned her descendants to carry the stain of original sin on their souls.

Introduction

Yet Pullman asks readers to question whether our assumptions about the nature of betrayal are wrong. What if there are shades of grey? What if one's disobedience comes from a place of ignorance? If a person unwittingly brings forth tragedy, do we still call this person a betrayer? Do we still level blame and judgment at her feet? Pullman says we should not. In an interview with Wendy Parsons and Catriona Nicholson, Pullman explains that the Fall is "completely essential. It's the best thing, the most important thing that ever happened to us, and if we had our heads on straight on this issue, we would have churches dedicated to Eve instead of the Virgin Mary" (3). Pullman explains that the essay by von Kleist gave him an idea which he later "stol[e]" (2) to become the central theme of his trilogy: the state of grace arising from innocence in childhood can be attained again after periods of change, loss, and growth. Whereas the Christian belief system is structured around the Fall and the loss of grace, which can only be granted to us "if we believe in God and then only if he chooses to bless us with his grace" (3), von Kleist suggests that the loss of grace as one moves through life is but temporary if one makes the effort to learn and grow. As Pullman explains, "We lose the innocence that we were born with, and then go on through life. But if we work hard, and if we train ourselves ... if we undergo all kinds of discipline, pain, suffering, and so forth, then the point is that we can regain grace" (2). He adds that the loss and gain of grace is "actually a more valuable thing to have" because this is the path to wisdom. Pullman concludes that this view is more positive and affirming than the "pessimistic and defeatist view" of Christianity (3).

As a writer of children's, adolescent, and adult fiction, Pullman frequently deconstructs commonly held viewpoints. Nowhere does Pullman more obviously deconstruct a worldview than in a trilogy that asks readers to redefine betrayal. With Lyra poised to become the new Eve, readers witness her unconsciously and consciously betray Roger and Pantalaimon. But do we then hold Lyra responsible and condemn her for her actions? Do we conclude that she has acted with malevolence and deliberately caused pain and suffering? No. Pullman makes that reaction impossible. We can only feel pity and sadness along with the character when she brings about tragedy, but we feel uplifted when she turns that trauma into growth.

Therefore, Pullman brings us to deconstruct our own assumptions about betrayal. We follow him and Lyra on the path from innocence to experience, gaining wisdom, as we stretch our minds in a new direction.

Embracing Change, Loss and Growth

As Linda Hutcheon notes in "Harry Potter and the Novice's Confession," those transitioning from youth to adult are affected by their experiences and by what they read. Pullman teaches us that "innocence is not a state of stasis to be nostalgically preserved; nor is experience only loss"; thus we, too, move from ignorance to knowledge through experiencing Pullman's stories, learning and adapting as we go along (175). By the conclusion of *His Dark Materials*, we see that betrayal may usher forth cataclysmic change: it is only because of those great losses that enormous change could occur and that Lyra could grow to aid humanity. A republic is born, and humans are free to make mistakes, allowing them to achieve the lost state of grace again and again. Regardless of the motive or lack thereof, betrayal brings forth opportunity. Pullman asks us to acknowledge that an act which initially produces great loss, pain, and suffering can become that catalyst that fosters change, growth, and wisdom. Without betrayers, we would simply cease to mature. A "fall" of some sort is the "the most important thing," because without it, we are not tested, and we lack the motivation to grow.

Philip Pullman is always open about the literature that inspires him, and he has admitted that Blake's *Songs of Innocence and Experience* have heavily influenced *His Dark Materials*. What many readers may not be aware of is just how much most of his "other" materials, the picture books for children, the novellas and novels for children, adolescents, and adults, reflect the journey from ignorance to knowledge. Pullman's trilogy has garnered so much critical attention that his many other magnificent stories have not been adequately addressed. Yet the path of growth figures so prominently that an examination of this theme in his body of work is not just overdue, but essential to understanding him as a writer. In this book, I have written about nearly every story Pullman has ever published. I chose to focus on the works that feature one or more characters facing a quest, trial, or betrayal, which has led me to exclude only a small number of selections that do not adhere closely to this theme.

I have aimed to bring to readers close textual analysis of the majority of Pullman's fiction in light of the themes of change, loss, and growth. I have divided the chapters into two parts, representing the stories of innocence and the stories of experience. William Blake's *Songs of Innocence and Experience* exhibit a strong shift in tone between the poems in his first section versus the second. The poems of innocence are more lighthearted, fun, and playful, while the poems of experience are more dark, cautious,

Introduction

and foreboding. I see the same shift occurring in Pullman's work. Pullman's characters in the "Stories of Innocence" part all encounter difficulties or trials as part of a quest. The foes they face may be more easily brought to justice, and they often come across many helpers, human or animal, on the path to complete their goals. The stories themselves are playful and lighthearted, and the characters come of age. Because happy endings abound, most loose ends are neatly tied. By contrast, the characters in the "Stories of Experience" part face tremendous difficulties and suffering, often attacked by individuals, groups, or even entire societies. These characters face an uphill battle in their efforts to achieve growth, and sometimes, they do not succeed. However, it is often in failing that they are motivated to make the most change and persevere, leading them to the path of wisdom and grace. Like Blake shows in his poems of experience, the world they face is darker, the endings are not always neat and tidy, but the characters mature by learning to accept uncertainty.

The first chapter provides a discussion of Pullman's revised fairy tales for children in *Mossycoat*, *Puss in Boots*, and *Aladdin and the Wonderful Lamp*. I identify the likely source text for each and describe the changes Pullman embedded in his retellings. The second chapter is on *The Firework-Maker's Daughter* and *The Scarecrow and His Servant*, both original fairy tales that reflect the quest story and the hero's journey, and in the case of the latter novel, a pretty hefty dose of *Don Quixote*. The third chapter analyzes a single text, *Count Karlstein*, the only novel Pullman wrote that was delivered in very different forms to the reading public. The various incarnations of the text are inspired by the German opera *Der Freischütz* and the Gothic tradition. The fourth chapter covers three shorter texts: *Spring-Heeled Jack*, a graphic novel, *The New Cut Gang's Thunderbolt's Waxwork* and *The Gas-Fitters' Ball*. All three texts have been inspired by the Victorian-era penny dreadful. For each, I provide a literary background for the content (if the text seems to have been influenced or inspired by other works)[2], a grounding in the work's style or genre, and a close reading of the elements of the text which fit the themes of change, loss, and growth.

The second half of this book begins with a chapter on the Sally Lockhart quartet. Because these stories are more sophisticated, more adult-centered penny dreadfuls, they are radically different in tone than those selections covered in Chapter Four, and Sally's journey to knowledge is more akin to true-life experience and less immersed in fantasy. Chapter Five covers two shorter works, *I Was a Rat!* and *How to Be Cool*, in which the interplay between realism, fantasy, and satire is prominent. The link between these seemingly divergent works is the exploitation of children or adolescents via incompetent and over-reaching individuals or groups in the fields of education, psychology, the media, and government. The seventh chapter is on Pullman's young adult novels *The Broken Bridge* and *The White Mercedes*, also known as *The Butterfly Tattoo*. These novels represent Pullman's foray into contemporary literature on teenage issues related to family ties, identity, and romantic love, and in them he thoroughly explores the psychology of human interaction from the perspective of the troubled teen, particularly one who must confront the aftermath of his or her parents' failures through infidelity, divorce, and abuse. Finally, the eighth chapter is on *The Good Man Jesus and the Scoundrel Christ*. In his re-imagination of the Gospels, Pullman depicts a protagonist who follows a new path to experience, creating a foil for Lyra and refining yet again his thoughts on the power of storytelling.

So much significant, provocative, intelligent commentary has been written on Pullman's *His Dark Materials*, while so little attention has been paid to the many amazing "other" materials Pullman has written over the course of his career. It is my hope that by treating Pullman's body of work with a similar respect and scrutiny that his readers will find that he has even more diversity and skill as a writer than his most ardent fans have proclaimed, and that this work will spark many more conversations about his contribution to the literary world. Furthermore, I aim to prove to readers that there is a silver lining to the cloud of betrayal.

While some infer that the focus on the path from naiveté to knowledge is ultimately pessimistic, Pullman disagrees. Robert Butler, in "An Interview with Philip Pullman: The Art of Darkness," asked him about his grandfather, the Anglican vicar who was responsible for Pullman's religious education. Butler wondered if Pullman felt a sense of "'loss'" or "'a sense of absence'" because he claimed to no longer believe in the stories his grandfather told him about God. Pullman's reply is revealing: "'Loss because there's something gone that I used to believe? ...I think it's a gain. It's a gain of a wider perspective'" (6). In the Arbuthnot Lecture, Pullman speaks of the importance of writing about "dark and gloomy" subject matter, insisting that "tragedy is uplifting, too, if it shows the human spirit at its finest" (38). Time and again, it is only through quests, losses, and betrayals that Pullman's characters can be tested; ultimately, most rise to the challenge and find reserves of strength and resolve they did not know they had. In this way, Pullman's stories are dominated by survival tied to the triumph of the will.

In Jack Zipes's introduction to Kathleen Ragan's *Outfoxing Fear: Folktales from Around the World*, he writes of the tale of Scheherazade and the "survival stories" she told to affect the king's actions. Zipes argues that she "civilized" the king by telling him tales about real people and their ethical problems (xix). Zipes wonders if folktales can become "remedies for sick kings and sick civilizations" (xx) and concludes that stories can have "a therapeutic effect" (xx). Reiterating that folktales were never meant to be solely for children, Zipes explains, "They are part and parcel of the fabric of every human being ... and were created by human beings to communicate and share experiences that can enable all people to survive in a dangerous world" (xx). Indicating that Ragan's collection was edited at a time when the world was in high conflict (post–9/11) and meant to look fear in the face, he states that tales of "overcom[ing] adversity" are typically penned to mimic universal and common life experiences across cultures (xxi). No matter the subject of the tale in question, the most important quality is whether or not the protagonist attains the ability to survive the trauma, for often death, literal or metaphoric, lies in wait otherwise. Fairy tales and folk tales, Zipes says, are much more realistic than we give them credit for being because they teach people about how to triumph over difficulties in their lives, giving them a sense of power and control that they must learn to master to grow (xxi). Lastly, such tales teach about the uncertainty of the future, for they often look characters' deepest fears in the face, teaching them to make friends with the enemy, to solve problems, and to become survivors (xxi–xxiii).

Is Philip Pullman a latter-day Scheherazade? Absolutely. In "Let's Write It in Red: The Patrick Hardy Lecture," he says, "We need to keep those old stories burnished and bright and new by telling them over and over again, and if we do we'll find that curiously enough we never get tired of them" (60). Stories of coming of age are universal; on some level, we all understand them. We have all walked the path and we have all been tempted to eat the fruit as Eve once did. We have all crossed the border and been expunged from Eden. It is what we do with that knowledge that dictates the course of our lives to come, and perhaps, in hearing the story of the path of another, the hope in ourselves grows, and like Pullman's protagonists, we rise to fight another day.

Part I

Stories of Innocence: The Quest and the Path to Maturity

"Who's going to betray her?"
"No, no, that's the saddest thing: *she* will be the betrayer, and the experience will be terrible. She mustn't know that, of course..."
— Philip Pullman, *The Golden Compass*[1]

As the quote above describes, Lyra must embark on her journey unaware of the role she will play in bringing about great change to all the worlds around her. She must play the part of the innocent, for if she knows ahead of time the difficulties she will face, she will naturally avoid that which she assumes may hurt or betray another. When Lyra is truly an innocent, she is not aware of the nature of her narrative; she has no basis on which to question the choices she makes. She lacks the knowledge and life experience on which to see the potential outcomes of her choices. As an innocent, she acts on impulse. As Pullman describes, "She was a sanguine and practical child, and besides, she wasn't imaginative. No one with much imagination would have thought seriously that it was possible to come all this way and rescue her friend Roger; or having thought it, an imaginative child would immediately have come up with several ways in which it was impossible" (*The Golden Compass* 247). As such, Lyra's mind and heart are open to all possibilities, and her journey is filled with moments that reflect the joys of discoveries made, answers revealed, and quests fulfilled.

The chapters in this part reflect the lightheartedness of innocence found in many of Pullman's literary works. Each text demonstrates the path from innocence to experience attained through characters charting a course, setting goals, embarking on their quest, and coming to a higher understanding of the world by the tale's conclusion. Whether the story is a picture book aimed primarily at children or a longer work assumed to be targeted towards an adolescent audience, the thread that connects them is the joy and happiness that can be found on the journey. Each work also reflects Pullman's penchant for complexity, illustrating his ability to engage audiences of all age levels, no matter the style of writing. Lastly, each maturing character is a comrade of Lyra, for all learn and grow as a result of their openness to the world and all it offers.

One

Mossycoat, Puss in Boots and *Aladdin and the Enchanted Lamp*
Fairy Tale and Folktale Re-visions

"Thou shalt not is soon forgotten, but Once upon a time lasts forever."
— Philip Pullman, Carnegie Medal Acceptance Speech[1]

W.H. Auden once observed that the fairy tales of the Brothers Grimm "'rank next to the Bible in importance'" (qtd. in Tatar xii). Though he is an unapologetic atheist, Philip Pullman has acknowledged that Biblical narratives have been essential to his storytelling, and *His Dark Materials* would not be so ground-breaking were Pullman's goal anything but a re-fashioning of the story of the Fall. Considering the number of times that Pullman engages his readers with fairy tale tropes throughout his body of work, one could conclude that he honors Auden's sentiments, deftly blending the sacred and the profane. Both religious parables and classic fairy tales, after all, explore the path from innocence to experience; thus, it is no surprise that while penning his epic, Pullman occasionally found time to craft his own fairy tales. Some are based on variants of which there are hundreds, if not thousands of predecessors, while others are original tales. All are presented in a variety of narrative styles, with tone appropriately shifting from rollicking, good fun to darker, dystopian moods. While other chapters in this work will briefly touch on fairy tale motifs, the central focus of this chapter is Pullman's fairy tale and folktale re-visions,[2] *Mossycoat* (1998), *Puss in Boots: The Adventures of That Most Enterprising Feline* (2000), and *Aladdin and the Enchanted Lamp* (2005), all variants of classic tales. By remaining true to the spirit of the tales while adding his own twists, Pullman joins the ranks of Charles Perrault, Giambattista Basile, the Brothers Grimm, Italo Calvino, and countless others who have sought to keep such stories alive for new audiences eager to follow along on the path to discovery and growth that the most memorable fairy tales and folktales promise.

In Kevin Paul Smith's *The Postmodern Fairytale: Folkloric Intertexts in Contemporary Fiction*, he delineates eight categories of fairy tale intertexts.[3] While Pullman has arguably dipped into every intertextual category in his body of work, he ultimately adheres to "re-vision" (10) in these three children's books. While the first two texts do not contain any author notes or introductory matter, Pullman provides an introduction to the third text, in which he discusses briefly the history of the tale of Aladdin, the points of which he left intact from commonly known versions, and the sense of honor and joy he feels from being one of a long list of storytellers who have offered a rendition of this centuries-old narrative. With his characteristic dry wit, Pullman explains, "it's important to add something new as well. If you can't bring something of your own to a traditional tale, leave it in the hands of those who can!" (n. pag.). In Jack Zipes's *Fairy Tale as Myth: Myth as Fairy Tale*, he contends that "the purpose of producing a revised fairy tale is to create something new that incorporates the critical and creative thinking of the producer and corresponds to changed demands and tastes of audiences" (9). Zipes asserts that the goal of any re-vision is enhancement and rectification (9–10). Hence all who have created variants of classic tales have sought to improve and clarify content and to reflect current morals and values of their audiences. Surely Pullman has followed suit. The question then becomes, what has he done to claim ownership of these centuries-old tales? By examining the probable source texts from which he began, we can determine which elements of the tales he kept intact versus those he enhanced or embellished to both make them his "own" and reflective of the late 20th- and early 21st centuries. Like the Brothers Grimm or Charles Perrault, Pullman, too, embeds a message in his fairy tale variants, and each of these tales is linked by their central focus on change, loss, and growth.

Mossycoat *(1998)*

The English tale "Mossycoat" is a variant of the ATU tale type 510, further separated into 510A ("Cinderella") and 510B ("The Dress of Gold, of Silver, and of Stars," also known as "Catskin") (Uther 293–96). However, the tale does not fit neatly into either sub-category. As Maria Tatar explains, the "Cinderella" tale type includes envy, stepmothers and daughters, and "domestic drudgery," while the "Catskin" tale type explores incest and the protagonist's flight from home in disguise (102). *Mossycoat* seems a hybrid of the two tale types: a form of a "skin" is given to the protagonist by her mother, but it is constructed of moss and foliage, not animal pelts. She is pursued by a lascivious man, but he is no relation. She is subjected to domestic chores, though not at the hands of an evil stepmother. In fact, her mother is a single parent, who encourages her daughter to find work in a castle in order to escape this man's advances. Later, she leaves a slipper behind, and the lovesick prince is able to find her easily with no stepsisters vying for his attention. Thus the English tale *Mossycoat* marries elements from ATU510A and 510B to create another variant of the tale type.

A traditional version of "Mossycoat," collected from Taimi Boswell, a gypsy, in 1915, charts a plot trajectory that follows the path from innocence to experience by opening with a 19- or 20-year-old girl who is fairly naïve despite her age. Her elder sister is unnamed and ignored after one mention, but her mother figures prominently, crafting a coat of moss for her daughter as the story begins. Approached by a hawker who falls in love (or lust) with her, she panics and begs her mother for assistance. Her mother instructs her to ask him for a gown of white satin with gold sprigs as a condition of her acceptance of his marriage proposal. When he complies, she asks for a second gown, this one the color of all the birds of the sky. After he delivers, she asks for a pair of silver slippers. Her fairy godmother figure, her mother, directs each request as a way to stall for time to enable her to finish stitching the mossy coat. Despondent that all the pieces are given to her and they all fit, the young girl is saved when her mother produces the finished "Wishing Coat," imbued with the power to transport her to any place she wishes while she wears it. Now called "Mossycoat," the young woman wishes herself to be transported to a large estate where she works in the kitchen. Since she is "a dam [*sic*] sight beautifuller [*sic*] nor what any o' dem [*sic*] was" (Boswell), she is instantly disliked and ridiculed by the staff. Given the most challenging work, covered in grease and soot, she is hit on the head with a skimmer. Despite the mistreatment, the master and mistress of the castle take notice of her and invite her to a grand ball (Boswell).

After declining the invitation twice, Mossycoat decides to put the servants under a sleeping spell so she can attend the ball. She attends the ball dressed in the white gown with her mossy coat underneath, using it to transport herself to the dance. The young master falls for her but she leaves and keeps her identity secret. The young man enlists his mother's aid in finding her, but they fail, and the servants' ridicule of her continues. On the night of the second ball, Mossycoat puts the servants under a trance and wishes herself to the dance dressed in the second dress and slippers. When she departs, the prince touches her foot and she loses a slipper. The next day, the prince is so lovesick that it is feared he will die if she is not found, and a search to find the one who fits the slipper ensues. When Mossycoat is found, the young man attempts an embrace, but he is halted by her until she changes into her white satin dress. Just when she is about to accept him, she tells him to wait again until she changes into the other gown. After telling the prince how she was able to transport herself to the dance and reveals the harsh treatment by the servants, the staff are promptly fired. The story concludes with the marriage of Mossycoat and the prince, who go on to have "a basketful o' children" (Boswell).

Pullman's variant of this tale, written in 1998,[4] is linguistically somewhat different than the version recorded by Boswell, though the plot is essentially the same. For one, Boswell's variant deviates frequently from standard English grammar and uses a significant amount of colloquial expressions. It also mixes tenses throughout: the frame story is told in the past tense, but the teller expresses isolated key events — the parts in which magic appears or the events that transpire at the ball — in present tense, creating an urgency and immediacy in the action. These linguistic and stylistic features lend themselves well to what is ostensibly better heard orally. By contrast, Pullman's variant is written with a more formal syntactic patterning, although it seems to nod in the direction of Joseph Jacobs' storytelling style with his use of "Well" to begin many sentences. Pullman himself has noted that his version reads quite differently if it is read to oneself versus spoken aloud, and he deliberately intended a bit of a poetic voice to shine through with his occasional use of trisyllabic meter ("Rags to Riches").

While Pullman's re-vision follows the essential plot structure of the likely source text, he explores a few characters in depth, fleshing them out to a greater degree than is typical with flat fairy tale dramatis personae. For one, Boswell only momentarily describes the hawker in a nearly flattering light; Boswell claims the hawker is "courting" the young woman,

One. Mossycoat, Puss in Boots *and* Aladdin

bringing her gifts, "dis [*sic*] thing and dat [*sic*]," "in love with her" and desiring to marry her. She is said to resist him only because she does not love him. In Pullman's variant, though, the hawker is a rube. Pullman describes him as "a nuisance" who "make[s] familiar remarks and wink[s] and pinch[es] the cheeks of girls too gentle to say no" (*Mossycoat* 7). Pullman even implies the hawker was jailed for his predatory behavior and has just returned to harassing young girls again upon his recent release (7). Pullman gives the hawker more offensive physical characteristics, describing him as "snaggle-toothed," "red-nosed," "greasy," "cocky," a man with "knobbly old fingers" who has no social graces and leers suggestively at young girls (8). When he propositions the girl, he eyes her up like a piece of meat (9). Unlike Boswell's protagonist, who is simply disinterested and "in a puzzlement" (1) about how to reject the man she does not love, Pullman's protagonist is frantic. She begs her mother to help her flee from this lecherous old "horrible" (*Mossycoat* 14) man. Since Pullman does not identify an age for his protagonist but calls her a "girl," the reader may assume she is younger than Boswell's protagonist. In fact, Peter Bailey, who works closely with Pullman as his illustrator, depicts her as a much younger girl on the cover of the text. Between her obvious younger age and the frightening description of the much older man, it seems that Pullman's re-vision recalls the spirit of ATU510B, implying that the much older man's sexual interest in such a young girl borders on pedophilia. Certainly his age is a central factor in Mossycoat's feelings of revulsion, for she seems to have no fear regarding the young master's pursuit of her and it could be argued that both men have somewhat predatory instincts to take possession of her.

Mossycoat's maturity comes with her successful passage through trials. While she is under her mother's protection, she lacks the ability to face conflict and act. Having no idea how to fend off the hawker's advances, she must ask for her mother's advice and follow her directions. Every action Mossycoat makes until she leaves home lacks self-direction and is triggered by fear responses. The coat, made by her mother, symbolizes the presence of the mother in her physical absence, acting as a talisman which both buffers her from the difficulties of the outside world and provides her strength and fortitude on her quest. While she is working at the grand house, her mother is not able to give her advice; having only her own wits, she relies on the coat for assistance. She may even face worse treatment in the kitchen than she did with the hawker, in that she is physically abused, but the strength of the coat as a symbol seems to keep her from regressing and wishing herself back home to her mother's sphere of protection, and instead, she faces the abuse and learns how to outsmart those who aim to cause her pain. Only after she has matured and advocated fully for herself is she properly positioned to become married, and the coat/mother accompanies her on that journey up to her betrothal. After this point, the coat no longer figures in the tale.

In "Rags to Riches in Fairytales," Pullman admits that both Bettelheim and Freud have lost their popularity, but he still finds "it can be both interesting and enlightening to read as if X is not only X but also Y." Asserting that the Cinderella story with its plethora of variants is at its core a tale of movement from childhood to adulthood, Pullman points out that the protagonist is always aided by someone on her quest, "always, in principle, an older female who has herself safely negotiated the perils of the journey towards maturity and whose task is to help the girl make the same passage." Bettelheim expounds on this theme further by stating that the path to securing one's identity is fraught with "hardships," "dangers," and "victories" (278). He argues that the heroine is "naïve and uninformed" at the tale's beginning but matures and thus "become[s] worthy of being loved," culminating, as many fairy tales do, with marriage (278). Bettelheim cautions, though, that tales ending in marriage often lack any instruction that would foster the growth of the individuated self within the context of a relationship. Most tales prepare the youth for the entrance into the marital union but offer little to nothing by way of teaching a person how to negotiate the intricacies of a shared life. If we look at the distinct differences between Pullman's characterization of the hawker versus the young master, we see that Pullman may be addressing a gap Bettelheim saw lacking. In comparing the hawker to the young master, Mossycoat views two different types of men, one of whom is much more "suitable" as a marriage partner.

Bettelheim explains that the root of all apprehension regarding marriage stems from fear about the sexual union, and that in youth, "what [one] experienced as dangerous, loathsome, something to be shunned, must change its appearance so that it is experienced as truly beautiful. It is love which permits this to happen" (279). Arguably Mossycoat is deeply offended by the hawker's age and sexual innuendo, yet she is not repulsed by the young master's age or his more passive tactics (his mother acts more strongly to find her than he does), and thus she chooses the man who threatens her less. However, it could also be argued that through the course of her trials in the kitchen that she has become much more capable in terms of handling herself in relation to others, and thus the young master represents an even lesser threat, allowing her to feel comfortable in accepting a union with him. In either case, it is clear that Pullman, who often makes reference to Bettelheim when he discusses fairy tales, might have had more than meets the eye in mind when he drew such a detailed picture of the hawker and Mossycoat in his re-vision. Of his heroine, Pullman says, "I like the attitude of the girl; she has that wonderful unearned arrogance that some young girls have, that completely flusters men" ("Rags to Riches"). Did she have such an attitude in the classic variants? Or did Pullman create a new type of Mossycoat that is more reflective of young women in the 20th century?

Puss in Boots: The Adventures of That Most Enterprising Feline *(2000)*

Designated as ATU545, *The Cat as Helper* tale type breaks down into 545A, *The Cat Castle*, and 545B, *Puss in Boots* (Uther 315–17). Jack Zipes indicates that Giovan Francesco Straparola is responsible for the first known literary version of the text with "Constantino Fortunato" in 1553, followed by Giambattista Basile's "Cagliuso" in 1634 (*The Great Fairy* 390; 394). Both Straparola and Basile's tales feature a female cat, while Charles Perrault is known for having popularized in 1697 a variant that features a male protagonist (397). Nancy L. Canepa discusses the prevalence of characters who manipulate situations to their advantage using trickery in *From Court to Forest: Giambattista Basile's* Lo cunto de li cunti *and the Birth of the Literary Fairy Tale*. Honing in on Basile's "Cagliuso," she notes that the character Cagliuso, who has achieved success only through the intervention of the cat as helper, remains ungrateful for the assistance: "this tale offers the cynical lesson (uncommon for fairy tales) that even such talent for intrigue as the cat displays has little chance of being valorized in a world where the principal players ... are all singlemindedly intent on one thing: acquiring or increasing their power and wealth" (163–64). Straparola's cat, the precursor to Basile's, orchestrates Constantino Fortunato's rise to power and wealth, but she is absent from the tale once the rise in status is effected (Zipes, *The Great Fairy* 393). When the story passed hands to Charles Perrault, Perrault's male cat is finally rewarded for his assistance by being made "a great lord [who] never again ran after mice, except for his amusement" (401). Of all three well-known variants, it is Perrault's to which Pullman most closely alludes, although as expected, he alters the tale to suit his own tastes, style, and audience.

Perrault's variant, titled "The Master Cat; or, Puss in Boots," presents a miller who bequeaths to his sons his mill, his ass, and his cat. The youngest son, in receipt of the cat, is despondent at his supposed misfortune, but the cat promises that all is not as it seems. Asking for a pouch and boots and using these items and his wits, the cat traps animals and gives them to the king, explaining that his master, the Marquis de Carabas, wishes to offer gifts. After several months, Puss tells his new master, the miller's son, to bathe in a river. Just as the king passes, Puss claims that the marquis is drowning. As the king's men save the so-called marquis, Puss's master sees the princess, who falls in love with him at first sight. Having told a group of peasants previously that a certain field belonged to the marquis, Puss is also able to pass off land as being owned by his young master when the king and his retinue pass by. Thus, Puss tricks the king into accepting his young master as the Marquis of Carabas (Zipes, *The Great Fairy* 399).

At this point in the tale, an ogre enters the picture. Because the ogre can transform himself into different animals, Puss uses this to his advantage. He tricks the ogre into turning into a mouse and then Puss kills him, claiming the ogre's castle for the young marquis. Having thus created a reputation, land, and stronghold for his young master, Puss convinces the king that his daughter should marry the "marquis" and they all live happily ever after, with Puss being named a lord. As is his pattern, Perrault ends his tale with two morals, the first of which speaks to "industry," "ingenuity," and "prosperity," the combination of which can lead to a great inheritance, while the second connects the miller's son and the princess through "good manners, looks, and dress ... inspir[ing] tenderness" (qtd. in Zipes, *The Great Fairy* 401).

Perrault's variant seems to encourage dishonesty as a fruitful means to gain wealth, position, and marriage, with no come-uppance for the perpetrators of falsehoods. Additionally, Perrault's protagonist does not appear to mature on his own and only achieves by association with Puss. Pullman maintains the core structure of Perrault's tale, but he improves upon it by fleshing out many sketchy details of plot and by charting the maturation process of the miller's son, producing a more dynamic character.

Unlike *Mossycoat*'s title page, which states, "Retold by" (Pullman n. pag.), *Puss in Boots*'s title page says, "Written by" (n. pag.), which might be an indicator that the tale that follows is significantly altered from its source text. Because Perrault's tale was evidently not intended for children, it may not have been important to him to create a full picture of growth for Puss or the miller. However, Pullman's plentifully illustrated picture book is obviously intended primarily for a younger audience, and this may play a part in presenting protagonists with a bit more integrity. Additionally, Pullman saw an opportunity to improve the villain in the text with his revision. Pullman states that *Puss in Boots* was initially a play commissioned for the Polka Children's Theatre in Wimbledon; he was asked to produce a fairy tale in the 1980s for them and he chose this tale to rewrite, paying particular attention to improving the character of the Ogre. He explains that when he rewrote the tale, he "discovered ... that the Ogre is a very unsatisfactory villain, as he comes in with no preparation or warning just before the end, so I improved the structure." The published book is "more or less" the same version of the story as his play,[5] and readers of Pullman's version will find that the alterations to the story improve characterization while illuminating the path of growth.

In *Children's Literature Comes of Age: Toward a New Aesthetic*, Maria Nikolajeva discusses the circular journey and its pattern of departure, adventure, and return to home that is an integral portion of most children's literature (79). Nikolajeva explains, "the purpose of the journey is the maturing of the child (protagonist as well as the reader), but the return home is a matter of security; whatever hardships and trials, the safe home is the final goal" (79). One way Pullman accomplishes this objective is to begin with a problem that Perrault's tale does not identify: the mill wheel will not turn, and the landlord, "Monsieur Ogre," is raising their rent. Therefore, the problem to be solved propels young Jacques forward. Linking the ogre to the miller's son as his landlord provides a more concrete reason for the ogre's animosity, and it is only through interactions with him that Jacques learns the reason the wheel is stuck: their father buried a bag of gold beneath it. Even though the gold is recovered, the ogre meets the same demise as he does in Perrault's version, removing the need to pay further rent. Consequently, Jacques and Puss admit that Jacques is not a marquis; however, Puss suggests the King make Jacques into a marquis by title, giving him the right to inheritance for his earlier good deeds. Pullman's Jacques is more driven by multiple goals: primarily, he wants to solve the family's money problems; marrying the princess is secondary, and he admits his true identity before marriage rather than keeps it secret, making him a more realistic active hero than Perrault's passive pawn in Puss's game.

By placing more obstacles in Jacques's path than his predecessors faced, Pullman gives him an opportunity to face trials and grow in self-reliance. To begin, Jacques takes it upon himself to leave and "seek his fortune" (*Puss in Boots* 2). Puss tells him that he has "wit" if Jacques has "courage," and he claims that together, they will persevere (3). Perrault's and Pullman's narratives dovetail here, when Puss takes gifts of partridges to the king and begins to create the amazing backstory of the Marquis de Carabas. Pullman's faux drowning scene and rescue resembles Perrault's, but once Pullman brings the king's daughter into contact with Jacques, the story becomes much more detailed. For instance, the Ogre desires to marry the princess, and his servants kidnap her and leave a note in which he threatens to eat her if anyone attempts a rescue (12). This conflict creates a reason for Jacques to prove his courage, and he promises the king that he and Puss will rescue her. They meet a Hermit on their journey, who tells them they must pass by the Ghouls on their way; he also reveals that the Ogre has magical abilities and suggests they ask him why the spring has lost its healing properties (14).

Prepared to meet the Ghouls, Jacques and Puss provide them with the Hermit's dream berries, which leads the Ghouls to assist them; in turn, they promise to ask the Ogre why the Ghouls cannot sleep (Pullman, *Puss in Boots* 15–16). Finding the princess imprisoned, Jacques and Puss convince her to ask the Ogre the questions. Taken by surprise, the Ogre reveals the answers that will help the Hermit and the Ghouls. The princess is also able to learn from the Ogre that the mill wheel is stuck because something is buried beneath (17–18). Having secured the information they need, Puss leaps out and goads the Ogre into changing into a crocodile, a hippo, and a mouse, and he is killed by Puss in the final form (19–20).

Returning to the castle, the trio assists the Ghouls and the Hermit on their way and retrieves the buried gold, allowing the wheel to turn again (Pullman, *Puss in Boots* 21–22). Having passed the trials by rescuing the princess and helping the Ghouls and the Hermit, they return to the king and disclose that Jacques is simply the miller's son and not the Marquis of Carabas. Because the king does not wish for his daughter to marry a commoner, Puss suggests the king simply declare Jacques a marquis. The king agrees and also names the "enterprising feline" Sir Puss. The Marquis and Princess marry and live in the Ogre's castle, while Puss lives out his days chasing mice and taking naps (23–24).

Nicholas Tucker, in *Inside the World of Philip Pullman: Darkness Visible*, describes Pullman's *Puss in Boots* as an example of "over-the-top pastiche" (59). Tucker admires Pullman's use of dialogue, illustration, and speech bubbles to convey a sense of playful fun in this children's book which was originally presented as a play for the Polka Theatre (59). Pullman achieves something quite sophisticated through the illustrations of the text that may not be apparent to younger readers: he moves from epic to polyphonic narration. Nikolajeva delineates four distinct periods in the development of children's literature. Period one encompasses folkloric adaptation of tales to make them more in line with children's interests (*Children's Literature* 95). Period two covers the rise of didactic stories created primarily for education (96). Period three establishes the canon of children's literature (96), during which epic narrative structure becomes the most prominent textual feature. Stories in this canon present a traditional plot trajectory with a clear conflict, movement towards a climax, and a solution, and are therefore considered "stable" stories featuring "a clear-cut message" (96). The fourth period in the evolution of children's literature is "polyphonic, or multi-voiced" (97). Arguably Pullman's *Puss in Boots* moves from epic to polyphonic narrative style through the emerging voices of ancillary characters heard only via speech or thought bubbles. As such, Pullman departs from the classic fairy tale narrative style in which the story is told in the third person by an objective narrator.

Nikolajeva asserts that polyphonic narration can potentially add a different layer to the text: "Manifold voices present their own ideas and viewpoints ... the writer's own voice disappears completely, and the novel becomes an endless discussion of various issues, a battlefield of ideas and existential questions" (*Children's Literature* 99). She explains that readers become more immersed in the characters' attitudes or feelings about the plot as opposed to connecting with the author's viewpoints. Readers therefore view the story quite differently, because the tale comes through one or more characters' filters, creating what Nikolajeva calls either a "subjective realism, or if you will, carnivalized realism, in the sense that we perceive reality *after* is has been reflected in the crooked mirror of the character's mind" (100). As an illustration, the first thought bubble in Pullman's text contains the phrase, "Little do you know, Master" (*Puss in Boots* 1), Puss's response in his own mind to Jacques's evident frustration over the presumed worthlessness of a feline inheritance. The thought signals to the reader before Puss even speaks that he is a thinking and rational animal with higher thought processes who is able to bring foreshadowing to the plot. Jacques's first thought bubble occurs when he and Puss begin to plan their strategy to find their fortunes. In the midst of starting their journey, Jacques wonders to himself, "But what about lunch?" (3). This query interjects humor during a very serious portion of the narrative, but it also addresses a basic need most fairy tale plots ignore: the need for characters to eat.

Hunger is also made prominent when the Ogre is introduced, for his thought bubble exclaims, "FOOD! Bring me food! Doesn't anyone understand how hungry I am? And where's that rent?" (Pullman, *Puss in Boots* 4). While Pullman could have simply commented that the Ogre was bloodthirsty and greedy, he chooses to imbue the character with his own voice as he plaintively makes his case presumably to the reader alone. The multifaceted personality of the Ogre is further exemplified in the note he sends to the King when his servants kidnap the princess. In it, he explains his rationale for stealing her, threatens to eat her if anyone tries to stop the marriage, and ends the note with a conciliatory P.S., stating, "When we are maried [*sic*] we will come and stay with you and you can come and stay with us" (12). Lastly, the princess, too, has more depth than the reader expects, for her initial thought bubble reflects relief that the Marquis de Carabas is single: "I'm so glad," she sighs (6), showing that she is more than just a pretty face but also a woman with an opinion.

When Jacques and the princess meet, their thoughts reflect that each is quite attracted to the other but they keep their feelings secret (Pullman, *Puss in Boots* 8). Their childish inability to interact directly persists when the princess thinks to herself, "When will he ask me to marry him?" while the prince, facing the other way (with the two characters separated in space by a large, heart-shaped topiary), says to himself, "I wish I dared ask her to marry me" (11). Through these illustrations and interior thoughts, readers are able to see a more true-to-life depiction of courtship. Unlike classic fairy tales in which a marriage proposal occurs after a single glance or an arrangement between kingdoms, Pullman's re-vision adds the element of realism through an honest rendering of the hesitation and fear implicit in the early days of a budding relationship. Thus Pullman's characters are more round than flat, differentiating his character types from their classic forebears.

The thought and/or speech bubbles also feature evidence of Jacques's maturity, a facet which is absent from earlier variants of the tale. Puss is certainly the stronger and more resourceful character in the first half of the story while Jacques is quite timid, but their traits seem to reverse partway through, showing character growth for Jacques. While on their journey to meet the Ghouls, Jacques holds back, questioning if they are going the right way, while Puss says, "Trust me!" (Pullman, *Puss in Boots* 13). Soon after, though, as they enter the area with the Ghouls, it is Puss who says, "I don't like this look of this..." while Jacques beckons, "Come on, Puss! Courage, remember?" (15). Character growth is an integral part of fairy tales, but it is typically a thematic growth, and not something shown so explicitly through character commentary. It is these facets of polyphonic narration that allow the reader to encounter the characters as dynamic and realistic.

Finally, Pullman's *Puss in Boots* illustrates the movement from innocence to experience. Considering again Perrault's tale, it may be argued that there is no growth whatsoever for the young miller's son, and Puss only grows into a more cunning trickster figure as the tale progresses. Yet Pullman's story illustrates a young man who is timid at first but who recognizes that he must push through his insecurities to gain confidence, and with the assistance of Puss, he undergoes a series of trials, many of which are additions to the classic tale, and by learning to aid others, he is finally able to earn his way to a higher position. He and Puss "save" the Hermit, the Ghouls, the princess, and his brothers. Only then does he earn the right to marry the princess, and they live in the Ogre's castle only after "*they'd* cleaned it up" (24; italics mine). Therefore, as Pullman takes his re-vision into the fourth period of the evolution of children's literature through polyphony, he also interjects a dose of didacticism to young readers, that happiness must be earned.

Aladdin and the Enchanted Lamp *(2005)*

In his introductory remarks to his re-vision of the Middle Eastern folktale *Aladdin or the Wonderful Lamp*, Pullman reflects on how honored he feels to be permitted to tell his own version of such an exciting classic.

Admitting that the physical setting of Aladdin is integral to the plot, he chose to keep it intact, but he also took delight in making the tale his own.[6] He suggests that just as this tale has been retold hundreds of times, it will be told again by many who come after him; he is but one in a long line of storytellers able to transmit its magnificence (n. pag.). Pullman's awareness of the ever-expanding list of folk and fairytale tellers is evident in his essay "I have a feeling this all belongs to me," a biographical sketch he wrote a few years before he began work on *His Dark Materials*. He muses that his storytelling impulse grew from childhood, when he told his brother invented stories every night with no idea in mind how they might end; later, he studied English in college but found that trying to write fiction gave him even more experience in laying out plots (qtd. in Beahm 18, 22–23). He immersed himself fully in storytelling when he began to teach during an era that was marked by significant classroom freedom, for he began a course of study for his students in which he would recount the Greek myths, the Iliad, and the Odyssey, to the point where he could recite the material by heart (26). "To tell great stories ... testing and refining the language and observing the reactions of the listeners and gradually improving the timing and the rhythm and the pace, was to undergo an apprenticeship" akin to Homer's process long ago (qtd. in Beahm 27). Pullman achieves the same in Aladdin, refining the language and the timing, streamlining the plot, and incorporating rich illustrations, all in an effort to bring a new voice to a well-known story.

The Middle Eastern folktale of Aladdin has many incarnations, but it first appeared in Antoine Galland's translation of *The Thousand and One Nights*, a text which found its beginnings in a manuscript of "The Voyages of Sinbad" which Galland acquired in the 1690s (Zipes, *The Great Fairy Tale* 827–28). Having published the stories of Sinbad in 1701, Galland continued to work on this collection by translating a 4-volume collection of works from Arabic to French. As Zipes explains, Galland both embellished the stories he translated and integrated eight new tales for which he had no source text, all of which was published posthumously in 1717. One of those eight tales was "Aladdin, or the Wonderful Lamp." Some of the new tales were oral in origin and recorded from Youhenna Diab or Hanna Diab, but the consensus among critics is that Galland was adept at literary creation himself and introduced a European influence into his re-visions of Arabic tales (828). Since Galland's published version of Aladdin, there have been countless re-visions, notably Sir Richard Burton's

One. Mossycoat, Puss in Boots *and* Aladdin

translation from *Favorite Tales from the Arabian Night's Entertainments* (1884). However, it does not appear that Pullman used Burton's variant as his source text — more likely, Pullman used Andrew Lang's variant, published in 1889 as "Aladdin and the Wonderful Lamp" in his *Blue Fairy Book*.

Lang's variant presents Aladdin, "a careless, idle boy" ("Aladdin") whose lack of motivation drives his father Mustapha to an early grave. An African magician who is supposedly Aladdin's long-lost uncle arrives and promises to assist Aladdin and his mother. He shows Aladdin a barren landscape with a flat stone and brass ring on the ground. When Aladdin tries to flee, the magician knocks him to the ground; he tells Aladdin to hold the ring while speaking his ancestors' names. With a passageway revealed, he instructs Aladdin to enter but to avoid touching anything but the lamp he wishes him to retrieve. Aladdin obeys but hesitates to hand the lamp over at the entrance; in fury, the stranger seals Aladdin in the underground cave. After two days buried alive, Aladdin prays, accidentally rubbing the ring the magician offered him before he entered the cave. This causes the Slave of the Ring to appear, and he is granted a wish. Asking to be free from the cave, Aladdin returns home to tell his mother of the false uncle's treachery. Because Aladdin and his mother worry about how they will eat, Aladdin's mother rubs the lamp clean, intending to sell it, and this causes the genie of the lamp to appear. Lang states that "they lived for many years" by asking the genie for sustenance.

Once Aladdin is a young man, he happens to see the Princess, the Sultan's daughter. Falling in love with her beauty, he asks his mother to secure the young woman's hand in marriage for him. His mother takes the fruits Aladdin once picked from the trees underground since they appear to be precious jewels, intending to offer them to the Sultan. Lacking the courage to speak, six days pass, and the Sultan asks the Vizier to present her to him (Lang). After she explains her purpose and offers the jewels, the Sultan agrees that Aladdin should marry his daughter. Yet the Vizier advocates for his own son, and he negotiates a three-month waiting period during which he hopes his son can amass more wealth than Aladdin. After just two months, though, the Sultan allows the Vizier's son to marry his daughter. Aladdin asks the genie of the lamp to put a stop to the nuptials, and the genie transports the couple to Aladdin's home; the bridegroom is forced out in into the cold while the princess is placed in his bed, where he "lay down beside her and slept soundly" (Lang). After two nights, the princess and her husband ask to be separated to avoid any further trauma, and their marriage is dissolved (Lang).

Aladdin's mother again pleads her son's case, and he is given a list of requirements to prove his suitability for marriage. The genie continues to furnish Aladdin with everything he asks for, even a palace for the princess. Eventually Aladdin marries the princess. Furthermore, he curries favor with people in the town, and though he is made a captain and wins many battles for the Sultan, he "remained modest and courteous as before, and thus lived in peace and content for several years" (Lang).

When the magician re-enters the picture, seeking vengeance, he brings a dozen copper lamps to town, asking passersby to exchange "'new lamps for old'" (Lang). Aladdin's wife's slave tells her there is an old lamp in the palace and she tells her slave to exchange it. With the lamp secured, the magician asks the genie to transport him, the Princess, and the palace to Africa. When the Sultan sees the palace missing, he orders Aladdin's execution, but Aladdin is given forty days' grace period to rescue his wife. Without the lamp, he is in despair, until he inadvertently rubs the magic ring again in prayer, and the Slave of the Ring comes to his aid (Lang).

Transported to Africa, Aladdin gives the Princess a magic powder which she uses in a drink to seduce and kill the magician. Reclaiming the lamp, Aladdin asks the genie to transport everything back to China. Just when the story appears to be concluded with a celebratory feast, the magician's brother seeks vengeance, and he travels to China and murders a woman named Fatima, whom he impersonates to gain access to the Princess. The Princess asks the holy woman if the palace lacks for anything, and "the false Fatima" tells her it needs "a roc's egg" suspended in the dome (Lang). When Aladdin makes this request, the genie flies into a rage and tells him that he has asked for enough and his wife has been tricked. Aladdin has the magician brought forward and stabs him to death, which removes all impediments to Aladdin's happiness, leaving he and his wife peaceful and content (Lang).

Pullman's re-vision follows the basics of Lang's plotline, but he creates more coherence, develops creative analogies, injects humorous incidents, and provides a more satisfying growth arc for the protagonist, better exemplifying the movement from innocence to experience. In an interview with Anita Vachharajani, Pullman says that he was drawn to this tale for its "wonderful shap[e].... As a jazz musician enjoys the sequence of chords in this or that time, so I enjoy the sequence of events in a classic fairytale

One. Mossycoat, Puss in Boots *and* Aladdin

and I love playing variations over it." Pullman thus remains true to many key elements of the tale yet tweaks it enough to make his mark with embellishments or subtractions.

First, Pullman adds and subtracts material, creating more coherence and a better sense of cause and effect relationships. He also removes some elements that do not lend themselves as well to what is ostensibly a book targeted to a younger audience — like *Puss in Boots*, Pullman's *Aladdin* is an illustrated book published by Scholastic's Division of Children's Books. For instance, Aladdin is punished with a beating when he simply doubts there is a garden, and it is the severity of such a punishment for his thoughts and not actions that leads him to doubt the Moor's claim of identity. Pullman alludes to this when he says, "Aladdin was no fool. He'd begun to suspect the Moor as soon as he got that clout on the head" (*Aladdin* 24). By contrast, older variants of the tale depict Aladdin as deluded and foolish until much later in the tale. In fact, Pullman's Aladdin ignores the Moor's instructions when he is underground in order to view the wonders about him, thinking to himself, "It's a shame to go straight back without looking around. I might never have another chance, after all" (22). It is only because Aladdin disobeys the instructions from the Moor that he finds the iron ring that later releases the jinnee who helps him escape. Thus, Aladdin must find the very object that will later aid him, where in other versions, the Moor simply hands the object over to protect him. Why would the very person who intends to betray Aladdin protect him?

Aladdin's powers of observation and clearer insight into others' behavior convince him to refuse to give the Moor the lamp, as opposed to other variants in which he simply cannot find a way to hand it over as his hands are too full. Additionally, his predecessors are not suspicious when the Moor loses his temper outside the cave, while Pullman's hero yells, "'You're no uncle!'... 'You're a sorcerer!'" (*Aladdin* 24). When Aladdin escapes, his mother also claims she never had faith that the Moor was truthful, showing that both mother and son are not as gullible as their forerunners (29). Arguably Pullman's Aladdin is a more realistic character who thinks things through and is more responsible for his own growth.

Whereas Lang's version states that many years pass over the course of the tale, Pullman's variant does not necessarily reveal that Aladdin ages. To illustrate, Pullman ends the second section of his narrative with "So Aladdin grew both in wisdom and in wealth" (*Aladdin* 35). The plot is streamlined hence, with Aladdin seeing the Princess Badr-al-Budur, falling

Part I: Stories of Innocence

in love, asking his mother to approach the Sultan to offer his hand in marriage with the offer of jewels, and his mother being given an audience with the Sultan at the end of the first day she visits (39–40). When the Vizier claims that his son Mahboob is promised to the Princess, a long waiting period is not negotiated to see which young man can produce more wealth; rather, the Vizier tells the Sultan to ask Aladdin immediately to produce forty treasure-bearing slaves (41–42). Aladdin offers the treasure and the palace the very next day. The three gifts are offered in a span of three days, making it more apparent to the reader that each gift builds on the last.

Most notably absent from Pullman's re-vision is the Vizier's son's short-lived marriage to the Princess. Even though Pullman's books are typically meant for audiences of all ages, it would seem appropriate that an illustration of Aladdin lying next to another man's wife be removed from the text entirely as its omission causes no problems in continuity.

The third part of Pullman's narrative brings the Moor back into focus, and he re-enters the story in much the same way Lang describes, but Pullman again streamlines what appears to be a two-part ending in Lang's variant into one unified whole in his own, by making Fatima the slave to the Princess who remembers the dusty lamp in Aladdin's rooms (*Aladdin* 55). Thus it is Fatima who unwittingly hands the lamp over, giving the Moor the ability to summon the genie and move the palace, with the Princess inside, to Morocco. When the Sultan finds out, he gives Aladdin but one day to rescue her (59). Before attempting the rescue, Aladdin enlists the aid of Fatima, who accompanies him to Morocco. Fatima is the one who gains access to the Princess, giving her the herbs necessary to lull the Moor into unconsciousness, rendering him incapable of defending himself so that Aladdin can successfully behead him (63–66). Thereafter, the story ends similarly to Lang's variant, with Aladdin using the lamp to return his bride, Fatima, and the palace back to their home land, living many years, "old and wise and surrounded by his many, many children and grandchildren, some of them almost as naughty as he had once been, but all of them brave, and beautiful, and greatly beloved" (71).

As for the descriptive elements of the tale, Pullman's imagery is lavish and at times even more intricately rendered than the beautiful illustrations by Sophy Williams. Probably the most stunning passage describes the wonders of the underground garden, where Aladdin views "a salamander wreathed in flames," an imp inside a glass bottle, "who beat the glass with his tiny fists and snarled with rage," a curious snake who ingested his own tail, and "a butterfly with a human face tethered by a golden chain no thicker than a hair" (*Aladdin* 22–23). Pullman also creates an unforgettable depiction of beauty in the palace which Aladdin "orders" from the jinnee; made of gold, lapis lazuli, onyx, and marble, filled with jasmine and roses, with windows constructed of gigantic diamonds, an abundance of wine and perfume through the air, and even "harps and lutes hanging in every room, so that when a breeze blows, music plays by itself" (49). Williams's illustrations are colorful and impressionistic, but in many instances Pullman's own words paint a livelier portrait in the reader's mind. Pullman also uses analogy liberally, particularly to describe the Moor: his "tears ran down his chest like rivers down a mountainside" (8); his "teeth ... pointed like a needle" (12); and his "legs set off like scissors" (16).

Pullman also interjects humor into a typically serious tale. For one, he places Aladdin's home "in the Street of the Oil Sellers ... Over the house of Shaheed the Nervous Poet" (*Aladdin* 10). In isolation this does not draw attention, but when the reader comes to the conclusion, he sees that Aladdin has become Shaheed's patron, and Shaheed is instructed to tell the very story that the reader just encountered, while Pullman proclaims, "Blessed be Aladdin, Prince of Publishers! May every poor writer of stories find a patron as generous and wise!" (70). Pullman also introduces tongue-in-cheek commentary through various asides, such as Aladdin's mother's revelation to the reader that her son's laziness is driving her to yearn to follow in her deceased husband's footsteps (7), or the Moor's quick and obvious shift in attitude from angry to kind when Aladdin comes near, or his comment, "'Once I have ... once *we* have the lamp, the world is ours!'" (19; italics original). Finally, equipping the Moor with "Turkish Delight" (64) when he is trying to woo the Princess, an obvious nod to Pullman's nemesis C.S. Lewis, is the crowning touch on the playfulness with his subject that defines much of Pullman's works for children.

Lastly, the embellishments to the text and the subtle alterations of plot lend themselves to featuring the theme of growth from innocence to experience. While every Aladdin moves from rags to riches, no matter the variant, most are simply lucky enough to be bailed out by others, ordinary people or magical helpers, and they end up rewarded not for their ingenuity or drive to discern good folk from bad, but for no apparent reason other than being in the right place at the right time. Pullman's reader is more satisfied to learn that Aladdin seems to mature at the conclusion of the tale. While Lang's Aladdin grows because time passes, Pullman's Aladdin learns how to read people, from the Moor to the deceptive goldsmith, and his wisdom grows as he takes part in his own education (*Aladdin* 35). He also learns when to enlist the help of another, such as Fatima, who is incredulous that he would deign to ask her help in rescuing the Princess. In this way, the tale is reminiscent of Puss in Boots, for both Aladdin and Jacques face more trials than their forebears. Furthermore, Lang's conclusion shows that Aladdin can be tricked yet again at the end of his journey while he still asks for more wealth, while Pullman's Aladdin never asks for more riches once he satisfies the Sultan's requirements for the Princess's hand. In fact, he puts the lamp in a safe place after asking the jinnee to transport them home and does not appear to use it again, preferring instead to rule the kingdom he inherits upon the Sultan's death with his Princess at his side. Thus on the path from innocence to experience, Pullman's Aladdin is a vibrant, dynamic, active protagonist responsible for many of his own accomplishments.

Conclusion

Pullman's fairy tale and folktale re-visions are a welcome addition to the vast number of existing literary variants, because as an accomplished storyteller, he enhances character depth, converting formerly flat characters into round protagonists. For this reason, such stories are better representations of the journey from innocence to experience. It is obvious that Pullman reveres certain elements of each classic tale because he chooses to keep much intact, and he admits that the retelling of fairy tales will not cease with his work. However, with these three re-visions he has made his mark as a teller of fairy tales for this age; though not (yet?) as prolific as Perrault, Basile, or the Brothers Grimm, he is a contributor to this vast array of stories that will live on for the ages. According to Pullman his latest work will be a new "Selected Grimm" for Penguin Classics, "a proper grown-up book" with 50 tales told "in [his] voice." While he is primarily working on his own translations, he is also adding his own touches: "Sometimes I deviate a little, or add a phrase or two to make it a little richer; sometimes I've added a detail or two to bring what seem to me two not-very-well-connected halves of a story more closely together; sometimes something florid or fanciful in the original encourages me to become even more florid or Baroque myself; sometimes I've left everything scrupulously

One. Mossycoat, Puss in Boots *and* Aladdin

alone, where it seems to me that the teller has it already perfect."[7] He further asserts, "I'm finding it a great purifier of narrative thinking, rather as a pianist relishes playing Bach's preludes and fugues as a sort of palate-cleansing discipline" ("Pullman's Fairy Tales"). Whether he is a jazz musician or a classical pianist, Pullman's melodious prose brings to the canon of classic fairy tales and folktales new compositions, both hauntingly familiar and yet enchantingly fresh.

Two

The Firework-Maker's Daughter and The Scarecrow and His Servant
Quest-Driven Tales

"Homer and the bards ... would have learned the stories and they would have told them, orally, again and again — refining their skills, finding a little bit that works, using it next time and embellishing it."

— Philip Pullman, *Talking Books*[1]

While the first chapter concerned three fairy tales Philip Pullman rewrote from classic sources, his books *The Firework-Maker's Daughter* (1995) and *The Scarecrow and His Servant* (2004) are original fairy tales painted from his own palette of colors rather than another artist's brush. In *The Firework-Maker's Daughter*, a novella, Pullman draws a picture of a young girl called Lila, an only child of a firework-maker, who desires to become more accomplished than her father. Told that girls are only to learn firework-construction as a hobby, Lila takes offense and embarks on a Campbellian quest to obtain the secrets she needs to become highly skilled at her chosen profession, and the story concludes with a grand fireworks show and her coming of age as she conquers her greatest fears and triumphs. *The Scarecrow and His Servant*, also a quest-driven tale, is a rollicking novel with a large cast of characters and a wealth of colorful scenes, and it centers on Lord Scarecrow, who is brought to life by a lightning strike, and Jack, his faithful servant, who follow a storyline that cleverly alludes to *Don Quixote*. Both tales also feature dual protagonists, a convention which Pullman perfects in *His Dark Materials* with Lyra and Will, although in both cases, one protagonist's growth is highlighted more than the other's.

The Firework-Maker's Daughter *(1995) and the Hero's Journey*

In his brief comments on *The Firework-Maker's Daughter*, Nicholas Tucker notes that Pullman's original tale is a mixture of "feel-good" entertainment undercut by more weighty concerns with precursors to themes and plot devices that follow in *His Dark Materials* (65–66). Tony Watkins discusses the genesis of Pullman's story in his book *Dark Matter: Shedding Light on Philip Pullman's Trilogy* His Dark Materials. Pullman once saw in a library a series of stage designs for a play by William Moncrieff named *The Elephant of Siam, or the Fire-Fiend*. Wishing to write a play that would allow him the chance to incorporate fireworks onstage, Pullman admits he has never read Moncrieff's text but set out to craft a story that would fit the title (Watkins 42; Birmingham Stage Company). In its earliest incarnation, Lila was not the daughter of a firework-maker but a princess who, in secrecy, became Lalchand's apprentice; he set out to teach her the skills of firework-making knowing the penalty was death if they should be discovered. Pullman's involvement with the drama was so intense that he even made the masks for the actors himself, explaining in the webpages for the Birmingham Stage Company that he kept the Razvani mask. Pullman wanted the play to live on after production, so he revised it into a novella, casting Lila as Lalchand's daughter, and he removed a custard pie fight to substitute a fireworks competition. Pullman reflects, "It was better like this, because something real and important — in fact, desperate — hangs on the outcome" (Birmingham Stage Company). Through the transformation from the play to the novella, Pullman ultimately understood what the story was about: "the making of art" (Birmingham Stage Company). It is only through Lila's journey that she learns she already has the three gifts necessary to become an accomplished firework-maker, making this story a Pullmanesque fairy tale, which "begin[s] in delight ... and end[s] in wisdom."[2]

"A thousand miles ago..." (Pullman, *The Firework-Maker's* 1) is the opening phrase of Pullman's playful narrative, offering a subtle change to the usual "once upon a time" declaration. Having lost her mother as a child, Lila is raised alongside her father Lalchand in his workshop where he creates beautiful fireworks. As she grows, Lila learns the tricks of her father's trade while showing a flair for her own inventions. One day, Lalchand notices his daughter appears soiled and unrefined, and he cries, "How am I going to find a husband for you when you look like that?" (3). His admonition generates such a strong reaction in Lila who is repulsed at the very idea of betrothal that the two suddenly realize that they view the world very differently from one another. This difference of opinion, brought about by gender and generational differences, pushes Lila into Campbell's first stage of the hero's journey, separation, both emotionally and physically from her father.

In *The Hero with a Thousand Faces*, Joseph Campbell describes the genesis of "the call to adventure," the first step on the hero's journey, which begins with either wonder or "blunder" (58). On one hand, a character may be tempted from her path by something which catches her eye and entices her to delve deeper into mysteries she has yet to face (58). Lila represents this type of hero, for she is lured to begin her quest when she finds that Lalchand has not taught her everything she wants to learn. On the other hand, the hero may also begin his quest due to a "blunder," a mistake, which accurately describes the second protagonist Chulak's involvement in the narrative. Servant to Hamlet, the white elephant who is fed mango-flavored Turkish Delight (Pullman's apparent nod to C.S. Lewis), Chulak is an entrepreneur who rents out space for advertisements on Hamlet's large frame. Crass as his actions may seem, Chulak's plan is to save enough money to run away with Hamlet for whom he has generous plans as he teaches him to sing in hopes he will someday be a performer named "Luciano Elephanti" (Pullman, *The Firework-Maker's* 8). Chulak sympathetically offers to help Lila discover her next step on her quest to attain the ultimate secrets of firework-making, and he asks her father for the secrets he has kept from Lila (8). In a gesture to the story of Aladdin, Lalchand accuses Chulak of being "dedicated to ... idleness," a "scamp" who will never actually carry out the steps to become a firework-maker himself, which is Chulak's cover story (9). Yet Lalchand easily reveals the secrets to Chulak, indicating the gender division to which he adheres when he is dispensing the wealth of his knowledge as an artisan: after all, a boy should know all he needs to become a skilled worker, even if he is a ne'er-do-well, but a girl should be shipped off to his sister's home where she could be brought up to become a dancer (3). When Lila learns that Chulak easily learns the secrets she covets, this pushes her to depart in anger, to self-ordain her quest. Chulak assumes he has just been a good friend, but he has unknowingly blundered, for this information puts Lila in harm's way as she leaves for her journey unaware of the trials she must face. Thus

Two. Firework-Maker's Daughter, Scarecrow and His Servant

Chulak also begins the hero's journey to assist Lila, but for a different reason than she.

Knowing then that Lila must travel to meet Razvani the Fire-Fiend in the Grotto at Mount Merapi, taking in hand three gifts which she must barter for the prize of the Royal Sulphur, Chulak sets off to aid Lila in her quest (Pullman, *The Firework-Maker's* 10). The division between Lila and her father is further widened when she hears that he so willingly gave his secrets to Chulak, and she vows that she will not forgive her father (13). Saying "He wants me to stay a child forever" (13), Lila sets forth on her quest and now adds physical separation to her emotional break from the man who single-handedly raised her, and as a parting shot, she even claims that she will put her father out of business when she learns the secrets of his trade (14).

Struck by the note she leaves with her signature, "Your ex-daughter, Lila" (Pullman, *The Firework-Maker's* 14), Lalchand panics, finds Chulak, and enlists his help to find her. In this way Chulak's role as a secondary protagonist is interesting, for while he has his own quest to follow, he aids both Lila and her father at separate yet complementary parts of the story. In this way, Chulak is reminiscent of Will in *His Dark Materials* who is a protagonist with his own quest, but who also acts as a donor or helper to the central protagonist Lyra. Armed with additional knowledge that Lila needs to complete her task in safety, Chulak and Hamlet set off in search of her.

On her way to Mount Merapi, Lila is daunted by the sheer size of the volcano "on the very edge of the world" (Pullman, *The Firework-Maker's* 18). While it seems she might refuse the call, the second step on the hero's journey, she only pauses. As Campbell reveals, "Not all who hesitate are lost. The psyche has many secrets in reserve" (*The Hero* 64). She nearly loses faith in her ability to prevail, but she reasons that "she had chosen to make the journey, and she could hardly turn back" (Pullman, *The Firework-Maker's* 18).

The next steps on the hero's journey are compressed into one event that begins when Lila comes across a group of comic, bumbling fishermen in a boat. Claiming to be Rambashi and his River Taxi, their boat is clearly painted "The Bloody Murderer" (Pullman, *The Firework-Maker's* 22) on its bow, which makes more sense to her when she is ferried partway across the river and turns around to see that the fishermen have transformed to pirates with the help of handkerchiefs tied over their mouths and "daggers

... made of wood wrapped in silver paper" (28). Though the men take her prisoner, Lila is more amused than scared by them, and she earns her place among them by saving them from a leaping tiger with the deployment of the Crackle Dragons she brought along for the trip (30). While Campbell's third step, "Supernatural Aid," often involves "a protective figure ... who provides the adventurer with amulets..." (*The Hero* 69), it could be argued that these men provide supernatural aid in an unorthodox way, for they bring out Lila's strength and show her that her "amulets" are within, and in this case, her primary tool of self-rescue is her sense of humor, as she faces her enemies down with a smile. Furthermore, in crossing a body of water, an obvious Freudian symbol of birth/rebirth/the unconscious, they assist her in Campbell's step "The Crossing of the First Threshold" (77), for "the regions of the unknown," such as desert, forest, and bodies of water, "are free fields for the projection of unconscious content" (79). Successfully confronting an element of "danger," however ridiculous, on the body of water, represents Lila's encounter with "The Belly of the Whale" (90). Having traversed the first leg of the hero's journey, Lila is prepared for initiation (97).

While Lila continues on her quest facing "the road of trials" (Campbell, *The Hero* 97), Chulak and Hamlet begin a parallel mission to Emerald Lake, where they meet a member of the faux pirate clan who writes "Eat at Rambashi's Jungle Grill" on Hamlet's side (Pullman, *The Firework-Maker's* 36). Chulak recalls he has an uncle of that name and later he is reunited with his relative and fed a satisfying meal before the ceremony of the full moon commences (39–40). It is Chulak, then, who completes the next stage of initiation, called "The Meeting with the Goddess" (Campbell, *The Hero* 109), for he must ask the goddess of the lake for an item to aid Lila in her trial. Nearly thwarted in his attempt by being forcibly removed from the shore for "defiling the lake" (Pullman, *The Firework-Maker's* 42), Hamlet comes to his aid by trumpeting in anger, which leads the goddess to question Chulak's intentions. The goddess delivers the flask of magic lake water to help Lila, but she warns them of the treacherous journey ahead (46–47).

The narrative returns to Lila's quest as she attempts to rest at night, but overcome by loneliness, she presses on to begin the arduous climb to the top of Mount Merapi. As Campbell explains, "Once having traversed the threshold, the hero moves in a dream landscape of curiously fluid, ambiguous forms, where he must survive a succession of trials" (*The Hero*

97). Lila's first hurdle occurs when she has partially ascended the mountain only to lose her footing and fall a great distance; she must resist the urge to give up and push onward despite missing one shoe (Pullman, *The Firework-Maker's* 50). As she climbs higher, she becomes so one with her purpose that despite "nearly cry[ing] out in despair" (50–51) she casts aside her food and blanket to drag her bruised and bloody body upward. She even comes to a point where she thinks she will perish, but "still she went on" (52). Campbell reveals that the hero may find that a "benign power" surrounds her, aiding her despite the extraordinary difficulties she faces (*The Hero* 97). Thus, a large rock dislodges from the mountain, revealing the entrance to the grotto that she seeks (Pullman, *The Firework-Maker's* 52).

Entering the realm of Razvani, Lila sees an empty room, and she falls to the ground assuming her journey has been for naught (Pullman, *The Firework-Maker's* 55). Yet she soon finds she is wrong as fire-spirits begin to fill the grotto, announcing with great clamor the arrival of the Fire-Fiend (56). Of course, Lila has made a grave error in judgment: she does not know what the three gifts are. Bent on her purpose to obtain the Royal Sulphur, she assumes she will receive if she asks. However, Razvani only laughs at her misfortune while he tells her she must prove herself by walking through flames, a task made easier by the use of the magic water from the goddess of the lake (who turns out to be Razvani's cousin) (58). In a scene that Nicholas Tucker says "anticipate[s] the haunted spirits later found in *His Dark Materials*" (66), Razvani shows Lila the ghosts who warn her of the consequences of approaching without the gifts. Scared yet undeterred from her path, Lila "would rather be a ghost than go back empty-handed and fail at the one thing she had ever wanted" (Pullman, *The Firework-Maker's* 60). She enters the flames and faces excruciating pain until she is startled by Hamlet's trumpet-call, announcing that he and Chulak have arrived to assist her. Thus Chulak's quest at this point is tied up in Lila's as he offers her the liquid from the goddess which enables her to walk to the center of the fire and remain unharmed (61).

Since Chulak's meeting with the goddess earlier satisfied that portion of Campbell's initiation stage, Lila's facing of the flames without assistance represents the "Atonement with the Father" stage (*The Hero* 126), for in a way Razvani is a symbol of Lalchand, the father who holds the secrets of his craft that will only be passed on to Lila if she proves worthy. As Campbell illustrates, initiation of the hero brings him into contact with "the

Part I: Stories of Innocence

techniques, duties, and prerogatives of his vocation" while he also learns to alter his personal connection to his elders (136). In other words, "He is the twice-born: he has become himself the father" (137).

Therefore, at the heart of the fire is Lila's first epiphany, which places her on the return path. The Fire-Fiend tells her that the sulphur is simply an illusion: "Illusions, Lila. Fire burns away all our illusions. The world itself is all illusion. Everything that exists flickers like a flame for a moment, and then vanishes. The only thing that lasts is change itself" (Pullman, *The Firework-Maker's* 62). With this amazing revelation, he vanishes to leave her in a barren cavern, but her journey is far from over. Reunited with Chulak and Hamlet, Lila finds that her father is threatened by execution for aiding in Hamlet's escape, and they all rush back to try to save her father. Just as in the beginning of the story when Lila is unsuccessful at obtaining the information she needs to succeed from her father, Chulak tries his hand at assisting her when her pleas for her father's life are ignored. The negotiation scene that follows is fascinating, as readers of *His Dark Materials* will surely make the connection.

Chulak tries to argue his case but is hit by Hamlet's trunk: "Hamlet had never done that to him before, and he rolled over in surprise to see the elephant giving him a special and particular look, and then he realized what he must do" (Pullman, *The Firework-Maker's* 70). Chulak proposes that he and the elephant share a special bond that allows them to communicate, thus the elephant has just told him he requests a private counsel with the king himself. Saying that "the white elephant is a rare and wondrous beast," the king accepts the request and will only speak to Hamlet (70–71). Hamlet then negotiates a deal with the king to save Lalchand's life (72). Pullman utilizes a similar scenario in *The Golden Compass* when Lyra appears before the imposing bear king Iofur Raknison and explains that she and Iorek have a special way that only the two of them communicate, all while Pan is nipping at her fingers much like Hamlet hits Chulak with his trunk. She also explains that Iorek must meet Iofur alone on the field of battle, where Iorek uses his trickery to gain the upper hand and vanquish the bear king, just as Hamlet reveals his mastery of speech to the king in Lila's story in order to convince him to offer her father a path that will save his life. In terms of the Campbellian monomyth, this plot point may symbolize "The Refusal of the Return" (*The Hero* 193), for even when the hero prevails in a great trial, the boon he brings is sometimes thwarted or refused. Evidently the story's progression relies on the joining of forces through dual protagonists to accomplish the hero's task, for it is Chulak's intervention that shows Lila her next step on the path.

Learning that they must win the firework competition to save Lalchand's life, Lila and her father begin to create a completely new fireworks show which wins the contest despite the stiff competition. The fireworks themselves are representative of the portions of Lila's journey, reinforcing in imagery the details of the plot. A common trope in fairy tales is the repetition of plot events in the latter part of the narrative. Often a character who is betrayed or victimized by another is placed into a situation in which the perpetrator is near and the victim has a chance to relate the trials of the quest in front of the villain. Pullman offers an interesting twist on the repeating narrative motif through Lila's symbolic fireworks display. To begin, early in the narrative Chulak allows the graffiti "Chang Loves Lotus Blossom *True*" to appear on Hamlet's side (Pullman, *The Firework-Maker's* 6). Consequently, the first part of Lila's fireworks display includes "little lotus flowers made of white fire ... [that] began to float across the dark lake like little paper boats" (86). Thus the lotus flowers represent the portion of Lila and Chulak's journey before they depart from home. The next leg on Lila's journey is the encounter with Rambashi and his men at the river. This is exemplified in the second part of her display, which "look[ed] like water, and it splashed and danced like a bubbling spring" (86). The third part of her journey involved a foray into the jungle. This portion is carried out in the third display of her show, in which "a carpet of living moss seemed to have spread itself across the grass, a million little points of light all so close together that they looked as soft as velvet" (87). Finally, the finale of her show culminates in a literal recreation of Razvani's Grotto, during which she uses her newly created "delayed-action fuses" to mimic the fire lights going on and off in the cavern while the stage is set for a visual representation in which Razvani himself seems to be present (88). This visual representation of the stages of Lila's journey up to this point is an innovative way for Lila to relive and to present to the crowd a summation of her quest leading naturally to her "crossing of the return threshold" (Campbell, *The Hero* 217).

Chulak completes the final step on his journey as he returns with Rambashi's Boys whom he has trained to be singers, putting him on his own path to self-sufficiency as he plans to tour with them (Pullman, *The Firework-Maker's* 91), while Hamlet fulfills his destiny by asking the lovely Frangipani to marry him after he explains the many trials he faced (93).

As Lila completes the final stage of the hero's journey, the return, with her winning of the competition and the saving of her father's life, she still wonders if she has truly completed her journey because she does not know what the three gifts are. In a scene that ties this text to the overall theme of this book, Lila's father explains that the gifts were in her all along, that they include "talent," "courage," and "luck" (96), and that the ultimate prize, the royal sulphur, is but an illusion, for "human beings call it wisdom. You can only gain that by suffering and risk — by taking the journey to Mount Merapi. It's what the journey is for" (96). Just as he would later do in *His Dark Materials*, Pullman creates a story in which two protagonists must aid one another on their own personal journeys to fulfill their own path to wisdom, a path that will be fraught with difficulties and trials, but which can be overcome with persistence and love (97).

The final portions of Campbell's' monomyth, "Master of the Two Worlds" (*The Hero* 229) and "Freedom to Live" (238), are bound up together in the conclusion of Pullman's story, for the dual protagonists must come back into their ordinary lives having traversed many obstacles that have forced their individual growth. Campbell speaks liberally of the concept of "transfiguration" (236), by which "the individual ... gives up completely all attachment to his personal limitations, idiosyncrasies, hopes and fears, no longer resists the self-annihilation that is prerequisite to rebirth in the realization of truth, and so becomes ripe, at last, for the great at-one-ment" (237). No longer fighting against invented goals, the individual learns to relax with groundlessness in his approach to life and death (237). Lila can be said to have embraced this worldview at the end of her journey in realizing that there is no "prize" to be gained in a literal sense, but in a figurative sense, the rewards of accepting illusion and change are limitless. As Campbell explains in the final portion of the hero's journey, the ultimate conclusion of the journey is to realize that there is no conclusion, for the prize can be achieved "through a realization of the true relationship of the passing phenomena of time to the imperishable life that lives and dies in us all" (238).

Does it seem reasonable that Pullman set out to imbue the play *The Firework-Maker's Daughter* with such weighty concerns? Not at all. It seems most likely that Pullman took the opportunity to create a magical, colorful, exciting display on the stage to delight his students and their parents. But it does stand to reason that somewhere in the back of his mind, active at work on *His Dark Materials*, Pullman was already working with the hero's journey and the path from innocence to experience, and so it is plausible that he lit a fuse on an idea, and when that idea shot high into the sky and burst in a shower of colorful sparks, some of those embers fell to the earth and instead of dying, took root in another tale about facing one's fears and gaining wisdom.

The Scarecrow and His Servant *(2004) and the Quixotic Quest*

While there is little written on *The Scarecrow and His Servant*, Michael Rosen's "Find me a leg" asserts that it "begins, travels and ends along the same lines as the first European novels did ... a picaresque with its lead characters owing something to *Don Quixote*, with flavourings from *Pinocchio*, *The Wizard of Oz* and *Candide*." As Rosen explains, the heroes of the tale, Lord Scarecrow and Jack his helper, are "locked together for mutual support ... rush[ing] from problem to problem, adventure to adventure, improvising as they go." Like *The Firework-Maker's Daughter*, Pullman's delightful story depends on the use of dual protagonists, each intent on his own quest while assisting on the mission of the other, although Jack is the dominant narrator and the story's events are told more frequently through his point of view. In fact, Jack's narration borrows quite liberally from Sancho Panza's style in *Don Quixote*, for both Sancho and Jack often reflect on the deteriorating mental state of their traveling companion. As Rosen and others have observed, Pullman has created his own picaresque for contemporary readers, while a nuanced reading of Pullman's novel reveals just how frequently he incorporates plot events, structure, and stylistic elements from Cervantes' epic. All this combines to form a quixotic quest that is completely original and yet, at least in early chapters, satisfyingly familiar.

In a personal communication with the author, Pullman explains the various pieces that inspired the text:

> There were three things.... The first was seeing a production of Leonard Bernstein's *Candide* at the National Theatre, and being very struck with the relationship between Candide and his servant ... the classic silly master/clever servant duo, and it set me thinking about other such pairs: Quixote/Sancho Panza, of course, and Bertie Wooster and Jeeves, and I thought that it was such an interesting relationship, and one we couldn't deal with realistically

anymore, because no-one except the very rich has servants. Another starting point was a book of sketches a friend of mine did of Japanese scarecrows, which can have any form: a red rubber boot up-ended on a stick, a little plastic aeroplane buzzing round and round, a Barbie doll tied to a balloon.... It was so inventive .... The third thing was a book of reproductions of drawings by the younger Tiepolo of the character Pulcinella, who alone of the Commedia del'Arte characters can exist as a multiple. There is only one Arlecchino, only one Pantalone, but there can be any number of Pulcinellas, with their silly long white hats and long noses, blundering about getting in each other's way, being sent to jail, being terrified by a chicken — a wonderful book. So the three things sort of got together and made the baby that is *The Scarecrow and His Servant*.[3]

Of all the various literary works, characters, and images that worked together as the catalyst for this engaging, delightful novel, the connection to *Don Quixote* is perhaps the strongest.

In *Crossover Fiction: Global and Historical Perspectives*, Sandra L. Beckett describes Miguel de Cervantes's *Don Quijote de la Mancha* (1605 and 1615) as "the most influential and emblematic work in the Spanish literary canon and a founding work of modern Western literature" (17). Though the work has been adapted countless times for children, Beckett admits that it was certainly never intended to be a "crossover" work; however, subsequent writers thought the overarching themes of the text could successfully convey "religious, patriotic, psychological, or moral values to children" (19). While Beckett contends that many classic crossover texts were created for didactic purposes (19), Pullman's *The Scarecrow and His Servant* seems to focus more on the facets of the adventure than on teaching lessons to young readers. However, with various allusions to Quixote in place in Pullman's narrative, one could argue that he has written a very loose adaptation of Cervantes' work that at the very least encourages those familiar with the classic text to make the connections. Of literary adaptations for children, Linda Hutcheon explains that writers of such texts "deliberately [write] on two or more levels" (175). When Pullman won the Whitbread Book of the Year for *The Amber Spyglass* in 2001, he said, "'I have always believed that children's books belong with the rest, in the general field, and the general marketplaces and general conversation about books'" (qtd. in Beckett 118). With the publication of his own Quixotic quest, he proves that all ages can appreciate a well-written tale of adventure with timeless themes.

Simon Dentith broadly defines parody as "any cultural practice which makes a relatively polemical allusive imitation of another cultural production or practice" (37), and he writes extensively of Cervantes' work as the impetus for parodic attacks on Romance, "the genre of wish-fulfillment, rules by coincidence and wonder" (55). If "the whole point of the novel [Don Quixote] ... is its attack upon the chivalric romance as a guide to life" (56), then arguably Pullman, in recasting the roles of Don Quixote and Sancho Panza, seeks to parody a classic parodic text. Yet as Dentith notes, often parody has the "paradoxical effect" (36) of breathing new life into the very form with which it plays. Dentith describes both "specific" and "general" parody, distinguishing between the two as the allusion to distinct portions of a preceding text versus the reference to a body of work or genre (7). Pullman utilizes both types of parody in *The Scarecrow and His Servant*, though the parallels to specific characters and plot events are more prominent than attacks on the genre, and his tale ends on a more positive note than Cervantes' tale; therefore, Pullman's tale more generally upholds the concept of the chivalric romance than debunks it.

Those familiar with Cervantes' *Don Quixote* will find strong parallels between the simple creature who wishes to be known as Lord Scarecrow and the famous hidalgo Don Quixote de la Mancha. In fact, Dierdre F. Baker's review claims "Brainless Scarecrow is more than a little like Don Quixote, and all his adventures have an edge of lunacy; it's the boy Jack, his loyal servant, who gives the story a core of sanity" (587). Maria Nikolajeva states that Pullman "...recycles the century-old figure of an animated scarecrow, turning it into a comical Don Quixote adventure with many philosophical overtones" ("Philip Pullman" 785). Physically, Quixote's patchwork armor and disheveled appearance is recalled in Lord Scarecrow's physical appearance, his head constructed from "a great knobbly turnip, with a broad crack for a mouth and a long thin sprout for a nose and two bright little stones for eyes ... a tattered straw hat ... a soggy woolen scarf, and an old tweed jacket full of holes, and his rake-handle arms had gloves stuffed with straw on the ends of them ... a pair of threadbare trousers, but since he had only one leg, the empty trouser leg trailed down beside him" (Pullman, *The Scarecrow* 5–6). Jack's first order of business is to find him a second leg, yet while Jack initially completes his frame, he sustains various injuries later which Jack must repair by replacing his arms with a pointing road sign and an umbrella, and his turnip head with a coconut. He is constantly losing straw, in need of so-called "operations" to bring him back to full function, much like Don Quixote whose body and armor are in constant need of repair.

Lord Scarecrow also has a Quixote-like presence about him, with a "rich and sonorous" voice (Pullman, *The Scarecrow* 5) and a chivalrous attitude that encourages a formality in his discourse with his enemies and a soft side for baby birds left by their parents whom he has a penchant for rescuing. Brought to life by a stroke of lightning, Lord Scarecrow is in fact so kind and courteous to all that most forget he is a scarecrow and believe they are talking to a "proper gentleman" due to his manner (15). Like Quixote, Lord Scarecrow describes himself as a great lord, "the lord of Spring Valley ... it all belongs to me" (32), and thus he appoints himself a sort of "knight errant" who asks Jack to travel with him as his "personal servant ... to accompany [him] throughout the world ... to attend to [his] needs.... [In exchange for] excitement and glory" (7). When Jack accepts Lord Scarecrow's offer, the two set off on a journey filled with risk and adventure much like the journey of Quixote and Sancho Panza.

Just as Cervantes' narration is often described through Sancho Panza's point of view, so is Pullman's story seen frequently through Jack's eyes. Like Sancho, Jack sees his traveling companion as potentially mad from early on. In fact, when Jack initially hears the cries of the scarecrow, knowing that scarecrows are not meant to talk, Jack wonders if he himself is going mad, yet he takes pity on the scarecrow, saying, "He looks madder than I feel" (Pullman, *The Scarecrow* 5). Just as Sancho Panza explains to Don Quixote, "Look you here ... those over there aren't giants, they're windmills" (Cervantes 64), Jack exclaims, "Master! Master! ... That's not a footpad — that's a road sign!" (Pullman, *The Scarecrow* 37). Despite Sancho and Jack's protestations, though, their fearless leaders attack the inanimate objects with vigor, and in so doing, both are injured.

Pullman's revision of the infamous Quixote windmill scene is particularly clever, for instead of a windmill with arms swinging vertically, he places Lord Scarecrow next to a four-pronged signpost with arms swinging horizontally, one of which "clonked the Scarecrow hard on the back of the head" (Pullman, *The Scarecrow* 36) and which keeps hitting him as it swings around. Quixote and Rocinante are dragged by the windmill to the point where Rocinante's shoulder is "half dislocated" (Cervantes 65); similarly, the Scarecrow "look[s] down in horror at his own right arm, which was slipping slowly out of the sleeve of his jacket. The rake handle had come away from the broomstick that was his spine" (Pullman, *The Scarecrow* 37). Furthermore, in the scuffle, the Scarecrow breaks one of the signpost's arms free, and he uses it as a new arm for himself (38). This is reminiscent of Quixote, who, after his battle with the windmill, "tore a dead branch that might almost serve as a lance, and fastened on to it the iron head that he'd taken off the broken one" (Cervantes 66). The details of Pullman's scene mirror those of Cervantes, yet they differ enough to be quite innovative and not purely derivative.

As the narrative continues, the portions told through Jack's eyes seem reminiscent of Sancho Panza's narration in that both characters find much evidence to come to the conclusion that they may be following a madman, but they are obviously taken by the charm of their companions, so that each excuses the element of madness, and sometimes each wonders if the madness has rubbed off on them. For instance, when they find a farmer who is willing to give them some food and a place to rest for the night, Jack is on his way to the barn when he hears voices coming from inside. Lord Scarecrow claims that he was in the midst of "telling these ladies and gentlemen about our adventures" (Pullman, *The Scarecrow* 65) and all Jack sees before him is a collection of "rakes and hoes and brooms" (65). When the Scarecrow continues his performance, suddenly "Jack's hair [is] standing on end" (65) because he believes he hears a rake speak. However, he rationalizes that tiredness has gotten the better of him, and he steps away from the thought that the Scarecrow may be mad. Later, when the Scarecrow professes his love for a broom, saying that he "worship[s] the ground she brushes" (68), and he asks for Jack to help him win her affections, Jack agrees to help him, even though he worries to himself, "He's got me believing she's alive.... I better be careful, in case I go as mad as he is" (75). Yet despite his misgivings about the Scarecrow's sanity, he helps him put the broom in position for the Scarecrow's serenade, thinking to himself, "This is a daft idea. Still, he's a marvel, the master..." (75).

The feeling of hesitancy or caution that is overcome by acceptance and loyalty is present throughout Cervantes' work, for despite his banter with Quixote over his madness, Sancho Panza is fiercely loyal and shows his true regard for Quixote when he meets someone new and describes his fearless leader: "a knight adventurer ... is someone who's being beaten up one moment and being crowned emperor the next. Today he's the unhappiest creature in the world, and the poorest one, and tomorrow he'll have two or three kingdoms to hand over to his squire" (Cervantes 123). In fact, both Sancho and Jack illustrate through their observations that "sometimes you go looking for one thing and you find another" (123), because while each begins his quest as squire or servant, with either a title or food and shelter in mind as goals, each grows during the course of the quest to understand that one's "hopes" (123) are more important than any other tangible reward.

In moving away from character doubling, one may find that there are many vignettes in Pullman's text that recall and alter events in *Don Quixote*. For instance, the Scarecrow falls in love with the broom and serenades her, only to find that she is engaged to a rake (Pullman, *The Scarecrow* 79). This tale of unrequited love is remembered by the Scarecrow throughout his quest when he periodically laments losing her, but it also pushes him to face great trials in spite of his loss. This is reminiscent of the tale of Cardenio, a story embedded within Quixote's narrative about a man who loses his true love Luscinda to another (Cervantes 234–43). Additionally, the tale of Master Pedro's traveling puppet show which Quixote destroys is evoked in Pullman's tale. Quixote is so caught up in the story of Don Gaiferos and his wife Melisendra that "he drew his sword and with one leap positioned himself in front of the stage, and with speedy and unprecedented fury began to hack at the hordes of puppet Moors, knocking some over, beheading others, wrecking this one, destroying that..." (Cervantes 666). Quixote never regains composure until he has ruined the puppet show beyond recognition.

Such a scene is alluded to in Pullman's story when the Scarecrow secures for himself a role as a prop in a play put on by a travelling company; he believes that the actors are actually brigands, and he attacks them until the scenery "came down with a screech of wood and a tearing of canvas, and in a moment there was nothing to be seen but a heap of painted scenery heaving and cursing, with arms and legs waving and disappearing and emerging again" (Pullman, *The Scarecrow* 52). The contrast between the scenes lies in a small detail: Quixote is an audience member, while the Scarecrow is a participant on stage; however, both are spurred to battle by the soldiers or brigands they mistake as true threats to the "actors" and each acts as the code of chivalry dictates, which leads to chaos and destruction. Quixote, for his part, argues his case, stating that if things have concluded differently than he intended, this is "the fault of the wicked ones who pursue me" (Cervantes 668), while the Scarecrow cries that he refuses to surrender and makes one final parting shot as he exits the destruction he wrought by freeing several caged birds while the bird-catcher is absent (Pullman, *The Scarecrow* 53).

There is also a clever nod in Pullman's work to a specific portion of

Cervantes' epic. In the prologue to Part I of *Don Quixote*, a poem appears called "Urganda the Unknowable" (Cervantes 18–20). An explanatory note on the poem by the translator reveals that its verse form is intentional, in that "the last unstressed syllable of each line [is] omitted, for the reader to fill it in" (Rutherford qtd. in Cervantes 984). The notes explain that this was a popular form of poetry in Spain when the novel was written (984). Pullman artfully evokes this verse form in his novel through the sentence patterns of the farmer with whom Jack and the Scarecrow stay the night. The farmer speaks but never finishes his thoughts, leaving them for Jack (and ostensibly the reader) to fill in. For instance, he asks Jack if he is looking for employment, then says "You couldn't have come at a better ... you know" (Pullman, *The Scarecrow* 62). He also fills in the empty words with non-words; to illustrate, "There's a dirty old pair of, umm, you know, in the woodshed.... There'll be a bite to, er, at sunset..." (62). In fact, the farmer's clipped phrases also link to his unwillingness to brand the Scarecrow as mad, but leave Jack (and the reader) to fill in that blank, when he says, "But — umm — he's a bit, er, well, isn't he? ... Then he's ... mmm ... is he?" (71). In fact, his style of speaking is adopted by Jack in this conversation (possibly because Jack, too, does not want to admit to someone else that his master is possibly insane), for Jack then says, "That's part of his cleverness. See when he's working, he never ... kind of thing ... there'd be no end of a — you know" (72). Just like the verse form in the prologue to *Don Quixote*, the omission of words encourages the reader to fill in the gaps but also encourages multiple meanings for the phrases while adding a sense of humor to the scene. One has to give Pullman credit for taking such a minor portion of *Don Quixote* and recalling it in such a clever and innovative way in his tale.

Thematically, the connections between Cervantes and Pullman are more broadly drawn, and they mingle flawlessly with the hero's journey and Pullman's recurring focus on innocence versus experience. In *The Power of Myth*, Joseph Campbell discusses the necessity of confronting situations that encourage growth of one's "higher nature" (130). Campbell states that Ortega y Gasset's *Meditations on Don Quixote* reveals the true conflict that "the last hero of the Middle Ages" faces is that the world has become mechanized and moved past the age of chivalry, and thus Quixote's "environment was no longer spiritually responsive to the hero" (130). Yet Campbell offers that Quixote was able to "save" the nature of his spiritual quest through the power of invention and transformation of his current world into elements that defy mechanization (130). Lord Scarecrow faces the same trial: he is a self-proclaimed gentleman farmer in a world where one large family, the Buffalonis, hold an immense amount of power and wish to "get hold of [Mr. Pandolfo's] land and divert all the springs and streams, and drain all the wells, and put up a factory to make weedkiller and rat poison and insecticide" (Pullman, *The Scarecrow* 2–3). Therefore, he, too, is fighting the forces of mechanization in an attempt to restore the image of the pastoral lifestyle to Spring Valley. Thus it isn't so much the individual battles of the quest that matter to each hero, but the ideological sum of the battles and their meaning to the hero's higher purpose, which is learning how to adapt his path to a world antithetical to his spiritual need.

Of course this notion ties in beautifully with the path from innocence to experience, for when each hero begins his quest as an innocent, he sees windmills or road signs and believes them to be brigands. Over the course of his journey, he learns to see things for what they truly are. This is his initiation, in which he might be said to face "the bottom of the abyss," at which "the darkest moment comes the light" (Campbell, *The Hero* 39). Of course in Cervantes' novel, Quixote reaches the abyss when he falls ill and his illusions are stripped away. Having lost his belief in chivalry which sustained him through his journey, he dies when faced with reality. He isn't able to "return" in the Campbellian sense to bring a boon upon his fellow man as death ends his quest. By contrast, Lord Scarecrow nearly dies when faced with treachery disguised by acceptance: having won in court against the Buffalonis, he is congratulated by them as a worthy adversary, yet he later realizes that the pats on the back were merely vehicles by which termites are delivered down his back, nearly destroying his body. Thankfully, those who support him rally to the cause and resurrect him from the edge, and he is able to continue on through his servant Jack's later years during which he recounts the stories of their adventures to Jack's children (Pullman, *The Scarecrow* 228–29), effectively making him a Campbellian boon-bringer.

The overarching narrative conflict in Pullman's novel centers on the ownership of Spring Valley and the "war" on the pastoral lifestyle by the dominating Buffalonis, who "get into everything" (Pullman, *The Scarecrow* 46). When the birds and the Scarecrow join forces to take the land back, they are faced with a tough court case and a judge who is himself a Buffaloni relation. With the lawyer and judge squarely on the side of the family who also makes up the United Benevolent Improvement Society, it seems that the land with its abundance will be lost to industrialization, pollution, and nepotism. Things appear to go the Scarecrow's way when he is able to prove to the court that his "inner conviction" (189) makes him the owner of the property. Furthermore, the paper which the Piccolinis witnessed Mr. Pandolfo sign designates that "Spring Valley with all its buildings and springs and wells and watercourses and ponds and streams and fountains [belongs] to the said scarecrow" (195) and even claims the Buffalonis are "a pack of scoundrels" (195), so the case seems solid. However, in a clever courtroom maneuver, the idea of ownership comes into play, namely, that the Scarecrow has been reconstructed throughout the tale from all new parts, making him quite a different scarecrow than the one to whom Mr. Pandolfo willed his land (198–200). Yet Granny Raven proves that portions of the Scarecrow (his pea brain and parts of his former turnip head) were ingested by Bernard the blackbird and by Jack, and thus he still exists, in a manner of speaking, which allows him to win the case (203–08).

One of the themes of *Don Quixote* is that of ownership and authorship, specifically, of truth and fiction in narrative. Through shifting narrative perspectives in the different sections of his novel and even subtle shifts when tales are presented within the larger narrative construct, Cervantes' work is about the blurring of lines between fact and fiction. It can be said that Pullman works with this theme in his novel through the court case and through the reconstruction of the continuously disintegrating scarecrow. By the time he appears in court, every single part of him has been "replaced," and he never does get his "brain" back (perhaps a clever nod to *The Wizard of Oz* lies here), but his personality and spirit remain intact. In fact, in the final operation of the book, the Scarecrow needs a new "spine" as his is termite-damaged. In a lighthearted twist, he is reunited with his long-lost love, the broomstick, whose "fiance the rake had left her for a feather duster" (Pullman, *The Scarecrow* 227), and who, like the Scarecrow, was "passed from hand to hand" (227) until she ended up attached to him both literally and figuratively at the conclusion of the story. Somehow the Scarecrow is able to lose all physical traces of existence but retain his inner conviction, reunite with his former object of affection, and gain ownership over all of Spring Valley because such an ending bears out the trajectory of the pastoral tradition. He is governed by two things: "Life and hope!" (136). As long as there are those who believe in him who keep these ideals alive, he is resurrected to live another day and tell future generations his pastoral tales. Quixote, by contrast, holds ownership over the pastoral world as long as he can keep those around him believing in the ideals of chivalry. When he becomes ill and no longer believes in such a world himself, the pastoral world comes crashing down, and the days of the knight errant and his squire must sadly cease. Clearly Pullman's quixotic quest, therefore, ends with a greater sense of hope and innocence that the days of old can persist in a new world, whereas Cervantes' work concludes with a more cynical vision.

Conclusion

When Pullman was writing *His Dark Materials*, he was frequently asked to reveal the form of his own dæmon. Pullman usually gave two different answers. Sometimes, he would say that it is useless to name one's dæmon because one invariably ends up proclaiming what one wants it to be rather that what it is; instead, one should ask one's friends to tell him or her because he claimed that those who knew us best would be more honest with us than we would be ourselves. His second answer to this question, though, was that his dæmon would be a jackdaw or magpie, because this bird has a penchant for stealing bright and shiny things. He said that as a storyteller, this is what he did — steal from other writers.[4] In *The Scarecrow and His Servant*, Pullman describes an incident during which Jack discovers that their bag has been stolen, and with it, all their food. The Scarecrow claims to know the identity of the culprit when he finds an owl pellet lying in the ditch. He initially tells Jack that the thief must have been an owl, yet he quickly changes his mind, and says, "It must have been a jackdaw, and he left the owl pellet to throw us off the scent. Can you believe the villainy of these birds? They have no shame" (Pullman, *The Scarecrow* 59). Jack agrees, "No.... None at all" (59).

Pullman tends to be quite self-deprecating in interviews, and as we have seen at the conclusion of Aladdin with his nod to those lucky enough to find a wealthy patron, he finds a way to poke a bit of fun at himself in many of his stories. Had Pullman simply taken the iconic scenes from Quixote and inserted them into his tale, we might agree he is a "shameful" storyteller; however, his adaptation becomes a new literary creation when such elements are crafted so intricately, and as we've seen in *The Firework-Maker's Daughter*, the presence of Campbell's monomyth is merely the structure on which he loosely bases his protagonists' journeys, while the details of plot and character are entirely new creations. Pullman's strength, therefore, in these quest-driven tales, is the way he honors old traditions while creating new works destined to be classics, both of which perfectly illustrate that the path from innocence to experience can be planted with the seeds of joy, laughter, and hope.

Three

Count Karlstein, or The Ride of the Demon Huntsman
The Influence of German Romanticism and the Gothic on an Evolving Text

> "The first children's novel I wrote was an adaptation of a story I'd done originally as a play.... I've rewritten it since then as a picture book, so it's had three incarnations. Maybe one day it'll be a T-shirt."
>
> — Philip Pullman, "I have a feeling this all belongs to me"[1]

With his characteristic tongue-in-cheek humor, Philip Pullman describes the genesis of his first children's novel, *Count Karlstein, or The Ride of the Demon Huntsman*, which exists in four incarnations, sans T-shirt. Beginning as a school play, the 1982 Chatto and Windus first edition of the text includes a frame story consisting of parts one and three told by Hildi Kelmar, a character, while part two is titled "Narratives by Various Hands" and presents the action from the point of view of several other characters (53). The next version, published in 1991 by Doubleday, resembles a graphic novel, featuring condensed narrative sections interspersed with drawings by illustrator Patrice Aggs. The point of view is primarily third person omniscient, and the chapters are reorganized to aid the shift in voice. The most recent version, published by Dell Yearling in 1998, removes the illustrations of the 1991 graphic novel but includes silhouette drawings by Diana Bryan; it also returns to the polyphonic narration of the first published version with few changes other than minor grammatical alterations or modifications to a character's name (i.e., using a character's full name in place of the first name only). A visual update incorporates different fonts to signal changes in narrative point of view.

Three. Count Karlstein, or The Ride of the Demon Huntsman

Through the various incarnations of one text, Pullman illustrates the point he often makes about the power of telling the same basic story via different methods. During his years in the classroom, he learned that a gifted instructor and storyteller knows many ways to reach his or her audience, and the distinct versions of *Count Karlstein* prove his point. It is tough to say one version of the text is "better" as such a decision is likely affected by personal preference, but arguably the multi-voiced narrative is the most complex. Because Pullman rarely creates variants of his own works,[2] these texts offer a unique opportunity to assess his range as a storyteller.

Complicating the number of variations on a theme by Pullman, further analysis proves that *Count Karlstein* is not entirely original. At the conclusion of the 1991 publication, Pullman includes a list of "Works consulted and ideas stolen from" (110). A compilation of 15 different literary pieces, works of art, films, and even a police handbook includes the opera *Der Freischütz*, by Carl Maria von Weber. Pullman is always quite candid about his influences, and in James Carter's *Talking Books: Children's Authors Talk About the Craft, Creativity, and Process of Writing*, Pullman says that his favorite 19th century music is Weber's opera (180). William Gray's "Pullman, Lewis, MacDonald and the Anxiety of Influence" addresses the concept of literary filiation as it relates to Pullman's work. Gray's argument concerns Harold Bloom's seminal work *The Anxiety of Influence* (1973), in which Bloom contends that lyric poets are never "self-contained" (qtd. in Gray 117). Gray asserts that Bloom's theory can be adapted to include writers of other genres than poetry, most specifically, to so-called "fantasy" writing, on the grounds that Bloom himself acknowledged this idea in his 1980 paper "'Clinamen: Towards a Theory of Fantasy'" (117). Bloom argues that in order for a writer to achieve his own voice, he "must necessarily *misread* a significant precursor" (qtd. in Gray 118). Gray cites part of Pullman's author's note in the acknowledgments of *The Amber Spyglass*, which reads, "I have stolen ideas from every book I have ever read. My principle in researching for a novel is 'Read like a butterfly, write like a bee,' and if this story contains any honey, it is entirely because of the quality of the nectar I found in the work of better writers" (Pullman, *The Amber Spyglass* n. pag.).

Taking together the fact that Pullman is so open about his influences or, as he calls it, outright thefts, and the fact that his very first novel for children includes a character "Zamiel," which is derived from Samiel in

Weber's opera, Gray concludes that Pullman's work is arguably linked to German romanticism (128). Furthermore, Gray notes that while Pullman has argued against placing too much stock in the intricacies of postmodernism, "some critics have found in his work an (inter) textually promiscuous postmodern pluralism" (119). The rest of Gray's piece considers Pullman's "anxiety of influence" as it relates to the work of MacDonald; however, he raises an intriguing point that will be discussed in depth in this chapter: what exactly is the influence of Weber's opera on Pullman's first version of *Count Karlstein*, and furthermore, how has Pullman reflected "textually promiscuous postmodern pluralism" in his revisions of his own novel? Lastly, how do these textual revisions bring character growth on the path from innocence to experience to the forefront of the story?

Carl Maria von Weber's Der Freischütz: The "Parent" Text

Der Freischütz[3] (1821), translated *The Freeshooter* or *The Marksman*, is considered to be "the work which defined and established German romantic opera" (Rahn 546). Utilizing a folklore motif, Carl Maria Freidrick Ernst von Weber (1786–1826) created a story which mingles elements of nature and the supernatural in a plot which concerns the battle of good versus evil. The protagonist, Max, makes a pact with Samiel, representing the devil, who provides him with magic bullets that will help him attain victory in a contest and win the object of his affection, Agathe (546). Weber's opera opens at a woodland tavern, where Max, a forester, has just lost a marksmanship contest to Kilian, a wealthy peasant. A procession forms as the villagers praise Kilian's skill until Max angrily grabs Kilian. When the head forester Kuno questions what is happening, Kilian says that they are only teasing Max for having missed the mark so many times. Kaspar, another forester, blames Samiel for Max's performance and instructs Max to "Go to a crossroads next Friday and call three times on the great huntsman" (Weber). Kuno quiets Kaspar but also tells Max that if he misses again in "the trial shot," he will lose the love of his life. The trial shot is a test to grant the "hereditary post of ranger" to the most talented marksman (Weber), a tradition handed down from Kuno's ancestor who made an extraordinarily challenging shot. Max laments his fate, realizing the stakes are so critical. Max says, "Invisible powers are angry/Dread

Three. Count Karlstein, or The Ride of the Demon Huntsman

foreboding fills my breast!/I could never bear the loss!" (Weber). Kuno tells him to trust in God as the huntsmen leave.

Once Max is alone, "Samiel enters, almost superhuman in height, dressed in dark green and flame colour with gold. His tall hat decked with a cock's feather" (Weber). He hides in the background as Max contemplates his position. Then Kaspar enters and "drops something from a flask into the glass for Max" and calls on Samiel for help (Weber). He gives the wine to Max and tells him they are alone. Max seems hesitant, but Kaspar implores him to drink, exclaiming, "Long life to our Lord the Prince! Anyone who doesn't subscribe to that is a Judas" (Weber). Encouraged, Max drinks and becomes somewhat altered, "like a light but malicious drunkeness [sic]" (Weber). Kaspar tempts him to shoot at large eagle above. Just as Max is about to fire, Kaspar says, "Shoot, in the devil's name! Ha, ha!" (Weber). Max makes the impossible shot and wonders how he did so, and Kaspar explains that he used a free bullet. If he wants another, he must go to the Wolf's Glen at midnight. When Max hesitates, Kaspar tells him he must master his fear and follow through or he will lose Agathe, while Samiel overhears this exchange.

Act II begins with Annchen, Agathe's cousin, nailing to the wall a portrait of Kuno's ancestor, which had recently fallen and injured Agathe. Left alone, Agathe worries about Max when she notices a storm off in the distance, "a clump/Of dark clouds, brooding and heavy" (Weber). Her mood changes when Max arrives with what she thinks are flowers on his hat, emblematic of him making the shot. However, she soon notices that his hat has a featherplume which "puts the lamp out," plunging the room into darkness (Weber). He is agitated, and she begs him to tell her what happened. He explains he has "fetched down the greatest bird of prey" and notices she is bleeding (Weber). They realize that the picture fell and hit her at the precise moment he killed the great mountain bird. He indicates he must leave again because he has shot a stag near the Wolf Glen that he must retrieve. Calling the place "the glen of terror" (Weber), Agathe begs him not to go, but he does.

Meanwhile, Kaspar and invisible spirits are in the forest. At midnight, Kaspar casts a spell and calls forth Samiel, who "comes from the rock" (Weber). Kaspar admits that his "term" expires the next day, but he can lengthen the term with a sacrifice (Weber). He tells Samiel to make him 7 bullets and direct the 7th free shot to Agathe, in hopes that "despair will make him [Max] yours" (Weber). Samiel agrees and says that either Max or Kaspar must be sacrificed, then he disappears. Max looks down onto the Wolf's Glen and works up his courage to enter. Max says to Kaspar, "I cannot turn back—my destiny calls!" (Weber). As he tries to climb down, Max is initially startled by his mother's ghost who warns him back, but the image of Agathe about to throw herself into the waterfall leads him back down as the darkness falls around him. Kaspar mixes the ingredients and casts the spell while Max watches him make the magic bullets, as everything around them shifts into a terrifying supernatural scene. As Samiel appears, the storm quiets, and Max and Kaspar are visibly shaken.

Act III begins in Agathe's room, where, dressed in white, she sing about goodness, devotion, and protection from the creator. She relates her symbolic dream to Annchen who provides a less ominous interpretation and a story about a relative's dream which came to nothing, but she is unable to quiet Agathe's distress. The bridesmaids enter and dance and sing around Agathe, telling her that the picture has fallen again. Annchen hands her a box which shockingly contains not a bridal wreath but a funeral wreath. Agathe reads this, too, as an ill omen, although Annchen claims that the boxes were simply mixed up (Weber).

The scene changes to the outdoors where everyone is assembled. Prince Ottokar is in attendance and eagerly awaits Kuno's choice of marksman. Ottokar tells Max to shoot the white dove; having seen the white dove in her dream, Agathe comes through the trees and tells Max not to shoot, for "the dove is me!" (Weber). Max makes the shot and Agathe and Kaspar fall while the onlookers exclaim, "He hit his own bride!" (Weber). Yet Agathe awakens, felled only by her own fear, while Kaspar dies, crying, "Heaven has conquered!/All's up with me!" (Weber). The prince asks Max to explain what transpired, and Max says that he shot four free bullets that morning and that he had been tempted by Kaspar, "turned from the paths/Of piety and righteousness [*sic*]" (Weber). An argument ensues about whether he should still win Agathe's hand, and Kuno and Agathe and the hunstmen and chorus beg for leniency. A hermit comes forward to say that love and despair often cause people to stray from the path. He says, "Who is to raise the first stone?/Who does not look into his own heart?" (Weber). He asks for the trial shot to be discontinued and for Max to serve a penalty for his actions, at which time he can reclaim Agathe. Prince Ottokar agrees, and the opera ends with the characters committing their love and trust in "the Father" and pledging to follow the path of the righteous (Weber).

Three. Count Karlstein, or The Ride of the Demon Huntsman

It is easy to see why such a piece would intrigue Pullman. Weber's tale centers on the classic battle of good versus evil, and the heart of it surrounds the pull of temptation and a deal with the devil. Incidentally, Pullman's *Clockwork, or All Wound Up*, may also have been influenced by Weber's work, for it, too, emphasizes a Faustian plot in which the character Karl resembles Weber's Kaspar, and a character named Prince Otto recalls Prince Ottokar at least in name.[4] Additionally, the power of Gretl's love in *Clockwork* saves Prince Florian, just as the power of Agathe's love assists Max in obtaining a pardon. Yet Pullman makes significantly more allusions to Weber's opera in *Count Karlstein, or the Ride of the Demon Huntsman*, and the following analysis will elucidate the elements he retained in his first published children's novel and its variants and then move on to interpret the texts in their own right. Since the graphic novel version of 1991 bears the closest resemblance to Weber's opera in plot progression, this text will be considered first. Then, the 1982 and 1998 editions will be measured together because there are few differences between them but vast distinctions from the graphic novel. No matter the version, though, Pullman was heavily influenced by German Romanticism and the Gothic tradition, and his latest revision to multi-voiced (and multi-font) point of view heightens the motif of the quest of the innocent and its impact on character maturity.

Count Karlstein *(1991 edition)*

Readers of Pullman's graphic novel edition of *Count Karlstein* immediately notice the structural features of the narrative. Containing nine chapters and an overture, the chapter titles are presented in the same grammatical structure, with a title, a comma, and an alternative title offered, such as "The Orphans, or The Deadly Oath" (Pullman 15) and "Love, or Sausages" (37). The overture is not titled in the same fashion; rather, its name is "The Wolf's Glen" (11), which directly references the location of the pact with Samiel in Weber's opera. The table of contents is followed by a two-page list of characters, many of whom are classified by name and some identifying characteristic, such as "Arturo Snivelwurst, Count Karlstein's secretary" (n. pag.). The list also includes various other objects that play a part, such as "A suit of armor," "Two elderly phantoms," "A wig-stand," and "A bearskin rug" (n. pag.). Illustrations are placed next to every

Part I: Stories of Innocence

"character" to identify each later in the text. One may conclude that Pullman is intentionally alluding to certain characters of Weber's opera (i.e., "German romanticism") through his character list while also referencing the Gothic tradition, by featuring personified objects that later play active if minor roles in the narrative.

In the few pages after the story ends, Pullman also delineates the works that have inspired him (110), while he also provides a list of "works referred to in the text" (110). Pullman's clever humor is evident here, for many of the sources are not real, and the authors include "A Governess" or "Another Lady" or "One Who Is Almost a Lady" (110); however, these works sound legitimate, and his characters familiar with gothic literature introduce the selections when they are pertinent to the plot. This blurs the line between fantasy and reality, which is one of the hallmarks of gothic literature, and it cues the reader into Pullman's extensive use of parody. He ends his text with two pages of advertisements, including an ad for "Zamiel Shoe Repairs: New Soles for Old" along with a few other ads that make reference to objects in his New Cut Gang books.[5] Thus, the structure of the text shows the influence of Weber's opera, the gothic tradition, parodic elements, and even intertextuality, all while setting the tone for a narrative presented primarily through comic-book style panels and illustrations.

Pullman's graphic novel begins with a meeting between Count Karlstein and Zamiel; Karlstein's wishes are granted for 10 years, in exchange for bringing Zamiel a new soul to avoid losing his own. The narrative then shifts abruptly to Sergeant Snitsch who announces the escape of a prisoner who goes by several aliases; he hopes the upcoming shooting contest will bring the villain out. Two sisters, Lucy and Charlotte, were orphaned when their parents died in a shipwreck, so they are under the care of their uncle Heinrich Müller, aka Count Karlstein. After a short interaction with their uncle, Count Karlstein decides he will sacrifice his nieces to Zamiel. Hildi, the maidservant, overhears him tell his plan to his secretary, Arturo Snivelwurst, so she informs the girls about Zamiel and urges them to escape. The next day, guests arrive for the contest, and the most interesting is a Miss Augusta Davenport and her maid, Eliza, who arrive so Augusta can explore and work on her experiments. Augusta has a robust personality and refuses to trifle with anyone who gets in her way, and she is arrested quickly after her arrival when she causes conflict for the Sergeant and his Constable who are trying to screen visitors for the escaped criminal. It

Three. Count Karlstein, or The Ride of the Demon Huntsman

quickly becomes apparent to the reader that Dr. Dante Cadavarezzi is the man they seek, though he outsmarts the police by saying he intends to help them find the criminal (11–36).

Meanwhile, Lucy and Charlotte, who have been trying to follow Hildi's directions to the mountain hut where Hildi's brother wanted for poaching is also hiding, become lost. Back at the Jolly Hunstman pub, Eliza runs into her lover Max Grindoff, from whom she has been separated. Max had spent some time in prison and was offered a position to help Dr. Cadaverezzi with his traveling exhibition when he became a free man. When the reunited Max and Eliza are told by Herr Snivelwurst that if they find the lost girls, they will get a reward, they are eager to earn the prize money so they can finally get married. When they set off to find the lost girls, readers learn that Miss Davenport has escaped and gone to see Count Karlstein herself to inquire about the girls she knew as students from her academy. Karlstein puts her off, claiming the girls are physically and mentally ill. She agrees to leave, but her suspicions are aroused, and she decides to search for the girls (Pullman 37–49).

When Herr Snivelwurst finds Lucy and Charlotte, he grabs Charlotte and locks her in a tower. Lucy escapes to the Jolly Huntsman where she finds Dr. Cadaverezzi, who gives her a position in his magic act because he has a soft spot for refugees. Back in the forest, Miss Davenport encounters Max, Eliza, and then Hildi; knowing that Hildi's brother Peter is a huntsman, she takes her silver bracelet, given to her by her long-lost lover Signor Rolipolio, and tells Hildi that Peter will know what to do. Hildi takes the bracelet to Peter and he crafts a silver bullet. Back at the Jolly Huntsman, Doctor Cadaverezzi performs and ridicules Count Karlstein to the audience's delight, but Lucy ends up in jeopardy again when she is recognized. A Genevan inspector identifies Dr. Cadaverezzi as the escaped criminal Luigi Brilliantini. In the chaos that ensues, Lucy is captured again by Count Karlstein and Snivelwurst (Pullman 50–72).

All this time, the others have been trying to rescue Charlotte; Max is almost at the top of the tower when the Count comes and takes Charlotte away. Finally trapped at the hunting lodge, the girls read a letter from Miss Davenport that tells them not to worry. Eliza, Max, Peter, and Hildi arrive at the lodge and Peter attempts a rescue via the balcony, but Max takes the musket and a silver bullet and shoots through the lock, freeing the girls. As the clock strikes midnight, Zamiel arrives, but since Peter, a huntsman, is with the group, Zamiel lets them go free. Instead, he goes

Part I: Stories of Innocence

after the true target, Count Karlstein, who runs away but is followed by Zamiel and his phantom hounds (Pullman 73–86).

The next day, the marksmanship contest is held, and Max clumsily misses the shot. However, Peter makes the mark, and thus becomes a free man because only free men can be Forest Rangers. Of course, there are still loose ends, such as Lucy and Charlotte's future, now that Count Karlstein is gone. However, the true heir to the Karlstein estate is revealed as a person who was abandoned as an infant, orphaned, and then became a soldier. The only object that can identify him is a half of a coin. Eliza happens to be wearing this artifact around her neck, because Max gave it to her when he proposed marriage. The two halves fit, proving Max to be the true heir to the Karlstein estate. Because this links him to the girls by blood, he and Eliza offer to take them in to keep them from the orphanage. The last loose end concerns Miss Davenport and her long-lost lover, Signor Rolipolio, but when she sees Dr. Cadaverezzi, she realizes they are one and the same. With these two reunited, all story threads are accounted for, and the tale ends with a final panel illustrating the future lives of the characters on a winter's eve, in the parlor, with everyone immersed in the stories of the demon huntsman Zamiel (Pullman 87–109).

The first allusion to *Der Freischütz* appears in the overture titled "The Wolf's Glen," in which Heinrich Müller, later known as Count Karlstein, blows a hunting horn three times to summon Zamiel, the Demon Huntsman, on All Soul's Eve (Pullman 12). Asking for an honorable name, accolades, and a wealthy estate, Zamiel tells Heinrich that he will have all he requests for 10 years, at which point he must bring him a soul to sacrifice or lose his own (13–14). While the terms of the pact differ between the opera and the novel, the motif of the pact and the identity of the "devil" character and location of his "lair" remain the same. From this point the stories differ significantly, but the threads of Weber's opera are taken up later with the climactic marksmanship competition and Count Karlstein's demise. Several of Pullman's characters double those in Weber's opera: Count Karlstein represents Kaspar; Max Grindoff and Peter Kelmar embody Max; Eliza epitomizes Agathe; Zamiel stands in for Samiel; Hildi Kelmar symbolizes Annchen; Herr Pistlpacker doubles Kuno. Pullman's final chapters concern the shooting contest which is similar to Weber's in that the prize given to the best marksman is the title of forest ranger; however, Pullman uses two characters to evoke one of Weber's characters. Early in Weber's work, Max is ridiculed for missing his marks. With

Three. Count Karlstein, or The Ride of the Demon Huntsman

Kaspar's encouragement and worry that he will lose the love of his life, it is he who makes the pact with Samiel to obtain the magic bullets to win the competition. Pullman's Max Grindoff, who is in love with Eliza, enters the competition, but his poor shooting skills are never remedied because he never makes a deal with the devil, so he does not win the competition and instead provides comic relief to the story. A second marksman must enter to win, and Peter Kelmar, who is wanted for a crime he did not commit, is allowed to shoot because he is a *free man* until the contest is over (97). Therefore, Peter as a character represents the *free shot* that Max takes in *Der Freischütz*. When he hits the mark, Peter then becomes a free man permanently, "because only a *free* man can be a Forest Ranger" (99).

While most of the character pairs are easily evident to readers, the pairing of Hildi Kelmar and Annchen is less obvious but worth exploring. In reading Der Freischütz, one may conclude that Annchen, Agathe's cousin, is the voice of reason and objectivity to Agathe's more fanciful and melodramatic persona. Hildi functions in much the same way though she plays a much larger role in Pullman's text, due to the complexity of his narrative, which contains a few plotlines that have no connection at all to Weber's opera. Like Annchen, who remains calm in the face of adversity, Hildi, a maidservant, acts as Lucy and Charlotte's protector and aids them in escaping from their uncle, Count Karlstein, who plans to sacrifice them in place of himself. Hildi is also nearly unshakable in the face of disaster, resourceful in her thinking, quick on her feet, and a rational and logical advocate for the safety of her young charges. Like Annchen, she is an atypical female character in a genre that is usually heavily populated by the damsel in distress type.

Aside from the allusions to *Der Freischütz*, Pullman's work is heavily influenced by gothic conventions. One gothic trope that stands out is his use of personification. All of the following objects "speak" in thought bubbles throughout the narrative: a tree, a book, a suit of armor, four mounted animal heads, two ghosts, a skull, a portrait, a wig-stand, an owl, a cuckoo clock, a bearskin rug, and a gargoyle (9). Typically the items provide warnings or commentary on the deceptive and untrustworthy characters in the narrative, and may function as the voice of the omniscient narrator or the voice of the skeptical reader. Interestingly, of all the personified objects, the book that speaks has the most intriguing monologue. The book is an invented gothic novel that Lucy is reading at the beginning of the story, titled *Amelia, or The Phantom of the Vault*. When Charlotte tells Lucy to look out the window, the book protests, "Don't interrupt!" (18), and when they both are distracted, it exclaims, "Oy! Pay attention!" (19). One wonders if the book is speaking to the girls, or to the reader, instructing her not to be caught up in fancy but to pay attention to the plot. When they finally get back to reading again, the book says, "About time, too. Here's Amelia and the Phantom kicking their heels, waiting to be read about.... Inconsiderate blooming readers..." (22). Since the reader of Pullman's text is temporarily distracted from the plot every time her eye falls on the words coming from a picture of a book inside another book, the reader herself is doubled and becomes like the girls, caught between the storytelling experience found in gothic fiction versus their harrowing real-life experience which may or may not be heightened by their exposure to the Gothic. As the girls' real life becomes more amazing and scary than the material they read, Lucy exclaims that their fate is worse than the fictional character Amelia's. The book shouts, "WHAT?" (25) and as the girls pack and wait for their chance to escape, the book is abandoned, left on the floor, and its last words are "Deplorable! Life imitating art! ... And they haven't even shut me properly!" (26).

In "Frightening and Funny: Humor in Children's Gothic Fiction," Julie Cross discusses the prevalence of works published in "the comic gothic" genre in the past few decades (57). She explains that much of the comic gothic meant for younger readers is quite sophisticated, depending on readers' ability to grasp elements of "irony, parody, genre convention, and 'higher' order cognitive forms of humour" (58). She discusses the divide between writers and critics who assert that children lack the sophistication to appreciate or understand higher level humor versus those who argue that exposing children to more complex material earlier may encourage them to understand it sooner than they are given credit (63–64). Indicating that "they have to work at the text" (64), Cross is evidently one who argues that young readers should be exposed to complex texts early and taught how to read such material (64). Pullman feels passionately about treating young readers with respect. So when Pullman created his cast of characters and anthropomorphized many in order to allow these objects to make comments both sarcastic and silly, was he doing so for his adult audience only? Not likely. As readers have seen in his children's picture books like *Puss in Boots*, he often works with illustrations to add both humor and an additional layer of narration, humor by which any younger

Three. Count Karlstein, or The Ride of the Demon Huntsman

reader could at the simplest level, be entertained, and at the more complex level, be educated about complexities such as irony and parody.

Cross adds that parody is also created in the comic Gothic by "the overt, intrusive, opinionated and often ironic narrator of melodrama" (70). Readers are exposed to irony through Pullman's chapter titles, which present an alternative heading following the first and mimic the style of the faux book names that Lucy and Charlotte discuss during their adventure. The girls' ability to remember all the plot lines and alternate titles for their favorite stories shows the hold the Gothic has over them, and the influence of this genre combined with their own near capture by the demon huntsman is so enthralling to them that the final panel of Pullman's novel shows the persistence of such obsessions even after his tale has ended. In the picture, a slightly older Max and Eliza sit in a parlor while Max is telling what appears to be their three children an embellished version of the story in which he "looked him [likely Zamiel] in the eye, and I took me musket, and..." (Pullman 108). Lucy is shown still reading the story of Amelia and the Phantom (109). Charlotte, sitting at a desk, has a stack of three pages to her left, while she writes on a new sheet with a quill pen "Chapter One" of the book *Count Karlstein* (109).

There are two ways one might interpret the stack of papers to her left; clearly the pile, a bit dog-eared, is the front matter of the text — the table of contents and list of characters (although it should be noted Charlotte has already shifted the narrative slightly in that the phrase "In the depths of the deepest" actually begins the Overture, not Chapter One). A second way to interpret that pile of papers is to say it is self-referential. It is common knowledge that Pullman has always written three pages per day, no more, no less. He prides himself on his discipline about his craft (Mountford).[6] Therefore, because Charlotte writes the book *Count Karlstein*, which Pullman himself altered through different styles of publication, just as she is already altering it slightly, Charlotte *is* Pullman. One final way to read this panel, though, is to suggest that Pullman may also be observing the action from up on the wall, for above Charlotte's desk are the mounted head of the stag and the boar, who say to one another, "Stories! They can't do without 'em!" and "Keeps 'em happy..." (109). Of course, Pullman is also noted for his copious commentary on the importance of storytelling. Cross says that writers who use parody in the comic Gothic do not attack the form but create "a playful imitation" of it (71). In this way, Cross concludes that "such texts are actually self-reflexive and foreground their own textuality, and this can ... provide young readers with a subconscious awareness of deliberately constructed literary devices" (71).

In an interview in *Talking Books* in 1999, when Pullman was asked which one of his characters he would most like to be, he replied, "Dr. Cadaverezzi ... because he's a showman, a magician, and a conjurer" (qtd. in Carter 180). Considering how much of Pullman himself can be seen through the use of personification in this novel, one can understand the connection. Dr. Cadaverezzi has many "disguises"; he goes by many different names, and he's seen as a trickster. Pullman himself is a trickster through this text, as he finds ways to let the various characters tell the story without there being an obvious authorial presence, but he interjects his opinions on the Gothic, on books, and on storytelling through the thought bubbles attributed to inanimate objects. Regarding both *Count Karlstein* and *Spring-Heeled Jack*, the subject of the next chapter, Pullman says that he "was just trying to be a film director in a way, and telling stories in pictures and words" (qtd. in Carter 193). He further explains that he even created "working pictures" for his illustrators on both of these novels because the pictures had to tell some of the story (193). Thus, the primary strength of the illustrated version of *Count Karlstein* is the use of pictures and monologue to tell a story behind the story, one which reflects Pullman's penchant for being a bit of a showman and disguise artist.

Count Karlstein *(1982 and 1998 editions)*

A glance through the published reviews of Pullman's *Count Karlstein* leads one to assume that his first full-length novel for children was virtually unnoticed when it was published in 1982 by Chatto and Windus. In fact, the illustrated 1991 edition published by Doubleday in London also stayed low on the radar. It was not until the 1998 edition published by Dell Yearling in the U.S. that the reviewers began to write about it and to praise the strength of Pullman's "first" children's novel, which accounts for why any reader who knows the earlier editions might be a bit confused. There are few differences between the 1982, 1998, and later reprints, with the most significant being a change in fonts. Because several chapters are told by different characters, the later editions use font changes to signal visually the narrative voices, although Patricia A. Dolisch's review asserts that the visual cues are not necessary because the characters are so "flawlessly drawn"

Three. Count Karlstein, or The Ride of the Demon Huntsman

(208). Otherwise, there are only occasional minor alterations, such as Hildi introducing herself as Hildi Kelmar instead of simply Hildi. The chapters are organized the same and the text is almost entirely consistent. One last subtle difference lies in the use of silhouette illustrations of characters in the later versions whereas the Chatto and Windus printing is free of illustrations. Because these editions are nearly identical, both will be contrasted simultaneously with the graphic novel version.[7]

Because Pullman originally conceived of *Count Karlstein* as a story told by many narrators, it is not as if by the third edition he "improved" the text. Rather, he simply departed from its style in the graphic novel to explore an alternative way to tell the story, and having done so, reissued a version that "restored" the polyphonic narration years later. This style of narration results in a richer, more complex, and at times, darker tale, because with events told from different perspectives, the text reads somewhat like a traditional Gothic novel, particularly in the chapters told by Hildi, Lucy, and Charlotte, because there is a wealth of physical description, creating a more chilling and enthralling atmosphere than the graphic novel's more light-hearted, fast-paced romp. There is also a distinct parodying of the melodramatic syntax of the Gothic in their narratives, most of all in Charlotte's sections. Additionally, the story is framed dissimilarly. The graphic novel is outlined by the story of Zamiel and Karlstein's pact with him. Therefore, the graphic novel has a plot-driven frame. The other versions, though, are enclosed by Hildi's narrative. By placing a character into the action and directing her to tell the story, the frame is character-driven. Hildi begins and ends with the story of Zamiel, but the primary account concerns Hildi's quest to save Lucy, Charlotte, and her brother Peter, all of whom face death or imprisonment. Because Hildi is focused on helping to save others, she emerges as the central protagonist while she plays only a small part in the graphic novel which lacks a central hero or heroine. Consequently, Hildi's struggle is made prominent, and readers may see her grow to learn who can and cannot be trusted to act in the best interests of the innocent.

Patricia A. Dolisch suggests that the book is "mined with almost every gothic device possible" and a good start for readers who have moved beyond the work of R.L. Stine but who are not yet prepared for Horace Walpole's fiction (208). In terms of his literary influences, Pullman certainly draws heavily from the work of Ann Radcliffe. Hildi provides a direct link to Radcliffe when she says that at night, Lucy and Charlotte often read

Part I: Stories of Innocence

"ghostly romances — *The Mysteries of Udolpho*, or *Zastrozzi*, or *Mathilda*" (Pullman 22). Many of the novels referenced in the text are inventions, but these three texts are real, and Radcliffe's *Udolpho*, the "most famous and most imitated of [her] six novels" (Botting 65), is parodied most frequently in Pullman's text.

Fred Botting's *Gothic: The New Critical Idiom* identifies several typical settings in Radcliffe's work, which include "dark forests and spectacular mountain regions populated by bandits and robbers" (64). Part of the reason that the 1998 edition comes in at 243 pages as compared to the 1992 edition's 109 pages derives from the long descriptive passages that render the beauty and terror of the harsh landscape. Hildi lacks Lucy and Charlotte's private school education, but her early exposure to storytelling with her brother and the material she likely overhears from two young girls well-versed in Gothic conventions has taught her romantic sensibilities, expressed beautifully in her reaction to the waterfall they come to in the forest: "A thick crust of spiky, sugary, bristly spears glinted and shone in the moonlight, all set about with a million tiny diamond-sharp stars of frost ... the little stream tinkled in a subdued sort of way, like a child put grumbling to bed too early for its liking. The world by moonlight could be lovely as well as threatening" (32). As Botting argues, Radcliffe's heroines tend "to overindulge their emotions, partaking too heavily of the cult of sensibility" (65); such characters become overly fearful, engaging in wild speculation, extremes of emotions, and react with astonishment, shock, or horror at their surroundings. A fine illustration of this Gothic device is seen in Lucy's description of the mountains. At first, she describes the grandeur of the moonlight, the crags, the cliffs, the precipices, and the carapaces. Then, she admits, "I do not know what a carapace is, but I am sure there were some" (Pullman 157). This bit of comic relief through Gothic parody, aimed at Lucy's overindulgence in both emotion and language, is followed by a passage that could have come straight from Radcliffe or Walpole: "The unearthly beauty of the scene — like some Vision from the works of Byron or Shelley — filled our hearts with strange longings. It was easy to believe, in that dreamlike setting, in the Spirits and Phantoms of folklore" (157).

There lies a subtle difference between Lucy and Charlotte's narrative passages; though both are strongly influenced by Gothic conventions such as the emphasis of certain words via capitalization or the tendency to evoke extremes of emotion in their descriptions of characters, events, and scenery,

Three. Count Karlstein, or The Ride of the Demon Huntsman

Charlotte, who is 10, sees the Gothic as something playful, while Lucy, who is 12, is much more serious (Pullman 28). It is Charlotte, for instance, who offers references to books that they have read as she makes connections between their plight and the trials of famous heroines, all from novels whose titles follow the same grammatical structure, such as *Marianna, the Captive of the Abruzzi* (111). Charlotte sees the Gothic in everything around her as she becomes the character of her own Gothic story, so it is no surprise when she is locked in a room that she investigates her surroundings, and after initially fearing a wig on a head-shaped wig stand, she dubs him Herr Woodenkopf and befriends him, treating him like a living being (114–18). It is likely that Charlotte becomes the writer or at least transcriber of Max Grindoff's narrative, for he explains that "not being very handy with the pen, I am speaking this to a certain young person who is writing it down for me" (123). Noting several times that he is being urged by the young person (a "she") to get on with his story, it seems most likely that Charlotte, the more natural, fanciful storyteller, presents Max's tale. Pullman's allusions to Radcliffe are evident in the more serious Gothic undertone evoked by Lucy, who is more succinct and matter-of-fact, while the more melodramatic, nearly comic conventions of the Gothic are shown through Charlotte, who overdoes the capitalization, often emphasizing two words to Lucy's one, and whose sentence structure is much more over the top. Lucy is adept at playing a role, but she confines her role-play to the time she is Dr. Cadaverezzi's assistant, preferring to remain in a state of melancholic realism in most other parts of the novel.

The same character doubling may be seen through Eliza and Miss Augusta Davenport. Eliza is the more fanciful of the two women, easily caught up in letting her imagination run away with her. Botting states that Radcliffe's heroines often react to that which they see and hear but do not understand by "conjur[ing] up images of ghostly supernatural forces" (64). Eliza does this when she exclaims to Miss Davenport that the girls are no longer living but "spirits.... Driven through the night ... because of a curse.... One of them was carrying her head in her arms ... beheaded ... a little girl carrying her own head..." (Pullman 144–45). A rational explanation, of course, is that Charlotte carries Herr Woodenkopf as a companion. In keeping with Radcliffe's style, "apparently spectral events are similarly explained after they have excited curiosity and terror" (Botting 64); Miss Davenport, a clear contrast in personality to Eliza, knows that a rational explanation lies beneath fancy (Pullman 145). Miss Davenport

Part I: Stories of Innocence

is a formidable woman who is quite rational and clear-headed, a welcome addition to the world of the Gothic, who may even strike the reader as similar to a heroine from a Jane Austen novel with her progressive observations about women and the world: "an English gentlewoman can rise above any circumstances, given intelligence and a loaded pistol" (104), she claims.

Miss Davenport represents the departure from Radcliffe's oeuvre, in that she moves beyond the traditional heroine of Gothic literature to embrace a life outside domesticity. Botting notes that often "the escape from confinement ... is no more than a prelude to a welcome return" (70), in that traditionally the pursued female victims encounter violence from within and without, and the resolved Gothic tale usually places them back where they began, albeit with an altered familial structure. It is true that Lucy and Charlotte must leave the realm of domesticity when their "home" is threatened by a corrupt and vile "parent" figure, and they return at the conclusion with a new parent figure in Max who is able to claim his rightful place as the new Count Karlstein. Eliza also is returned to "home" by being able to marry Max after the story ends, become the Countess Karlstein, and bear four of his children. However, Miss Davenport, who becomes Signora Roliopolio, strikes out of the domestic realm by opening a new school for girls (Pullman 241), where, ostensibly, they will finally become educated in the things she deems appropriate: building fires and killing and butchering animals (142). In addition, this "learned lady" is known for her great expeditions all over the world (241). She also inspires Hildi to write their story down for future generations. Through Miss Davenport, Pullman shows growth, not necessarily of an individual person, but of a literary genre and the changing position of women.

In "Making Nightmares into New Fairytales: Goth Comics as Children's Literature," Laurie N. Taylor states that "the Gothic traditionally subverts normative values by presenting large family histories (often personified in aging mansions and castles) and then showing those family structures to be corrupt or failing, often through ... orphaned children" (196). She further cites Anne Williams' work which asserts as a literature of subversion, the Gothic tends to argue against oppression via gender and class (197). The heart of Pullman's tale concerns two orphaned sisters under the care of their wealthy uncle who is corrupt and evil. Karlstein's lawyer initially establishes that he may not be the rightful heir to his title and castle because the true heir was stolen as a child, raised as an orphan, then

Three. Count Karlstein, or The Ride of the Demon Huntsman

apparently lost after he became a soldier and fought in the Battle of Bodelheim (Pullman 10). Frustrated that the matter is not at rest, Count Karlstein asks his lawyer, "If evidence is all you want, can't you manufacture some? Eh? Make it up?" (9). His disregard for law or moral authority is evident when he devises the plan to offer his nieces as "human prey" (24) to Zamiel, who is permitted to hunt on his lands every year with impunity but who he must offer a human sacrifice to on the tenth year. Nicholas Tucker's brief analysis of *Count Karlstein* indicates that he "represents the type of mean, self-centered ruthlessness Pullman particularly loathes in real life" (58). The corrupt family structure is further shown through the addition of Frau Müller, Karlstein's wife, who is not present in the graphic novel. She is just as ruthless and unkind as he, and while it is not apparent if she knows the details of his bargain with Zamiel, she participates with zeal in the mistreatment of the servant class and the nieces placed in their care. She is directly responsible for Hildi's firing as a maidservant: "Frau Müller was at his side, speaking swiftly, pointing at me. He looked up and his eyes seemed to flicker ... with enormous undischarged anger" (Pullman 70).

Count Karlstein demonstrates a great deal of oppression towards gender and the servant class through his treatment of Hildi Kelmar. For instance, he calls her or other female servants "hussy" (Pullman 10; 41), "wench" (132; 196), or "slut" (196). Often, Hildi fears that Karlstein may physically assault her (10; 42) if someone else is not present, which leads the reader to assume that he has indeed lashed out at her before. After Frau Müller speaks to him about Hildi's supposed interference in the girls' welfare, he strikes her with a stick, throws a heavy object at her, and then fires her; she remarks, "the spot was tender for weeks afterwards" (70). Frau Müller also participates in abusive behavior, though her tactic is to threaten and punish as opposed to direct physical abuse. She claims, "I'll have you tanned" (65) and requires Hildi to spend hours completing meaningless tasks to waste her time, such as cleaning all the silver and putting it away (67). She also makes condescending comments about Hildi's servant class with "Your trouble is, you don't know your place.... You've got ideas above your station" (61). These facets of the flawed familial structure and the prevalence of class-based and gender-based oppression do not come through as keenly in the graphic novel, which leads the reader to view the traditional novel as a darker narrative.

Nicholas Tucker explains that there is a subtle biographical connection between Hildi Kelmar and Pullman himself, for Hildi begins by reminiscing about how she and her brother Peter loved stories, "stories of hunting for him and tales of terror for me" (Pullman 3), just like Pullman who once enthralled his brother with tales he invented for him at night before they went to sleep (Tucker 57). Tucker points out that Hildi is similar to many other Pullman heroines: "Hildi is tough, brave and extremely resourceful.... [With] a strong sense of right and wrong" (58). Through the window readers have into her personality, readers see her enormous sense of loyalty to Lucy and Charlotte because she acts as their self-proclaimed protector even though she is not much older than they. Despite the abuse she takes from all authority figures in the text (not just the Karlsteins but also Herr Snivelwurst and Sergeant Snitsch), no matter what befalls her, she has spirit and drive to continue on her quest. She is compassionate and altruistic; she often remarks that she is afraid someone will become distraught, or worse, cry, and she tries to diffuse volatile situations to prevent others' misery. Because she has a strong sense of morality, she is intuitive and has insight into the actions of the more nefarious characters, which bears out when she overhears grand confessions that confirm her worst suspicions. She is guided by goodness and in setting things right, but she is not entirely consistent in characterization, for when things become most dire, she finds something inside herself she has never felt before: "I had to search my memory before I came up with the word that fitted. And that word was *vengeance*" (Pullman 191). The passion stirring in her that is strong enough to make her want to face Count Karlstein for his acts marks a departure for her in terms of character traits, revealing her complexity.

 Hildi takes a much more active part in moving the plot along, for she participates in many events that are unique to the novel version. For one, she leads the girls on the first escape, taking them to the hermit's cave for shelter, but on finding it occupied, on to the mountain guide's hut where she ensures that they are warm and secure before she leaves early the next morning to throw Count Karlstein off their trail by claiming that they have run away in the night and must be leaving the country. Later, she steals the key to the tower room where Charlotte is imprisoned and puts it into her soup, so that when Frau Müller delivers it, Charlotte can make her escape. Hildi also looks out for her brother Peter and keeps him hidden from the authorities until the marksmanship contest. She provides some comic relief when she pushes Herr Snivelwurst into the river, and she also is present (but hiding) to hear Count Karlstein's ideas about suddenly doing good works for others just because he thinks he will gain something from it, and for the final claiming of his soul when Zamiel comes for him. Because she is present for so much of the action and so heavily involved in the tale, she emerges as the protagonist, fighting for good to prevail over evil. Unlike Charlotte, who becomes the storyteller at the conclusion of the graphic novel, Hildi becomes the storyteller (and by extension, the voice of Pullman himself), when she reveals, "It was Signora Rolipolio's idea to write the story of what happened, and she would have me do the bulk of it — but then, I suppose I saw more of it than anyone else" (Pullman 242). Through the trauma that Hildi endures, she finds that if she just keeps standing up and fighting, goodness will prevail. This is evidence of her maturity as she moves on the path from innocence to experience.

One final way that movement occurs on the path from innocence to experience comes not from what any individual character learns but from what the reader herself learns. As Pullman moves farther from his more lighthearted fairy tales and magical realist novels for younger readers, and into slightly darker stories, one may see that he begins to introduce social commentary. The chapter featuring a police report filed by Sergeant Snitsch provides an apt illustration. One one hand, the report functions as pure slapstick humor and comic relief; on another, the undertone of the chapter suggests a subtle social criticism that Pullman begins to bring forth more frequently in his later works. The more Pullman begins to bring in social commentary, the more that his texts educate and enlighten the readers themselves, drawing them along the path to maturity and a more adult way of looking at the world.

Julie Cross explains that writers of the Gothic often interject slapstick or farce into a story to help younger readers deal with the darker elements portrayed in the text, because "the humour acts as a generally socially sanctioned form of transgression" (62). The placement of Police Report Number 354/21 in the larger context of the novel is likely intentional, then, for Hildi controls the narrative leading all the way up to the police report except for a short departure to feature Lucy's narrative; thus, the tone of the text for over the first third is fairly dark. Sergeant Snitsch's report comes in at just the right moment to lighten the mood, and with the style of writing and bumbling ineptness shown through the events recorded in the report, the mood is changed briefly before the narrative changes hands again. Sergeant Snitsch reveals himself as utterly incompetent; his report is on Dr. Cadaverezzi, whose name he fails to spell correctly no less than twelve different times. Each time he also spells it differently from all the others, coming up with hilarious alternatives, such as "Crackanutsi" (Pullman 95), "Calamatipsy" (97), and "Crackawhipsy" (100). He has quite the self-congratulatory attitude towards his own skills, often touting the evidence of his many awards and commendations, which are obviously honorary titles with no meaning, as evidenced by the fact that he apparently received the "Ernest Stuffelbaum Plate for Memory Training" (98) and yet his transcription of a conversation between Dr. Cadaverezzi and Lucy, which he claims is exact, bears no similarity to either Lucy's or Dr. Cadaverezzi's syntax but sounds suspiciously like his own (98–100).

Sergeant Snitsch further takes credit for designing a bracket to hold his helmet, noting that the drawing of the bracket is enclosed, but then he provides an asterisk which indicates "Drawing now missing" (Pullman 96). He indicates that the supposed criminal got away since his constable was too busy eating a meat pie, and so the doctor's cabinet instead is apprehended in his place (94–95). When investigating the cabinet, he sprays himself in the eye with ink (95), and he ends up with a half-eaten piece of cheesecake on his head when his constable puts it inside his upturned helmet to hide it (97). On his way to apprehend the criminal, he steps into a bucket and falls on his way out of his hiding place (100). In the midst of trying to effect the arrest, he and his constable are actually handcuffed by the supposed criminal and his accomplice (102), leading the inspector to "[express] his surprise that two grown officers of the Police Force should be beaten by one little girl" (103).

It would seem that Pullman interjects this humor into the story to lighten the otherwise somber mood. The same pattern is followed a few chapters later, when Max Grindoff's narrative also provides a bit of comic relief in its very scattered telling. But there is also another level to the meaning of this section for the reader. If the reader, too, is to be guided on the path from innocence to experience, the reader must learn along with the characters that those who initially seem to be the protectors of others are not always what they seem. Tucker states that in this novel, the "younger characters come over as pleasant, courageous, and happy to do the right thing. But they are also vulnerable to those older people who want to take advantage of them" (58). This is a theme to which Pullman consistently returns, and as will be shown in the following chapters, he

Three. Count Karlstein, or The Ride of the Demon Huntsman

moves in the direction of creating darker, more nefarious authority figures for whom the ends justify the means — any means necessary. What readers find in this novel is that the characters in positions traditionally seen as protectors and nurturers are anything but that, and instead, those on the lower social scale emerge as more kind and compassionate protectors of the innocent. Just as many writers of Gothic fiction show a serious and a satirical side to their plots, there is a serious and satirical side to the characters, for Count Karlstein's inappropriateness as a caretaker is shown in a very serious light (readers find, after all, that he has murdered before), while the police officer's inappropriateness as a protector is shown in a humorous light. In either case, the reader comes to the same conclusion as Hildi and other characters: not all who hold power can be trusted.

Conclusion

Count Karlstein, or the Ride of the Demon Huntsman, is an incredibly rich text that has escaped extended analysis until now. From the piece that inspired it, Carl Maria von Weber's *Der Freischütz*, to its first incarnation, to the graphic novel, then nearly back to its former state, the novel is both inspired by the Gothic tradition and a departure from it. It is also a text that showcases Pullman's talents as a writer who can entertain readers of all ages as he deftly moves between two distinctly different genres in telling altered versions of the same story. Further, he indicates that the story itself must be told again and again, with subtle changes each time, through the concluding panel of the graphic novel and even the questions raised by the authenticity of the "narratives by various hands." Here is the story of the demon huntsman and the characters who encountered him, but the story changes, ever so slightly, depending on the teller. Behind the curtain, of course, is Pullman himself, the master storyteller, reminiscent of the character he claims he would most like to be, Doctor Cadaverezzi: "Doctor Cadaverezzi ... captured his audience completely. They all knew, now, that he was a trickster — that if you turned your back on him, he'd pick your pocket; but it didn't seem to matter, as they were all in a high good humor. And he did it so well, with such a delight in his own tricks, that you couldn't help but enjoy it" (89–90). Perhaps the wisdom that readers gain from these texts is the knowledge that a story retold, never grows old.

Four

Spring-Heeled Jack and *The New Cut Gang*
Thunderbolt's Waxwork *and* The Gas-Fitters' Ball: *Narratives of Orphaned, Displaced, and Dispossessed Children*

> "In one way there's nothing so inconvenient in a story as a mother and father. As Jane Austen might have put it: It is a truth universally acknowledged, that young protagonists in search of adventure must ditch their parents."
> — Philip Pullman, "Darkness Visible: An Interview with Philip Pullman"[1]

In *Literature for Today's Young Adults*, Nilsen and Donelson list seven characteristics of the "best" adolescent literature, covering such necessities as a fast-moving plot, a wide variety of genres, and an eye toward issues that most interest and relate to young adult lifestyles (25–33). While each characteristic is described in a declarative, third-person statement, only one characteristic is delivered in the form of a heartfelt plea: "Please, Mother, I Want the Credit" (26). Nilsen and Donelson explain that adolescents become empowered through what they read by observing protagonists who are forced to act on their own, with little or no adult guidance. Perhaps the character's parents are missing, deceased, estranged, or otherwise incapable of providing leadership, care, or love. Often the adolescent finds other role models, either in the form of friends, teachers, unrelated adults, or a related but much older adult, such as a grandparent. Yet the absence of one or both parents places the adolescent into the unique position of having to take on "more" than the typical member of an intact family unit, which fosters exposure to difficulties which must be overcome (26–27). Therefore, when the character succeeds over what seem to be insurmountable odds, without the assistance of a mother or father, he or she becomes a source of inspiration for the reader who grows in wisdom and empathy.

Philip Pullman is no stranger to the motif of the parentless child. Over half of his published novels feature characters who have lost one or more parents to death, illness, neglect, disinterest, work or family obligations, or separation. In an interview with Kerry Fried for amazon.com, Pullman says that he and Peter Dickinson, another writer of children's and adolescent fiction, have discussed the unusually large number of children's book authors who have lost one or both of their parents when they were very young. Diane M. Duncan has explored this phenomenon as well concerning both Pullman's and fellow writer Michael Morpurgo's parental losses (271). Linking Pullman's mother and father to Mrs. Coulter and Lord Asriel in terms of similar personality characteristics (273), Duncan speculates that the loss of Pullman's father and his "ambiguous relationship with his glamourous mother" have affected his storytelling in both *His Dark Materials* and his fiction in general (272).[2] Duncan also points out that Pullman's heroes are frequently "fiercely independent girls who are intelligent and remarkably resourceful, and with an insatiable appetite for adventure and self-knowledge" (274). Such characteristics of independence, willpower, and curiosity with which Pullman imbues his protagonists demonstrate that he has evolved the typical patterning found in children's literature concerning orphaned children.

Melanie A. Kimball's "From Folktales to Fiction: Orphan Characters in Children's Literature" links a study she did of 50 folktales about orphans to 19th and early 20th century literature about children which shows a series of "universal elements" between each (558). Calling orphans in folktales and literature "the eternal Other" (559), Kimball contends that such characters are symbolic of both individual and community isolation (559). One of the many cogent points Kimball makes about orphaned heroines in folktales and literature is that they tend to overcome obstacles based on their virtues as opposed to their wits, which orphaned boys seem to have in great supply (561). Pullman does not make such a gender-specific distinction in terms of the progress of his orphaned characters: whether female or male, he shows both as resourceful and resilient, evidence that the gender of the protagonist is not as important as the character's individual traits and ability to overcome obstacles. Ostensibly, Pullman's work is therefore more relevant for our time, because both female and male readers need heroes with which to identify: as Kimball explains, "when orphans succeed against all odds, their success ultimately becomes ours" (559).

While a study of almost all of Pullman's fiction could be completed concerning his treatment of orphaned, displaced, and dispossessed children, this chapter will focus on three texts that contain the most similarities to one another in tone and style. All three books pay homage to the "penny dreadful," also known as the "schilling shocker," a type of popular pulp fiction available in the Victorian era, "full of wild and dramatic incidents and bloodthirsty savagery and hairbreadth escapes" (Pullman qtd. in Court). Pullman's *Spring-Heeled Jack*, a graphic novel, fits the penny dreadful genre with the inclusion of the infamous urban legend himself after whom the book is titled, but also for its melodramatic plot and tongue-in-cheek humor. The adventures of the New Cut Gang, as presented in *The Gas-Fitters' Ball* and *Thunderbolt's Waxwork*, also fit this genre with their focus on several young amateur detectives, working together to help solve crimes and learn the difference between authority figures who need their help versus those who seek to harm them. In all three books, the tone is light-hearted and generally optimistic, with page-turning narratives that feature an underlying sense of humor and whimsy.

Spring-Heeled Jack: A Story of Bravery and Evil *(1989)*

First published in 1989, Pullman's *Spring-Heeled Jack: A Story of Bravery and Evil*[3] is a graphic novel that concerns three orphaned siblings, Rose, Lily, and Ned, who have lost their father in a shipwreck and their mother to her death a short time after. With only a locket by which to remember their mother, the children live in dismal conditions at the Alderman Cawn-Plaster Memorial Orphanage, which is run by two ne'er-do-wells, Superintendent Killjoy and his assistant Miss Gasket, who are concerned only with packing in as many orphans as they can to ensure a steady paycheck. The novel opens with the siblings' escape from the orphanage and their quest to sell the locket to gain money for tickets to sail to America. However, a chance meeting with the super-villain Mack the Knife thwarts their plans, resulting in a fast-moving narrative in which

Four. Spring-Heeled Jack *and* The New Cut Gang

all three children are alternately caught, trapped, or held back from initially completing their journey, but with the aid of super-hero Spring-Heeled Jack and several human (and non-human) helpers, the children are freed and reunited with their long-lost father.

While the text is primarily presented in the style of a graphic novel (and shall be referred to as such in this chapter), like the second version of *Count Karlstein*, there are many paragraphs interspersed between the illustrations. Pullman explains in *Talking Books* that the writing process is similar for the semi-graphic novel and traditional novel, yet he tends to "describe [the picture] in the same way one would do stage directions for a play" (193). Like several of his other works, *Spring-Heeled Jack* was originally a play he wrote for his pupils when he was a teacher (Tucker 61).

Concerning the inspiration for this exciting narrative, the chapter opening epigraphs provide one set of clues, for they read like a literary and cultural compendium of Pullman's favorite works. With references to Dumas's *The Three Musketeers*, "a Western," Janet and Allan Ahlberg's *The Jolly Postman*, Dickens' *Sketches by Boz*, and Prokofiev's *Peter and the Wolf*, to name a few, Pullman sets the tone for each chapter with a quote taken verbatim or presented and then tweaked ever so slightly. In fact, as Pullman himself triumphantly notes on his website, "This is the first book in the world to feature a quotation from itself," for Chapter 11 begins with an epigraph by Pullman in the same book that reads, "Meanwhile, back at the orphanage..." which he then uses a few inches down to begin the chapter (84). The range and, to a lesser degree, the content of these epigraphs recalls his list of "works consulted and ideas stolen from" in the second version of *Count Karlstein*—for instance, both the epigraphs and list contain references to works of literature, film, and opera, and both also cite Janet and Allan Ahlberg's *The Jolly Postman or Other Peoples' Letters*, one of his favorite childhood books. Later, of course, Pullman used illustrations and epigraphs in a much more serious way to head up the chapters of *His Dark Materials*. The Knopf boxed edition from 1995 to 2000 utilizes Pullman's own pen and ink drawings to help the reader visualize the themes of each chapter in *The Golden Compass* and *The Subtle Knife*, while epigraphs from Blake, Coleridge, The Bible, Milton, Dickinson, Keats, and others allude to Pullman's greatest literary influences while quite seriously foreshadowing the content of each new chapter in *The Amber Spyglass*.

While it has been established in the past three chapters that Pullman is often heavily influenced by other works and either creates his own variants of them or alludes significantly to what inspires him, *Spring-Heeled Jack* provides a departure from this storytelling mode because the influences are confined to the epigraphs, while the story is primarily inspired by Pullman's own childhood fascination with comic books and adventure tales and the genre of Victorian pulp fiction. In his essay "I have a feeling this all belongs to me," Pullman describes the day he received a Superman comic from his stepfather, a life-altering experience: "I devoured it and demanded more.... Those poorly printed stories on their cheap yellowing newsprint intoxicated me, enthralled me, made me dizzy with passion.... It was the first stirring of the storytelling impulse" (qtd. in Beahm 17). Pullman explains that his goal as a young boy was not necessarily to become Batman, but to "brood over [his] world" and to construct stories about him (17). The impulse to tell adventure stories to his brother, making them up as he went along, took root in Pullman at a young age and surfaced later in *Spring-Heeled Jack*, a sort of Batman for the Victorian era, "a mysterious character with special powers who would suddenly appear out of the murky London night to aid the victimized" (Andronik 42).

In "A Well-Heeled Villain," Bruce Heydt explains that Spring-Heeled Jack was one of the first urban legends to surface in reference to a September 1837 series of crimes in London (4).[4] Heydt explains that those who insisted they saw the man himself described him as very tall, "as much as 10 feet high," complete with black helmet, cape, tunic, pointy ears, orange eyes, and claws, whose abilities included spitting blue fire and leaping over tall buildings and walls (4). What became an urban legend persisted for at least 40 years with people claiming to have seen this man as far away as New York City (4). While Heydt notes that there were large-scale hunts for Jack the Ripper, there were not for Spring-Heeled Jack, and he assumes that this was due to the latter's status as a penny dreadful character, a "comic book supervillain" (4). Unlike Jack the Ripper, Spring-Heeled Jack became a character in penny dreadfuls *after* he was said to be real, but later the supposedly "real" character and his fictional namesake merged, leading him to be relegated to the status of urban legend and not worthy of protracted criminal investigations (4).

A simple internet search for "Spring-Heeled Jack" yields numerous articles on "sightings" of the urban legend. What is clear from these articles, whether they are credible or not, is that Jack was believed to prey on innocent men and women, but children do not appear to have been victims of

Four. Spring-Heeled Jack *and* The New Cut Gang

his attacks. Pullman deconstructs the legend, altering the personality of the man who was known for attacking the innocent into a superhero who instead *protects* the innocent, targeting the evildoers to stop them in their tracks or to punish their misdeeds. Pullman even takes the time to establish Jack's notoriety as a savior of the innocent when he reveals that Polly, one of the children's helpers, had been assisted by Jack before the narrative began when he protected her from thieves (*Spring-Heeled* 37). Polly's familiarity with him leads to her immediately rendering aid after Jack relates the plight of the orphans to her. Yet Pullman may also be suggesting that Jack has not aided children previously, for Rose, Lily, and Ned have no idea who he is when they first meet him: "The girls looked up at the stars and saw — The devil? Well, if he wasn't the devil, then who the devil was he?" (13–14).

While it could be argued that sheltered Victorian children would not recognize a super-hero/super-villain that their parents and elders might, Pullman imbues his young protagonists with qualities that their peers would probably have lacked in their time: resourcefulness and independence. Children growing up on the streets of London would learn such qualities for the sake of survival early on, but Rose, Lily, and Ned come from a middle-class background and are only recently orphaned. Therefore, they are either surprisingly self-sufficient for children who have not had to get by on their own wits until now, or they are willing to risk their safety regardless of lacking the skillset to take care of themselves simply because their current living conditions are so dreadful. Once their parents are gone, there seems to be no end to the exploitation they face, whether it is at the hands of the nefarious creatures running the orphanage for profit or a gang of criminals who think nothing of tying up a child and chatting openly about physically harming him. Yet despite the children's collective strength, they must be assisted by others to prevail. Pullman's remarks on the relationship between children, adults, and bullies are enlightening. He relates that when he was young, he had to ask for his grandfather's help when he had problems with other boys at school. His grandfather, a former boxer, showed him the way to defend himself. He says rather than spending time trying to understand where bullying comes from, which is the job of adults to learn, that children must learn how to protect themselves. Yet he is quick to point out that when bullies begin to use harsher methods, like guns or knives, this changes the game ("I have a feeling" 19).

Part I: Stories of Innocence

What Pullman does, then, in *Spring-Heeled Jack*, is to resurrect a popular urban legend and place its central character in the context where he must assist a true group of underdogs: orphaned children. But Jack doesn't go about his business alone; Polly, Jim, and even Spangle the dog also assist the children; the intervention of multiple helpers shows the children they must grow to discern who is worthy of their trust. Through their own resiliency and wits, coupled with the assistance of others on their journey, the children are able to bounce back from tragedy and grow in confidence and wisdom. If one views this book with an eye towards the themes of change, loss, and growth, the children must first lose their parents and lose their home in order to meet those who are true advocates for them, which gives them the ability to mature, and as a result, they are then rewarded for being able to come back from their loss when they are reunited with their father at the end. As Kimball states, the typical non-orphaned protagonist usually gains independence and separation from parents as a reward for completing his or her quest; however, the orphaned protagonist often achieves a sense of place in the world and is able to make him or herself a home after successfully undergoing trials (563).

In regards to the trauma that the children must face that becomes the catalyst to their growth, certainly the loss of their father to a shipwreck while he was on a quest to find gold in Australia is an exotic counterpoint to the dismal conditions in which they find themselves after they also lose their mother.[5] Because Pullman's novel begins by dropping the reader immediately into the children's escape from the orphanage, readers are given a crash course in "why the orphanage is a horrible place for children." The orphanage serves "porridge ... as thin as the blankets, and as cold as the smiles on the guardians' faces" (Pullman, *Spring-Heeled* 6). The location alone is a dark and dreary place, where "only alley cats and criminals had any business," the East End of London, where the children are forced to sleep in a doorway of Fog Row, "the dirtiest, dankest, miserablest spot ... only a spit and a stride from ... garbage cans" (7). As a great fan of the 19th century, Pullman took on a part-time lectureship at Westminster College, Oxford, where he taught a class on Victorian novels (Watkins 41). Watkins says, "He [Pullman] is particularly drawn to the Victorian East End ... a seedy area" (41) and it becomes an oft-used location in his fiction. And yet despite the physical setting in which the children have been forced to live and escape, it is clear that they face greater horrors from the adults around them who mean to exploit them for personal gain.

Four. Spring-Heeled Jack *and* The New Cut Gang

Paramount among those exploitative authority figures are Superintendent Killjoy, aptly named, and his assistant Miss Gasket. Both are motivated solely by the wish to adhere to "Clause 44" of the rules and regulations of the orphanage, which states that their beds must be completely full for them to be paid. Just to clarify, a footnote appears below the clause description, in Pullman's authorial voice, which says, "In other words, if they didn't cram as many kids as the place would hold, they didn't get any wages" (*Spring-Heeled* 19). Kimball states that in stories about orphans, the trend is that orphans, by and large, must face some level of mistreatment or "hostility" from their keepers (562). In fact, the primary obstacles on an orphan's quest are other characters (563). Cruelty is often inflicted by relatives — either blood or step-relatives, employers, or the supernatural (563–64). As a man and woman working together, Killjoy and Gasket serve as surrogate parents, but of the crass and uncaring variety. Their rule even governs the way the children sleep, which is in a "regulation posture" (Pullman, *Spring-Heeled* 19). Killjoy and Gasket's interest in money over anything altruistic pushes them to require all jewelry be handed over to them and entices them to go after the escaped children in an effort to retrieve the locket. When they comb every portion of London in an effort to find Rose and Lily, "they [are] only bothering because of the locket, of course" (40). Mr. Killjoy also is obviously cheating with his accounting practices, made clear by his efforts to work on the books only when no one can see what he is doing and to lock the books away (20).

The other adults desiring to exploit the children for personal gain are Mack the Knife and his crew of criminals. Unlike Spring-Heeled Jack, whom the children do not recognize, Mack the Knife is a notorious figure known for grisly murders, and the children immediately plead for their lives when he attacks (Pullman, *Spring-Heeled* 9). However, Mack explains that he is also only interested in the locket which can be pawned to buy a meat pie and brandy (10). Seeing an opportunity to bargain with the children, Mack kidnaps Ned and offers to return him in exchange for their mother's locket. When Mack takes Ned to his hideout, Mack's gang immediately wants to beat him up, but Mack sees him as a bargaining chip in his schemes: "'This little feller's going to make us a lot of money'" (29). So Mack is also intent on exploitation of children for his own gain, and yet, when compared with the machinations of Killjoy and Gasket, one wonders, who does more damage?

Killjoy and Gasket, for instance, go to much greater lengths to mistreat the children than Mack the Knife. While Mack simply ties Ned up and goes off to play his violin (Pullman, *Spring-Heeled* 31), intending to wait until the girls hand the locket over so he can trade his prisoner for booty, Killjoy and Gasket much more frequently use trickery and brute force to gain control over the children. First, they deliberately lie to Polly Pickles, the pub worker who, at Jack's request, hides the girls. By telling her that they represent the "Happy Smiles Sunshine Villa Home for Lost and Impoverished Little Children," Killjoy disarms Polly enough to encourage her to hand the children over. In fact, he and Gasket are so persuasive with their false caring and love that Polly says, "'I'll have to believe you, you being in your position and me being in mine, and the world being what it is'" (45). Polly's comment reflects the classism inherent in the exchange as well. Using their position in society as leverage, Killjoy and Gasket regain possession of the girls, only to delight in revealing that they used lies to get what they wanted (46). After the two then capture Lily but lose Rose, Gasket dupes a kind-hearted policeman into trying to arrest him so that she may regain possession of Rose (59–60). Lastly, they make the ultimate exploitative act when Jim and Polly pose as the girls' long-lost parents in an attempt to "adopt" them and care for them. Rather than be overjoyed that two of their charges are about to be given a better life, Killjoy and Gasket scheme and produce a set of questions that only the parents could answer in an effort to stop Jim and Polly, two very caring people, from being able to take the girls away. With the temporary loss of Ned, the orphanage is short one child, and unless they can find another "urchin," they will not be paid (85). If they lose Rose and Lily, their numbers will be down by three. Thus, they sacrifice the well-being of the children for their own personal gain. It is only the intervention of the superhero Spring-Heeled Jack at this point that stops their final betrayal of the children.

While Pullman's novel concretely demonstrates the forces that orphaned children are up against, it also offers much hope for salvation by way of those who come forward to care about the downtrodden. First and foremost is the superhero Spring-Heeled Jack, who swoops in to save the day, but Jack is not without helpers. His past relationship with Polly indicates that she only must be told the children's plight to jump to their assistance, and she enlists the aid of her fiancé Jim, a courageous man who helps without hesitation, even conquering temporarily his fear of heights to take Rose to the roof to hide (Pullman, *Spring-Heeled* 58–60). When

Polly and Jim's assistance proves to be no match for the deceit of Killjoy and Gasket, they decide to pose as the children's parents, in a way trying to replace what they see as a dysfunctional and harmful parental unit in the two running the orphanage.[6] There are other characters who assist the children, too, in more indirect ways, such as the captain who sends Jim on the errand which puts him in contact with the case belonging to their father, or Casey Wilkins, the pastry cook and former ship's carpenter who urges Jim to defy his fear of heights by thinking back to his days climbing a ship's rigging (53). Such characters, major or minor, provide a counterpoint to those who hold the view that children are disposable, and part of the children's growth lies in knowing whom to trust. Because the children lack a home in the traditional sense, they must find something that replaces home on their quest, and the characters looking out for them become their extended family as they embark on their journey.

Melanie Kimball discusses the concept of "home" in her essay on folktales and children's literature. She states that orphans find that leaving home to go on a quest is easier for them than other heroes because they lack a true home. "What the orphans seek, in fact, is a place to belong to and the right to be there" (563). Knowing that the orphanage the children have been kept in for 18 months is not a home, they leave with their mother's locket that they intend to sell to buy tickets for America, a place which represents the hope of a new home. However, there are two ways that a home is created, either by them or for them, on their journey. One way is through the intervention of helpers, as discussed above, who help create a home for the children until they find it again by being reunited with their father. The other way is through what they create themselves, which is emblematic of their growth: they create the concept of home through their relationship with the dog.

The children adopt a dog they call Spangle, in the midst of their escape: "Spangle was quite happy to go with them. There wasn't much love where she came from, and the children had some to spare" (Pullman, *Spring-Heeled* 7). Even though they lack a physical home, they do retain the emotional feeling of "home" through their love and affection for one another, so much so that they can widen this circle of compassion to rescue a dog in need of attention. Spangle functions as an animal helper, sniffing out where Ned is kept after his capture, biting at the gang members, and then later "sav[ing] the day" when Mack the Knife comes back with vengeance in mind and she attacks him: "Her little teeth were snapping, and her little paws were scratching, and the growl that came out of her throat would have done credit to a werewolf" (73). Spangle operates in many different places the same as she would were the children living in a residence; she guards the children to the best of her abilities and attacks those who attempt to hurt the children. In essence, her home is wherever at least one of the children is. To the children, of course, their ultimate home, or ultimate "reward," is to be able to sail for America. When Spring-Heeled Jack comes to their rescue at the story's conclusion, and they assume that they are going to America after all, Rose and Ned show evidence of character growth and wisdom when they ask if the children left behind in the orphanage can be given Spangle to make their lives happier. The illustration of the children in the orphanage on page 95 shows them looking through a railing on the landing, yet it also looks deliberately institutional, as if they are imprisoned. Rose and Ned show maturity and empathy through the decision they make to leave what has come to be known as "home" to them, their loyal dog, so that they can give over this gift to the orphans left behind. "Leaving Spangle was even more difficult than facing up to Mack the Knife. But after all, he [Ned] and Rose and Lily were going to be free now, and none of the others were" (98).[7] Evidently the children have learned that they carry the concept of "home" with them and no longer need their animal helper to solidify this awareness for them, but having grown in empathy, they recognize that the children they are leaving behind in the orphanage lack the concept of home. Therefore, they offer Spangle to them as a way to pass on the stability that they have gained. It is an act of kindness that only comes with maturity.

As for the text's resolution, it is clear that evil is punished and good is rewarded, which makes this novel a story of innocence for Pullman. Kimball states that death usually comes to those who punish orphans in folktales (566), and it could be suggested that Killjoy and Gasket face a metaphorical "death" in that both are going to lose their positions as head and second-in-command of the orphanage, and it is suggested that Polly may now replace them (Pullman, *Spring-Heeled* 112). Kimball also notes that there are times that an evil character is redeemed and becomes good or at least is put on the path to changing for the better (566). This may be true for two characters: Mack the Knife is seemingly defeated when he and Spring-Heeled Jack exchange stories, competing to see which one committed the more atrocious deed.[8] However, thrown into the river, his "scorched" soul "cool[s]" and he comes out of the water, ready for vengeance, but Jack strings him up from a tall building until Mack says he will do anything to "be good" (Pullman, *Spring-Heeled* 75). Finally, a minor character, Filthy, is shown from his entrance to have a conscience. In what may be a preview to a character's dæmon later in *His Dark Materials* (Tucker 62), Filthy is accompanied by "an odd, bedraggled little creature like a mournful moth, or like a secondhand angel ... invisible to everyone except us" (Pullman, *Spring-Heeled* 38). This creature is a manifestation of Filthy's conscience[9] and it is quite bothersome to him throughout the story as it makes him feel guilty when he acts inappropriately. Despite his best efforts to "lose" his conscience, as the other gang members have already done (39), Filthy's conscience is persuasive, so much so that in the conclusion of the novel, he is moved to get rid of the money he wrongfully attained earlier by paying the organ grinder and the pie man (110–11). Thus, the novel projects the idea that even those who are wrong can embark on the right path if they are frightened enough or if they listen to the sound of their inner voice.

The New Cut Gang: Thunderbolt's Waxwork *and* The Gas-Fitters' Ball

Thunderbolt's Waxwork and *The Gas-Fitters' Ball*, published in 1994 and 1995, are two significantly lesser-known Pullman works that also deal with the subject of displaced and dispossessed children.[10] Yet what makes the New Cut Gang books different from *Spring-Heeled Jack* is their focus on a larger group of child and adolescent protagonists, most not related by blood, who band together to solve crimes and support one another in a world that does not always seem conducive to the nurturing of children. Each novel focuses on a central protagonist's story: the first book centers on Sam "Thunderbolt" Dobney,[11] a 10-year-old boy who gets his name after he knocks out a rival gang leader named Crusher Watkins after Watkins insults Thunderbolt's mother (Pullman, *Thunderbolt's Waxwork* 15); the second book features Benny Kaminsky, the 11-year-old leader of the New Cut Gang whom Tucker says is "dreamy, often living in a world of his own..." (64). Other characters include Bridie Malone, a 13-year-old girl, and her 6-year-old brother Sharkey Bob, as well as Angela and Zerlina, the Peretti twins, who are a little younger than Thunderbolt. Just as in *Spring-Heeled Jack*, the youths living in the same time, place, and culture find that their world can be divided between those outside the gang who can be trusted versus those out to exploit or simply mistreat the innocent, and the growth the youths achieve comes from learning how to discern the difference.

In "Penny Dreadfuls: Late Nineteenth-Century Boys' Literature and Crime," Patrick A. Dunae identifies the characteristics and controversies surrounding the penny dreadful or penny blood, a term for juvenile fiction in Britain which moved into the vernacular around 1840 (133). Noting that religious, political, and journalistic leaders were known to connect the mass distribution of cheap sensationalized fiction to juvenile crime, Dunae explains that "the tales were also considered to be a threat to society, not only because they glorified physical aggression, but because they seemed to encourage disrespect for authority" (134). The penny dreadful underwent changes over the years; the first, aimed at adults, were much more violent and presented the "bizarre" and "heinous," such as "Varney the Vampire, Spring-Heeled Jack, and Sweeney Todd" (133–34). However, the turn of the century was marked by low-level periodicals aimed at boys alone, and these were considerably tamer by comparison (134). Those most opposed to the publication of this cheap fiction were convinced that readers of the lower class, who were supposedly already "inclined to criminal activities" (136), would be further egged on by reading of the fantastic exploits of young criminals. Yet the assumption of the penny dreadful readership is itself a controversial point.

John Springhall's research, published eleven years after Dunae's, asserts that a more "well-spoken" middle-class youth read the penny dreadful than the lower-class ruffians sometimes depicted in the stories. "Whether in the school, the office, the warehouse, or the workshop, youngsters could participate in the criminal yet exciting escapades of homeless orphans without having their own life-styles radically altered.... Penny dreadfuls[12] thus provided a romantic escape from the uneventfulness of their readers' everyday lives" (224). Springhall makes a distinction in his essay between the English penny dreadful and the American dime novel; of the former, he states that plots tend to buttress conventions in society such as the figure of the wealthy, unethical upper-class peer (225). Written by anonymous, middle-class writers, these serials were then published by "déclassé publishers" who wished to earn accolades "within the existing social order" (226). Often the characters themselves were middle-class and prevented from attaining their rightful place in society due to the interference of the immoral aristocratic character type. The reader, often middle-class as well, would empathize with characters forced to face difficulties and overcome them (226).

Nicholas Tucker explains that Thunderbolt Dobney of Pullman's New Cut Gang is reminiscent of William Brown, a character in stories by Richmal Crompton. According to Tucker, both boys are "always coming up with unlikely ideas, disrespectful of adult authority ... given to switching between grinning cheerfully, scowling in contempt or sighing in despair" (63). The difference, Tucker explains, is that William lives well, while Thunderbolt lives in poverty (63). While it is clear that Pullman's New Cut Gang is comprised of youngsters of the lower-class, and therefore may depart from the conventions of the penny dreadfuls Springhall discusses, Tucker over-simplifies Thunderbolt's attitude towards authority. In fact, Thunderbolt is the most conscience-driven of all the children and shows respect towards certain adults while also coming across as more reserved and introspective than other members of the gang.

For instance, in *Thunderbolt's Waxwork*, Thunderbolt exchanges a piece of rubber for a piece of lead that came from a statue, now destroyed, of King Neptune (Pullman 1). His goal in making the trade with a schoolmate is to add to his menagerie of "curiosities" (1), but from the point he takes possession of the lead, his conscience begins to bother him as it is technically stolen property, because the statue had been erected and then dismantled for its lead (52). Later, when his father is arrested and Thunderbolt works to clear his name, he is distressed that he himself is technically a criminal, making it likely that his own guilty feeling spurs him on to do the "good" deed in helping to save his father.

While Thunderbolt and his father are not openly demonstrative with their affection for one another, they have a good relationship that benefits from a mutual appreciation for the others' interests. Thunderbolt does most of the cooking and Mr. Dobney creates his inventions: "there was nothing nicer than sitting by the fire of an evening with the kettle simmering and the brass Buddha gleaming on the mantelshelf and Mr. Dobney reading scandal out of the paper while Thunderbolt arranged his Museum" (Pullman, *Thunderbolt's Waxwork* 12). It is precisely this easy camaraderie between father and son that makes it that much more difficult for Thunderbolt once he begins to suspect his father of having created counterfeit coins. At first, he cannot accept the idea that his father is a criminal, but once he is able to openly wonder if his father is guilty, he cannot banish the thought "Though it made him feel hot and heavy, as if he was ill" (24). Every time he tries to rationalize that his father cannot be responsible, another fact comes back to haunt him, such as the Buddha his Uncle Sam stole and the piece of stolen lead he possessed, evidence of criminal theft through his family (25). By the time Mr. Solomons, the baker, tells him what happens to forgers (hanging) and he learns how coins are counterfeited, he is nearly sick with worry that the batteries in his father's workshop are proof that his father is guilty: "Thunderbolt could hardly hear; there was a kind of roaring in his ears" (27). Finally, when his father is taken away by the police, Thunderbolt is convinced his father is the forger, and it will take Benny and the others to get to the bottom of the mystery.

Despite the fact that the gang sets out to clear Mr. Dobney's name, Thunderbolt still struggles with his conscience. As Bridie explains, the only person Thunderbolt trusts in the world is his father (Pullman, *Thunderbolt's Waxwork* 34), and when his trust is temporarily broken, Thunderbolt becomes despondent and withdrawn. When he tells the others about new information regarding the fake coins, he gets "quieter and quieter," worrying he will only end up giving information that might further hurt his father's case. "What he really wanted to do was shut his eyes and hide in the dark for ever" (42). But his own guilt at his illegal possession comes back to haunt him in the midst of trying to scheme to help his father. When Bridie suggests giving their new information to the police, Thunderbolt feels "a drizzle of fear" at the thought, worried he'll be found out for his petty crime (47). In fact, he has "spasms of criminal guilt" over the lump of lead (52).

Once Mr. Dobney is free from prison, Thunderbolt's tearful reunion with him speaks volumes about his feelings for his father. He is angry at himself for thinking his father could ever do anything wrong, angry at his father for not being open about his activities, and disappointed with himself for avoiding the police all over that stolen piece of lead (Pullman, *Thunderbolt's Waxwork* 107). Their embrace over, they "pretend he hadn't been crying" and head home to eat (107). The standard penny dreadful protagonist probably did not expend so much energy battling his conscience, trying to decide whether he could trust his father, or focusing on a piece of lead he traded an item to obtain to put in his collection of curiosities; thus the narrative focus on Thunderbolt's conscience illustrates Pullman's penchant for creating tales with more multi-layered characters.

In subverting the patterns that emerged in penny dreadfuls of the

Four. Spring-Heeled Jack *and* The New Cut Gang

past that presented either orphaned and lower-class children or upper-middle-class children, Pullman's group of urchins are lower-class, but all come from intact, caring families. Thunderbolt's mother has died — but he is very close to his father and watches over him (Tucker 63), and the other children all come from families with one or both parents present. While there are technically no orphans in these novels, the children seem to have the run of Lambeth, the setting for the action, and seem to interact with their families only at meal-time. Therefore, they are more or less on their own for the majority of their day. It is true that only Thunderbolt takes his education seriously; in the first adventure, he spends time learning vocabulary words and doing homework, and in the second, he is tutored by Miss Honoria Whittle in trigonometry. As for the other children, "The gang should have been at school, but most of them regarded the School Board as the slow-witted opponent in a delightful game, and played hookey at the slightest opportunity" (Pullman, *Thunderbolt's Waxwork* 33). Likely their skipping school, having a hangout, and appearing in public in a group causes the police and others to assume they are miscreants, up to no good. Yet their "crimes" are essentially pranks and amount to little or no harm. In describing the books himself on his author website, Pullman says, "They're funny (I hope) tales about the children ... a mixed bunch of vagabonds and rascals in late Victorian Lambeth, and their adventures among the petty crooks and the showmen and the market traders of the time."

Like G. K. Chesterton, who wrote "A Defence of Penny Dreadfuls" in 1901, Pullman may also be making his case in their favor. In the midst of the furor over fears that such texts would encourage crime, Chesterton wrote that "There is no class of vulgar publications about which there is, to my mind, more utterly ridiculous exaggeration and misconception than the current boys' literature of the lowest stratum" (1). Pointing out that "the magisterial theory" (2) states that the availability of cheap fiction creates youth crime, Chesterton argued that literature by writers such as Scott, Byron, Stevenson, and Wordsworth also presented outlaws and pirates in a favorable light, yet no one felt the need to attack those works. Proclaiming that "literature is a luxury; fiction is a necessity" (1), Chesterton contended that there was a true need for the penny dreadful to delight the average man: "...these great gaudy diaries of his soul ... [constitute] a plainer and better gospel than any of those iridescent ethical paradoxes that the fashionable change as often as their bonnets" (3). Many years later, in "Dawkins, Fairy Tales, and Evidence," Pullman makes a similar argument when he reflects on whether or not magic and fairy tales can have a "pernicious effect" on young readers (Dawkins qtd. in Pullman 1).

Pullman's essay concerns remarks that the scientist Richard Dawkins made on a news program during which, in talking about his intention to write a children's book, he wondered what the effects of magic and fairy tales on youth would be. Pullman then asks, "So: do children believe what they read in stories, or don't they? And if they do, in what way do they believe it?" Pullman offers that children think of this as a form of role-playing. He relates that he and his friends would read comic books or listen to the radio or see films and then act as if they were the characters they grew to love, fully aware that they were not the characters themselves, but simply pretending. He further discusses how this made him feel: "What was my mind doing? I think it was feeling a little scrap, a tiny fluttering tattered cheaply printed torn-off scrap of heroism.... That intensity of feeling is what both fuels and rewards childhood play.... Exhilaration, heroism, despair, resolution, triumph, noble renunciation, sacrifice — in acting these out, we experience them in miniature, or as it were, in safety" ("Dawkins, Fairy Tales"). It seems that this is the feeling that Pullman intended for readers of his New Cut Gang books, for rather than show the band of children as hooligans bent on destruction and crime, he creates a group of playful and shrewd youngsters who seem more interested in solving crimes than committing them. If anything, the tales showcase how adults assumed to be upright citizens may in fact be hiding evidence of their own criminal behavior, and that children assumed to be villains may be working to clear the names of the innocent or assist others in need of help.

As far as the actual criminal wrongdoings of the group, the children often take part in crimes in an indirect fashion. One example can be found in a storyline originating with the twins Angela and Zerlina. In *The Gas-fitters' Ball*, both have made bets on Dick Smith proposing to Daisy Miller with Snake-Eyes Melmott, a local bookie who is betting against their marriage, and so they try to increase their odds of winning the bet by trying to teach Dick romantic gestures that he can make towards Daisy. The problem is that through their interference, Dick grabs the hand of Mr. Horspath, Daisy's other suitor, assuming it is Daisy's hand, and the two men get into a fight, and Dick is arrested. Later, the twins help Dick to escape from prison. Therefore, they commit a crime in effecting a prison escape, but they also do so because they believe this "good" deed makes up for the earlier "bad" deed, for it was only due to their advice that Dick grabbed the wrong hand which began the fight. What seems clear through these and other examples is that the children become involved in situations where criminal activity of some sort occurs, but their intentions are usually good and in the end, of course, the "right" people are arrested and the "innocent" released.

The primary activities of the New Cut Gang fall into several categories: assisting others who have some sort of "dream," freeing the wrongfully accused from arrest or jail, and getting to the bottom of real criminal mysteries and finding the real perpetrators of crime. Michael Anglo's *Penny Dreadfuls and Other Victorian Horrors* explains that "glorifying villains, endowing criminals with noble qualities they never possessed, and casting murderers, thieves, and outlaws as heroes of romance was ... common" (30) in the era of the penny dreadful. Obviously Pullman's cast of characters and their activities do not entirely fit the stereotypical penny dreadful.

In each novel, a character is revealed who has a dream or wish. In the first novel, Dippy Hitchcock, a kind older man who sells roasted chestnuts, reveals that he would like to be featured as a waxwork in the museum, and the children decide that they can honor him by accomplishing this task. Thunderbolt says, "'They don't make waxworks of hot-chestnut men' ... only Kings and criminals" (*Thunderbolt's Waxwork* 3). Dippy explains that he once attempted to be a pickpocket, but he "'had to give it up on account of me conscience'" (3). Despite the fact that he is a legitimate businessman and the children do not take part in any significant criminal activity, they are presumed to be criminals by the domineering Mr. Rummage, who yells, "'I will not have vagrants and costermongers on my property!'" (4) Of course, Mr. Rummage is later revealed to be the very adult no one should trust as he is responsible for passing the counterfeit coins. Because the children and Dippy are insulted by Rummage, they later dress Dippy in a suit and make him up to look like a department store dummy; since the professor running the museum rejects the mockup of Dippy that they construct for the museum, they come up with the scheme to have Dippy pose as a waxwork in Rummage's store window, a stunt that veers out of control when Dippy becomes inebriated by having drunk "horse reviver" to keep his courage up (77–79). Despite the twists and turns, by the end of the story, Dippy's visage is commemorated in the Chamber of Horrors in the Waxworks Museum (113), and thus the children help an ordinary man become extraordinary.

Part I: Stories of Innocence

In the second novel, the character Dick Smith dreams of asking Daisy Miller (a clear nod to Henry James) to marry him, although he is socially inept and falls apart any time he is near her. It is true that some of the children have made bets on them getting together and stand to gain if they can pull this off, but they are also motivated to assist Dick because like Dippy, he seems to be an adult in need of courage. Thunderbolt even becomes caught up in the romance of their union as he "(a sentimental soul) was looking forward to the kiss" (Pullman, *The Gas-fitters'* 8). At the bandstand and the Music Hall, the kids are nearby, coaching Dick through what to say and how to act to show his affection for Daisy, but he mixes up their advice and his words and fails every time, culminating in being arrested after the Peretti twins convince him to grab what he thinks is Daisy's hand and "cover it with burning kisses" (67), an action which results in a fight between the men when he assaults Mr. Horspath by accident. After freeing Dick from prison and dressing him in disguise for the Gas-Fitters' Ball, the children finally find a way to give him his confidence and attract Daisy to him, and by the end of the story, Mr. Horspath is revealed to be the one who stole the silver, and Dick proposes to Daisy and she accepts (118).

Besides helping two characters to gain courage and attain their dreams, the children also help to save the wrongfully accused. Mr. Horspath, the Deputy Manager at the Gasworks, accuses Dick of having stolen the silver from the gas-fitters' hall; despite Dick's poor attempts at winning Daisy's heart, Horspath sees him as an adversary and an obstacle he must remove from Daisy's life, and so he devises a plan to put him away for good, but Benny discovers that he is the one who actually committed the crime. The children's intervention also ends up proving that the infamous criminal of Lambeth, Sid the Swede, is nothing other than a pillowcase thief. Additionally, in *Thunderbolt's Waxwork*, Benny works to help free Thunderbolt's father, whom the children think is arrested for counterfeiting coins, but who is being held for not paying his debts. Through the gang's efforts to prove Thunderbolt's father is not guilty, they discover Mr. Rummage is the true criminal and they also are able to earn a reward, which Thunderbolt uses to pay his father's debt and free him from prison. These acts of intervention to save the innocent or at least, the harmless, are reminiscent of those towards the conclusion of *Spring-Heeled Jack*, where the children show compassion for others; certainly they are not the acts of the typical penny dreadful protagonist.

Four. Spring-Heeled Jack *and* The New Cut Gang

The gang's approach to crime-solving is led by Benny Kaminsky, their fearless leader who himself has a fascination with Mr. Sexton Blake, the famous detective. Tucker explains that Pullman is known for his love of Sherlock Holmes,[13] and that Blake, a fictional character, is reminiscent of Holmes (63). E.S. Turner's *Boys Will Be Boys*, written in 1948, was "a breezy popular history of generations of English penny dreadfuls and boys' papers" (Springhall 223). Turner devotes a chapter to the persona of Mr. Sexton Blake, about whom a seemingly endless supply of boys' books were written by over one hundred writers (128). There is no definitive answer to the question "Who invented Sexton Blake?" but a writer named Hal Meredeth, which may be a pen name, is sometimes credited (129). Referred to as "the office-boy's Sherlock Holmes" (127), Blake appeared from the 1890s onward in publications all over the world (128). Though Blake was popular on his own, he drew more of a following when he was given an assistant to help him fight crime, much like Holmes's Watson. In fact, Turner states that "an errand-boy reader could more easily project himself into the narrative by imagining himself to be Blake's assistant. So arrived Tinker" (134). In addition to several references to Blake in the New Cut Gang books, Benny is said to have a low opinion of Tinker: "Tinker's main duties seemed to consist of running about with messages, of handing Sexton Blake his magnifying glass, and of getting hit over the head by crooks, and Benny regarded him with patronizing scorn" (Pullman, *The Gas-Fitters'* 36). Thus Benny, as a fictional character, projects himself into the "tales" of Blake by imagining he is his assistant. In fact, Benny takes credit in the first novel for having done some work for Blake (Pullman, *Thunderbolt's Waxwork* 34), and Benny's fascination with him evolves into mimicry, when he rips a page from his textbook to make notes about the four clues he has discovered that eventually lead him to find the true criminal (Pullman, *The Gas-Fitters'* 38–39).

While Pullman pays homage yet again to the "blood-and-thunder" penny dreadfuls of the Victorian era in his Sally Lockhart series, as will be covered in Chapter 5, there is a clear distinction between that series and the New Cut Gang series. While the New Cut Gang books are filled with youthful shenanigans, petty crime, and humor, the Sally Lockhart series is marked by much more serious crimes, larger-scale deceptions, "adult" concerns, and a much more serious tone. In fact, Tucker calls the new Cut Gang books a "junior version of the Sally Lockhart novels" (62) that reflect a "wish-fulfillment world," where the ever-resilient New Cut Gang are able to discover clues that everyone else misses and in the end, save the day (65). Thus, the New Cut Gang follows the path of innocence to achieve growth, while Sally Lockhart must walk the path of experience.

Conclusion

The novels discussed in this chapter feature characters moving from needing assistance to prevail to being able to stand on their own without superhero or adult intervention. Pullman's *Spring-Heeled Jack* depicts an urban legend/comic book superhero as one helper, with other kind adults and a dog as secondary helpers, while the *New Cut Gang* books feature children who find some adult helpers and others who are villains. In every case, the penny dreadful style which featured fast-paced narratives with a plethora of somewhat disjointed plot events is used to pay homage to a literary form that Pullman admired as a youth. Yet in this group of texts, Pullman's child and adolescent characters are not as criminal-minded as their ancestors, most of their behavior is harmless, and the stories focus on the path they take as they learn that their innocence sometimes sets them up for exploitation by adults who do not have their best interests at heart. All the characters grow through their experiences to become more aware of the nuances of adult behavior, and this leads to them becoming experienced. Yet overall, these novels reflect Pullman's stories of innocence, for the tone, plot events, and settings reflect quest-driven stories where the focus is centered more on the fun aspects of youth as opposed to the darker elements that Pullman exposes in his stories of experience. As readers will see in the next chapter, the darker elements prevail with a focus on corruption and mistreatment by social institutions and government structures, placing other characters into a world where it is not the innocent path that awakens them to experience, but the path of betrayal and trauma that affects their maturation process.

Part II
Stories of Experience: Betrayal and the Path to Maturity

> "My heart, Will..." she groaned, and clung to him, her wet face contorted with pain.
> And thus the prophecy that the Master of Jordan College had made to the Librarian, that Lyra would make a great betrayal and it would hurt her terribly, was fulfilled.
> — Philip Pullman, *The Amber Spyglass*[1]

As the quote above reveals, Lyra becomes the great betrayer to the dearest part of her world, Pantalaimon, her dæmon, her own dear soul. Through Lyra's passage, she learns that she must often play the role of the betrayer, but until the part of her journey where she must visit the land of the dead, she is not conscious of this role. She acts in the best interests of those around her in innocence, only to find that her actions set other actions into motion which result in the betrayal of others, such as Roger. For Lyra to truly reach wisdom and grace and achieve her higher purpose in bringing about great change to the worlds around her, she must betray with full knowledge of what she is doing. As the boatman explains to Will in *The Amber Spyglass*, "It's her misfortune that she can see and talk to the part she must leave" (282). This means that Lyra must become experienced. It is only through her journey that she has truly been able to understand what it means to separate from one's dæmon; she has developed empathy and understanding for those who have lost their souls. But now, she must willingly tear her own away. She must do so in full knowledge of the sacrifice, that to achieve a greater good, something has to die for others to be reborn. As Philip Pullman elucidates in "The Elementary Particles of Narrative," one "can find yet another elementary particle underlying [*His Dark Materials*], and that's the one in which two things that are closely bound together split apart and go their separate ways. That little pattern turns up over and over again in the story — quite without my intending it to; I only saw it there when the story was finished" (145).

The following chapters reflect the darker side of Pullman's fiction: the stories of experience. Despite the fact that some are tempered with humor and lighthearted moments, each piece has a darker core that speaks to the difficulty of passing through the path to maturity when losing something precious becomes the only way to grow. Whether the text in question is a children's book, young adult fiction, or a work penned for an adult audience, Pullman ties his darker works together by this common theme. As such, the characters in these selections are Lyra's compatriots at the climax of her journey and onward, when she must put aside childish things and learn to act as an adult. Fraught with peril, pain, and anguish, these characters must learn that the only way to reach the light is through the darkness.

Five

The Sally Lockhart Quartet
Socially-Conscious Penny Dreadfuls

> "I wrote each one with a genuine cliché of melodrama right at the heart of it, on purpose.... And I set the stories up ... with the most convincing realism I could manage.... There are many more such hackneyed situations awaiting my attention."
> — Philip Pullman, from his official website[1]

If we accept the theory of parallel universes, then there is more than one ending to *His Dark Materials*, for in a universe juxtaposed with Lyra's own, Lyra decides not to return to her Oxford, but instead enters another, and in that world, she grows up to become Sally Lockhart. After all, Lyra and Sally have much in common. Their stories commence with the belief that they have been orphaned; their journeys reveal their true parentage; their dear animal companions, mirrors of their souls, are brutally severed from them, metaphorically or literally; and the great loves of their lives are also lost forever soon after their relationships become intimate. This is all to say nothing of their extraordinary similarities in personality, such as independence, stubbornness, tenacity, resiliency, and empathy for those less fortunate. The Sally Lockhart quartet includes the novels *The Ruby in the Smoke* (1985), *The Shadow of the North* (1988),[2] *The Tiger in the Well* (1990), and *The Tin Princess* (1994). With the publication of *The Golden Compass* in 1996, one might wonder if Pullman was working with a prototype of Lyra for more than a decade, as if he decided, in *His Dark Materials*, to go back and imagine what a younger version of his heroine Sally might be like if she were living in a slightly altered time and place. The two women are classic Pullman heroines who live in worlds that are anathema to women, the poor, the uneducated, and minorities, and both heroines rise up against significant personal trauma to come to the aid of those in need. Despite the many rich connections that exist between Lyra and

Sally, which could be explored in depth in another study, this chapter is concerned primarily with Sally, her compatriots, and their dramatic journey from innocence to experience. The path on which Sally and her friends find themselves is reinforced by the gothic and penny dreadful conventions of a more sophisticated variety than Pullman has used previously, and the destination culminates in an updated version of the Victorian historical thriller that highlights a social and political consciousness.

Claire Squires provides some brief reflections on the Sally Lockhart quartet in her book *Philip Pullman's* His Dark Materials*: A Reader's Guide*. She claims that the stories can be seen as precursors to Pullman's epic, for they feature the exciting escapades of a group of self-reliant, courageous, and resilient young people on a quest to vanquish evil (13). Linking the novels' setting to that evoked by Wilkie Collins, Charles Dickens, and Leon Garfield, Squires states that the characters must face questions of identity, maturity, gender roles, and morality in the face of varying levels of incompetence, indifference, and pure malevolence as they attempt "to defeat wrongdoing, to protect the disadvantaged" (14). Squires compliments Pullman's "refusal to provide happy endings" (14). She especially notes that the final novel concludes "with a violent scene of twisted love, where innocence and experience collide in a dreadful fate" (14). Additionally, Squires points out that Pullman included a prototype for the dæmons on which he would later rely so heavily in *His Dark Materials* when he crafted Ah Ling's servant Miranda, seen initially as a supernatural figure and later revealed to be a trained monkey who attends to his needs but who also reflects his own "brooding, sick, [and] malign presence" (14). Finally, Squires discusses the importance of storytelling in the quartet, which reaches its peak when Daniel Goldberg quiets an agitated crowd and staves off a riot by engaging them in the power of narrative, a scene which is evoked more than once in *His Dark Materials* when Lyra enthralls others with her own narrative prowess (14).

In spite of the many links which arguably exist between Pullman's epic and these forerunner novels, though, the books are beautifully written and stand on their own as wonderful examples of Victorian historical thrillers with a twist. Sandra L. Beckett's *Crossover Fiction: Global and Historical Perspectives*, explains that Pullman has always been a significant player in the world of crossover fiction, not just in *His Dark Materials*, but also through the Sally Lockhart books. Beckett notes that the focus on "serious issues" such as patriarchal attitudes, the drug-infested underworld, and anti–Semitism make the texts relevant and exciting for both adolescent and adult audiences (116). Beckett also describes how Pullman has become an outspoken advocate for crossover fiction, insisting that young people should read so-called "adult books" as he did in his youth (22). She argues that no matter how much he integrates fantasy in his stories, he remains highly attuned to realistically portraying human emotions (138). While her remarks are directed towards *His Dark Materials*, the same could be said for the Sally Lockhart texts. Despite the gothic and penny dreadful conventions that lay the foundation for the setting and style, at the heart of each novel lies the psychology of realistic human dramas, reminding readers that emotional struggles are timeless. But before reflecting on those enduring difficulties, we must consider the foundation of the series.

Textual Awareness of Penny Dreadful and Gothic Conventions

In *Penny Dreadfuls and Other Victorian Horrors*, Michael Anglo explains that publishers seized the opportunity presented by advances in literacy and printing methods to produce vast quantities of "cheaply produced escapist literature" in the 1830s and 40s (11). Interested primarily in turning a quick profit, the publishers often printed contributions from unknown writers without acknowledgement or deliberately committed theft from reputable authors of Gothic and popular fiction (11). The books were targeted towards a mature audience, but between the cost, the size, the sensational titles, and the illustrations, the material also attracted a younger crowd (11). In fact, Pullman recognizes the variation in readership of penny dreadfuls early on in *The Ruby in the Smoke*: when Sally first enters the offices of Lockhart and Selby, she sees an elderly man, the porter, "reading a sensational story of the sort known as a penny dreadful" (3). Yet the moment that young Jim Taylor is introduced, he accuses the porter of having stolen his "*Union Jack*" (4). E.S. Turner's *Boys Will Be Boys* indicates that the penny dreadfuls put out by Edward Lloyd were proven to be aimed at a dual audience. In fact, he explains that Thomas Frost recorded in 1860 that if there was speculation about whether a work would achieve popular success, Lloyd would first "'try it out on the office boy'" (20).

As the primary aficionado of the penny dreadful in Sally Lockhart's

Part II: Stories of Experience

world, Jim, an office boy himself, is frequently reading a thriller or reminiscing about the plot of a story as he meets similar situations in his own life. In fact, the penny dreadful often provides inspiration for solutions to problems Jim encounters. One day, he comes up with an idea to help Sally, and he reflects, "It was a penny dreadful idea, but a good one.... After all, here was something straight out of *Stirring Tales for British Lads*, or *The Adventures of Jack Harkaway*— the penny dreadful once again proving to be a sound and accurate guide to life" (Pullman, *The Ruby* 113). Jim further spreads the gospel of the penny dreadful when he frequently offers copies of them to others. He uses "a tattered copy of *The Skeleton Crew, or Wildfire Ned*" as a bargaining chip to try to obtain information from a messenger boy (139); he tells Sally and Fred that they need to portray infamous murderers such as Sweeney Todd and Spring-Heeled Jack in their stereoscopic photographs (141); he gives Fred a copy of *Boys of England* (141); and when he tracks down the gang who has been caring for Sally's daughter Harriet, he offers Bill, who has recently learned to read, "a pile of penny dreadfuls" in addition to expenses incurred as a thank you for the gang's assistance (Pullman, *The Tiger* 401).

Interestingly, Jim takes his affection for tales of adventure full circle by becoming a writer himself during the course of the quartet, but he faces some scrutiny along the way that is not unlike the charges leveled at the writers of sensational fiction in the Victorian age. A humorous incident in *The Shadow in the North* symbolizes this tension surrounding the popular fiction that took its ideas from established Gothic literature. Jim has been trying to attract the attention of a theater owner with his work, and his creation *The Vampire of Limehouse* is returned, accompanied by a note from, of all people, Bram Stoker, who manages the Lyceum Theatre. Stoker's note identifies Jim's melodrama as a "farce" and Stoker asserts, "I feel that vampires, as a subject, are played out" (97). Jim's defensive response is "'It's a bleedin' tragedy, that one. Farce, my arse'" (97). Undeterred, Jim continues to read and write, and when he is injured and recuperating in Trembler's home, he passes the hours "reading sensational novels, losing his temper at the thinness of their plots, writing a story of his own, tearing it up in a fury" (353). As Jim's character deepens, his tastes change, and in *The Tin Princess*, Pullman writes, "He [Jim] also wrote stories for the shockers and the bloods ... though he had higher literary ambitions than that" (26). Jim's dream of becoming an established author is revealed at the conclusion of the quartet when he tells Adelaide

Five. The Sally Lockhart Quartet

that he intends to pen "a serious, proper, historical, scholarly book" about the events of the past few months, the treaty and many betrayals that took place in Razkavia (282). In more ways than one, Jim Taylor represents Pullman himself, who may have initially been inspired by the Victorian blood-and-thunder tales, but who stretches their boundaries while still keeping many stock devices intact.

E.S. Turner reflects on the essential premise of 19th century plots: a villainous, manipulative relative or legal guardian orchestrates the stripping of the protagonist's birthright (19). Descending from the Gothic, this plot device abounds in the Sally Lockhart quartet. First of all, Sally is meant to receive 10,000 pounds upon her father's death and is denied this birthright and financial security, and so she must peddle her services as a manager and accountant to Rosa and Frederick in exchange for food and shelter. She was also to receive the Ruby of Agrapur, but like the money, it has gone missing and she must piece together the clues of its whereabouts after the journal that Major Marchbanks gives her, which reveals its location, is stolen. Later, when she finds that Major Marchbanks was actually her father, she loses more than the physical objects that were her birthright: she must also come to terms with the emotional anguish that results when she learns that she is not descended from the good and honest Captain Lockhart, but from a man who was an opium addict who sold her for a gem (Pullman, *The Ruby* 210). The loss of one's birthright, symbolized in an inheritance or a connection to someone by blood, is standard fare for the Gothic novel, and it is a tragedy that affects more than just Sally.

In *The Tiger in the Well*, Sally's daughter Harriet is the character nearly denied her birthright. Though Harriet is such a small child that she cannot properly function as a protagonist, her birthright is threatened when Mr. Parrish, a pawn in Ah Ling's sick and twisted game, attempts to use the court system in England to remove Harriet permanently from Sally's custody. Mr. Parrish also attempts to seize her business and assets; thus, Sally's entire livelihood is threatened. Since Sally's lover Frederick, the father of her child, dies immediately after Harriet is conceived, Sally is a single parent and Harriet her only living relative. By attempting to kidnap Harriet for his own purposes of revenge, Ah Ling nearly succeeds in denying Harriet her future birthright. In fact, until the conclusion of the novel, it appears as if Harriet will either be captured and forced to become Ah Ling's personal servant, or remain in the gang of street urchins who inadvertently end up caring for her (400–401).

Birthright is also denied to various characters in *The Tin Princess*. In being caged and hidden away before the tale begins, Leopold is presumed dead and therefore denied succession to the throne, because he married without monarchial approval. Prince Wilhelm, the next in line to the throne, and his wife Anna are shot, denying their rule, and then later Wilhelm's brother Rudolf, who is assassinated during his coronation ceremony, is also denied the chance to live out his days of leadership over the kingdom of Razkavia. Furthermore, Adelaide, who assumes power as queen when her husband dies, must flee the country at the story's conclusion, and thus she, too, is denied her rights, not by birth, but by union through marriage, as the story ends with "the annexation of the Kingdom of Razkavia by the German Empire" (275) and an implication in the papers that Queen Adelaide has disappeared along with "several valuable items from the Treasury" (276). In fact, the novel culminates in a character's reflections on usurpation, when Becky tells the recently returned Sally Lockhart, "It's all been for nothing. The *betrayal* ... Adelaide worked so hard for so long, and she was nearly there.... And all the time, there was someone working away to undermine it" (285).

Another convention of the Gothic is the larger-than-life villain, and Pullman creates four prominent antagonists in the four texts, all of whom are possibly more complex and multi-dimensional as characters than their Gothic predecessors. Jackson, Coats, and McGillis's introduction to *The Gothic in Children's Literature: Haunting the Borders* discusses some of the typical traits of Gothic villains, who "attract us because they are flamboyant and irrepressible. Their desire refuses to be contained. They are audacious.... They are, in that psychoanalytical sense, both ourselves and our 'other'" (13). Jackson, Coats, and McGillis also explain that the Gothic villain may be termed a destroyer or creator (13). Pullman's villains are more complex due to the subtle nuances of their malevolence, their motivations and their own struggles. As Jackson, Coats, and McGillis reveal, traditional Gothic fiction "maintains that evil is undeniably evil ... and its corruption must be as forcefully and completely expelled as possible. Nowhere is there any suggestion that evil might simply be misunderstood, or forgivable" (7). Yet Pullman's villains are all described in such depth, and the additional revelation of their motivations shows that while they are indeed evil, there are catalysts behind their actions. Part of Sally's maturity comes from being able to empathize on some level with her persecutors.

Mrs. Holland is undeniably a force of pure hatred. She is manipulative, self-serving, and able to control men twice her size to do her bidding. It is one thing to see her blackmail a criminal into committing more crime on her behalf, but another to see her gross negligence and mistreatment of Adelaide, the young, fearful child who trembles at the mere sound of Mrs. Holland's voice. Mrs. Holland's primary threat to Adelaide is to tell her that if she does not obey, she will find herself buried in the garden with the other little girl who was murdered by Mrs. Holland. It is heart-wrenching to see such a young child living in fear of being mutilated by her employer, staring fixedly at the patch of earth where she believes "the last little girl" has been interred (*The Ruby* 126, 129). Mrs. Holland also exposes this young girl to the ravages of opium addiction by forcing her to sit with Matthew Bedwell while he enters the "nightmare," prompting him to talk and taking down his ramblings should he say anything of value about Sally or the ruby, and even lighting the pipe for him when he starts to come out of his drug-induced haze.[3]

Despite the many atrocities committed by Mrs. Holland in the name of claiming the ruby that was promised to her, she is nearly humanized at the end of the story when she comes face to face with Sally and explains Sally's true parentage and the reason she has a connection to and a right to the jewel. One almost feels sympathy for her when she says to Sally that she was once young and beautiful: "'You look at me now and you think I'm old and ugly, but twenty years before the mutiny — before I married — I were the loveliest lass in the whole o' northern India. Pretty Molly Beckwith, they used to call me'" (Pullman, *The Ruby* 212). It was her beauty that attracted the maharajah, and she gave herself to him, only to be rejected. His dismissal of her encourages her need for vengeance, and from the moment she allows the men in to murder him, she is forever changed, willing to murder again if it means she can claim the ruby she was once promised (212). Her one-track mind is so intensely focused on that ruby that she leaps into the water after Sally discards it, committing suicide in the process (213). Thus Mrs. Holland is more interesting than the typical villain because readers understand she was once a very different person who was betrayed, and instead of choosing a higher path, she chose the path of hate and malice. In her last moments, she even appears to regress to her youthful state, "laugh[ing] and toss[ing] her head like a young girl ... [saying,] 'My beauty. My pretty Molly'" (213). Her final performance is marked by madness.

The same trajectory can be shown in villain Ah Ling's progression.

Part II: Stories of Experience

Known in *The Ruby in the Smoke* as Hendrik Van Eeden, he is described as a physically imposing man, strong, blond, and sunburned, of mixed race. He changes drastically in physical appearance from the first novel to the third, in which he makes his comeback. When he threatens her life in *The Ruby in the Smoke*, Sally shoots him, but his body is never found (223). When the third novel begins and the custody of Sally's daughter and her entire livelihood are threatened by a man she has never heard of, the reader wonders fairly early about the identity of the man behind Mr. Parrish. Ah Ling is mentioned briefly with the words, "Whether she'd killed him or not she didn't know, for she had fled in horror at what she'd done, and no body was ever found" (Pullman, *The Tiger* 15–16). It naturally follows that a person shot and left for dead might return to enact vengeance, especially if that person has a ruthless criminal past. In his essay, "Let's Write It in Red: The Patrick Hardy Lecture," Pullman explains the difference between surprise and suspense. Surprise means the reader has no idea what might be coming and is therefore shocked by it when it happens, while suspense enters the narrative if the reader has some idea of what may happen but does not know when it will occur (58). Ah Ling's reappearance falls into the suspense category, for the reader probably suspects that he is the man trying to take everything important from Sally, but the reader also is not quite sure because his physical appearance is so drastically altered from what it had been in the past. As it turns out, Ling was paralyzed by Sally's bullet and he has little remaining quality of life. Blaming her for his sorry state, he seeks revenge by attempting to take her business, assets, home, reputation, and respectability, but all of that may pale in comparison to what he wants to do with her daughter. Because he is paralyzed, he has a trained monkey, Miranda, who feeds him and helps to care for him. Ling's goal is to kidnap Sally's daughter Harriet and train her to become the replacement for Miranda and his manservant, Michelet, a role which would effectively make her his personal slave. All of this would be sufficient reason for Sally to want to kill him, and when they are trapped in the collapsing building with the lift broken and the water rising below them, Sally has every opportunity to allow him to die in front of her eyes. Yet she overcomes her feelings of revulsion because she knows that it is she who imprisoned this villain in his useless body: "'No, I never intended this, Ah Ling. You didn't deserve this. But I did it'" (351). Her realization urges her valiant attempt at rescue, but he dies despite her efforts (370–71).

The Tin Princess presents a few villains of varying degrees, but the most interesting and multi-layered one is Carmen Ruiz. Because her husband, Leopold, married outside his social class (and ethnicity), she is seen as a blight on the monarchy, and Leopold is removed and kept caged away from the public eye rather than allowed to publicly embarrass the family. Meanwhile the two are reported to have been murdered. As the story opens, Carmen is in the beginning stages of her revenge, intending to murder the potential successors to the crown, with the intention to free her husband and reclaim the throne which is rightfully his. She succeeds in murdering Rudolph, but she does not realize that Adelaide, his wife, will claim the throne, and this sets off a chain of events whereby she wants Adelaide dead as well. By the time Jim figures out who she is and finds her, her complexity comes out, because he notices that she is very likely borderline insane, and yet, he understands why her mental state has deteriorated. Like the other villains, she has lost something significant and has been turned evil by the circumstances of her life and the trauma she and her husband have faced. Carmen appears to have drowned, only to come back at the conclusion of the novel and attempt to kill Adelaide in her fury, and Adelaide subsequently kills her in self-defense in what may be one of the strangest conclusions to a series ever written that nearly screams "sequel needed."

Finally, Axel Bellmann, the villain of *The Shadow of the North*, is a very cold, calculating, intelligent man who is incredibly complex. Of all the villains, he is the one Sally respects most, if only because she comes to admit to herself that many of the points he makes about his motivations bear out in the real world. Axel is the architect of the steam gun, and if he is to be believed, his intentions are initially noble, in that he wants to construct many steam guns in order to keep the peace. He believes that simply knowing a weapon of mass destruction exists will keep people in check — that no wars will break out, and people will live in harmony because they know the consequences of refusing to keep in line. Further, he knows that creating large-scale weapons, especially in countries that lack sufficient jobs, schools, and resources, is a way to bring those things to the people. He makes an impassioned speech to Sally in which he explains the ends do justify the means. Yes, he is responsible for the sinking of the steamship Ingrid Linde and the collapse of the Anglo-Baltic company, but in his mind, those who perished were acceptable sacrifices incurred to bring his stolen plans to fruition, so that a far larger number of people could survive and thrive as a result of his bringing work to impoverished areas. When he makes his case to Sally, she claims initially that people would never agree to his radical ideas. But he tells her that they would agree to make weapons even knowing the potential cost, and she has to admit to herself that he is right, that as long as people have money in their pockets and a roof over their heads, most do not care if their paycheck comes from a ruthless man interested in attaining power above all else (329–32).

It is likely his strange idealism and his truthfulness that Sally finds almost attractive. Axel is the one villain whom Sally seems to respect, evidenced by her reflections on him even after he has been brutally killed by his own gun. He is the serpent to her Eve, in that he is able to cloak his malevolence in idealism, which is seductive and enticing to her. When he asks her to marry him, it appears that Sally is entranced by him. After all, he refers to her as his equal, which for the time, would be unheard of (she has heard this before only from Frederick Garland). As it turns out, she tells him she accepts only because it means that she can ask him to show her the gun, and her intention is to shoot the gun, destroy it, and die in the explosion. She may or may not intend to kill him. In the end, he is killed by his own gun while she survives. But she holds in herself some measure of respect for him as a villain, because later she compares him in a favorable light to Ah Ling. Perhaps what she found attractive in him was those qualities much like her own: independence, resourcefulness, and drive. Certainly for these reasons, Axel Bellmann is not the stereotypical Gothic villain but an altogether more complex character.

Thus, the penny dreadful and Gothic conventions that permeate the Sally Lockhart series provide an underpinning in terms of genre and setting, bringing to readers familiar patterns evoked in novels of this era. Yet as critics have noted, Pullman updates the Victorian historical thriller by introducing some 20th century conventions and concerns, the first of which is a feminist heroine.

Sally Lockhart: A Victorian Era Feminist Heroine

One of Sally Lockhart's most attractive qualities is her fierce independence. Unlike the classic Victorian woman of her time, she defies socially-prescribed roles for women in a plethora of ways. She is like the typical Pullman heroine in terms of her resiliency, tenacity, and self-reliance, but she is unlike the women of her era for whom domesticity reigned. It is difficult to know how accurate a person she might be if she were real, or if Pullman has simply applied the qualities of a more modern-day heroine to a character living in the past in an effort to make a larger point in exposing the difficult realities that invariably faced women should they attempt to be more independent than their age would allow. In terms of literary realism, he provides enough of a backstory for Sally to lend some credence to the idea that a woman raised such as she would naturally grow into a woman used to defying convention.

One of the first shocking discoveries that Sally makes at the conclusion of *The Ruby in the Smoke* is that the man she believed to be her recently deceased father, Captain Lockhart, was in fact a friend of her real father who took custody of her when she was a baby. Her real father, Major George Marchbanks, was an opium addict who amassed great debts, and he traded Sally to Captain Lockhart for a priceless ruby when she was very young. Captain Lockhart, being a bachelor himself and an atypical father, allowed Sally many liberties women of her time were denied, thus "her knowledge of English literature, French, history, art, and music was non-existent, but she had a thorough grounding in the principles of military tactics and bookkeeping, a close acquaintance with the affairs of the stock market, and a working knowledge of Hindustani" (Pullman, *The Ruby* 14). She can also ride and shoot and carries her own pistol, a gift from her father, whose timeless advice to her was to "'keep [her] powder dry'" (148). Such skills do not serve her when she enters the home of Mrs. Caroline Rees, her father's second cousin, to live and work after Captain Lockhart dies, and her Aunt Caroline admonishes her for her lack of accomplishments (16–17). Yet it is precisely those skills that prepare her to have the wherewithal to leave her aunt's home and secure for herself a place with Fred and Rosa Garland in exchange for becoming their accountant and business manager. Regardless of the fact that Captain Lockhart was not her blood relative, it was his unorthodox methods of raising her and the lack of a mother figure that are responsible for Sally's unusual abilities when she is thrust into the world without a guardian.

While it would seem believable that Sally would come to her teens in possession of a different skillset than most women, it would seem unlikely that those around her would so readily accept her for who she is. In fact, most do not, but it becomes clear that she chooses her friends quite wisely. Sally is not one to fall back into the use of feminine wiles (because she frankly has not had much practice in using them and feels awkward summoning up the damsel in distress persona) and she is direct and forthright with those she meets. It stands to reason that she instantly feels a kinship with Fred and Rosa Garland, because their backstory, too, is unconventional. Both are seen as mavericks for their career choices — Fred is a budding photographer and Rosa an actress — and they are all but disowned by their father and thrust into the world with no one to rely on but one another. Sally's immediate perception upon meeting them and their assistant Trembler is that *"they don't think of Trembler as a servant. And they don't think of me as a girl. We're all equal. That's what's so odd"* (Pullman, *The Ruby* 85; italics in original). So it is not as if Pullman is rewriting history in terms of showing women in a different light than was possible, but he has chosen to focus on the story of a small set of characters who are outliers and therefore find camaraderie.

Sally is a breed apart as a young woman in Victorian England, and her independence begins to shine in *The Shadow in the North*. In the introductory remarks to the Masterpiece Theater production of this novel, actor Alan Cummings jauntily observes, "Sally Lockhart has her own business ... and it's not a dress shop." The only other woman in Victorian England, he says, with a job, is the queen herself, who is the model of domesticity, yet he says, "Sally sees nothing blissful in domesticity." As this novel opens, Sally has established her own business as a financial advisor, even though she retains ties to Frederick Garland's photography business. It is interesting to note that in rewriting this novel, Pullman changed the opening to hone in on the struggle for women to find emancipation. The original first chapter, which was quite melodramatic, encompassing the scene in which Mackinnon is being threatened in his dressing room, is exchanged for a fleshed-out description of Sally's meeting with a female client, a former teacher, who gave her life savings to Sally to invest. This investor is alluded to in the original version of the text, but in this second version, the teacher's story and her interests in women's rights are placed front and center. Upon losing her investment in Anglo-Baltic, Miss Walsh asks Sally to investigate if there is a way she can recoup her loss, and she says, "I have a lifetime's interest in the emancipation of women, and nothing pleases me more than to see a young lady such as yourself earning a living in this enterprising way" (Pullman, *The Shadow in the North* 7). Later, Sally makes reference to Bellman's factories and the "dangerous working conditions in them," to which Miss Walsh replies, "Girls with necrosis of the jaw.... There are some wicked ways of making money" (9). Such commentary makes for a less exciting opening than the original melodrama, but it sets the tone for the book and warns the reader that there are larger social issues afoot than the typical penny dreadful fare.

In terms of Sally's personal life, she finds herself in a difficult position regarding her connection to Frederick Garland. It is clear that she has deep feelings for him, but it is also evident that she sees marriage as an instant ticket to domesticity, something she seems to abhor. In terms of Frederick's offer of marriage, her feeling is that "she'd never marry anyone else, but she wouldn't marry him. Not until the Married Woman's Property Act was passed" (Pullman, *The Shadow in the North* 14). Even though Sally trusts Frederick, she rails against the legal ramifications of marriage regarding her personal property and business. She believes having to relinquish her rights is "intolerable" (14). But more than the issue of property rights, she is quick to criticize Frederick any time he appears to be protective of her, almost as if she believes she will lose the ground she has gained emotionally as a self-sufficient woman if she gives in to her femininity. When Frederick asks her to move her residence so he can keep watch over her, she explodes in anger, saying that she has a pistol and her dog, and "[she doesn't] need to be shut up in a fortress and guarded" (189). Frederick has every reason to worry about her and as he says and proves with his actions, he is not like other men. But her reaction is to close down when he offers to help, even if it puts her life in jeopardy.

Later in the novel, with the loss of her beloved dog Chaka, Sally seems to change a bit in her thinking. Understanding that she might have died alongside her dog, she finally grasps that connecting with Frederick and allowing her true feelings to surface does not make her weak. Interestingly, though, the scene in which she expresses her love for him is entirely orchestrated by her. Unlike the typical Gothic or penny dreadful heroine, Sally makes love with Frederick on her own terms. She initiates the act by leading him to her bedroom, and she asks him not to speak until they consummate their relationship. Later, she explains why she was so insistent that Frederick not speak. She claims that she was afraid he would ask her to marry him, and "you wouldn't have seen that I brought you up here because I wanted to, and not because we were going to get married. D'you see? I wanted to do it. I wanted us to be like this" (Pullman, *The Shadow in the North* 291). This is evidence that Sally claims power over her sexuality in desiring for Frederick to know that she was a willing partner who was not simply sleeping with him in gratitude for a marriage proposal, but instead, she is a woman who wants to freely give her virginity to someone she truly loves. It is only after this act that she accepts the proposal of marriage, saying that she thought all along that her career would be over if she married, but since she lost Chaka, she now sees that she can have both Frederick and her career in her life (291). The real tragedy, of course, is that just after she reconciles her independence with her desire for a partner, she loses Frederick in the fire. And yet she gains in that she becomes pregnant with his child, which later leads to other advances in her growth.

A final way that Sally differs from the typical Victorian women of her time lies in her initial unsuitability for motherhood. Sally first encounters a situation in which she is expected to be motherly in *The Ruby and the Smoke* when she and her friends rescue Adelaide. While Rosa has a natural affinity for childcare, Sally stumbles, completely unsure of herself and awkward: "Sally wanted to help; but she couldn't discover how to express the kindness she felt" (Pullman, *The Ruby* 130). Sally is more effective as a teacher or role model than a caregiver, as evidenced in *The Tin Princess*, where she is only physically present for a small part of the story's action but evidently a constant presence in the minds of the female protagonists who find her inspiring. In the brief time Sally and Adelaide are together in Adelaide's youth, Adelaide is in awe of Sally and unable to find a way to connect to her. This measure of respect is evident later in *The Tin Princess* when Adelaide reflects on her lowly beginnings and her rise to a prominent position, and she remarks to Becky, "I'd love to feel that she [Sally] was proud of me ... I think if she approved, I wouldn't mind what anyone else thought" (*The Tin* 138; italics original). Becky, too, thinks of Sally as a role model: "Becky was fascinated. If you were a single woman, you needed great strength of character to have a child and remain respectable. She found herself looking forward to meeting this gun-toting female desperado Mrs. Goldberg [Sally's married name], and finding out how she did it" (17). Despite Sally's obvious public strengths, though, she harbors feelings of inadequacy that she must face and overcome.

Thus, the more significant way that Sally's worries about motherhood manifest lie in her connection to her daughter Harriet. At the end of *The Shadow in the North*, Harriet is a connection to the man Sally loves who has passed, a symbol more than a reality, precisely because she has not been born yet. In *The Tiger and the Well*, though, Harriet is still a largely symbolic figure in Sally's life, because Sally appears to have put her business

Five. The Sally Lockhart Quartet

front and center while Sarah-Jane raises her child for her. Sally is not an absentee parent by any stretch, but she does not know the first thing about taking care of a child. She spends her days at her consulting firm, and her time spent with Harriet is relegated to play or bedtime: "Shortly afterward, Margaret left for the station, and Sally went up to Harriet. They had an extra long time together; Sally held her close and sang her all the nursery rhymes they could remember, and then offered to play a special game ... but only Jim could play that properly; so Sally blew out the candle" (*The Tiger* 41–42). It is only after she flees alone with Harriet that she is forced to face what to this point might have been her greatest fear: caring for the basic needs of a small child.

In Roberta Seelinger Trites' *Waking Sleeping Beauty: Feminist Voices in Children's Novels*, Trites defines the feminist children's novel as one which focuses on self-discovery by female protagonists, who are pushed to become introspective by the realization that "some form of environmental pressure has made them aware that they are not upholding socially sanctioned gender roles" (2). Trites explains that scrutiny may come from a variety of sources, which includes "self-doubt," and this is probably the factor that most affects Sally. Pullman generally stays with his third person omniscient point of view throughout the Sally Lockhart series, but the exception is made just after Sally loses "everything." When she is holed away for the night in a sparse rented room, the point of view of the text shifts to an internal monologue scribed in a notebook in which Sally writes to calm herself, and the passage is marked by anxiety and doubt: "I don't know what to do. I don't know enough about washing her and feeding her, and I certainly don't know how we're going to manage, but many women do, after all.... What am I going to do? ... Am I going to have to stay like this for the rest of my life?" (*The Tiger* 133). To that point, Sally has always been able to take care of herself through her unorthodox skills and ambitious drive. But when she no longer has Sarah-Jane to mother her child for her, she is thrust quite abruptly into a world she does not understand. Interestingly, her fearful monologue moves from the unknown, concerns about how to adequately care for Harriet, to what is more familiar to her, getting to the bottom of the legal mystery that surrounds her.

Sally fights an uphill battle in becoming a mother figure because the job is so alien to her, a truth which may have been perfectly normal for some Victorian women but which would never have been spoken of. She tends to move by instinct, addressing problems as they occur rather than obsessing over being the perfect mother. When Cicely Corrigan, Sally's maid, meets Sally at the British Museum, Sally allows Harriet to "relieve herself into the gutter" (Pullman, *The Tiger* 162). Cicely initially reacts with shock, but as she watches Sally, she thinks to herself that somehow this act shows Sally's strength (163). As much as Sally initially identified with the upper class, the losses she has experienced and the poor women and children she has observed have humbled her to such a degree that she acts with alacrity to solve a problem, even if it means debasing herself in public. So it is not as if Sally's maturation includes growing into the typical Victorian mother when she lacked this quality at the beginning of her journey, but it does include learning how to overcome self-doubt. As Trites reflects, "the character who uses introspection to overcome her oppression almost always overcomes at least part of what is oppressing her. Feminist children's novels, ... then, constitute a triumphal literature" (3).

Betrayal, Trauma, and Loss

The typical sensational Victorian story was enthralling and over the top with an "often incongruous plot" (Springhall 234), fitting in some ways the genre of romance with a so-called "glamorized" lifestyle of the street urchin (238) and "strict attention to Manichaean opposites, poetic justice, and happy endings" (245). Springhall asserts that the plots of such tales buttressed established standards of propriety, social standing, and politics rather than questioning or undermining the status quo (225). The penny dreadful-influenced novels in Chapter Four of this study of Pullman's work certainly reflect minimal questioning of the norm, with only minor exceptions noted. However, it is clear that Pullman's agenda in the Sally Lockhart series is quite different. By reinventing the penny dreadful and injecting a feminist heroine with sympathetic supporters, Pullman sets the stage for subversion. Through various betrayals, trauma, and losses, Sally and other characters grow to learn that the world in which they live is corrupt and in need of serious ongoing attention and change; further, the characters realize that they themselves may in fact be part of the problems, and they must come to terms with keeping hope alive in a world where the notion of one person being able to make a significant difference may pan out, but it just as likely may not. In short, Pullman's blood-and-thunders are about more than excitement and lurid details; they are just

Five. The Sally Lockhart Quartet

as much about the way that loss can become the greatest teacher and inspiration to individuals to attempt to make a difference.

Nicholas Tucker is one critic who has written a fairly extensive analysis of the Sally Lockhart quartet in his book *Inside the World of Philip Pullman*. Tucker focuses much more heavily on the detective story origins for Pullman's narratives, but he also agrees that Pullman alters the typical detective story by imbuing it with an awareness of political and social concerns (31). Tucker has many terrific insights on the series, but there is one claim he makes which is easily refuted. He contends that these stories take "romantic license" because the characters' "kindness and generosity never see[m] to come at any real cost in terms of subsequent emotional or financial problems" (34). On the contrary, there are innumerable costs to Sally and others.

The most obvious example lies in the consequences to Sally, Fred, and their friends that occur as a result of their assisting Isabel Meredith. Isabel is a most tragic figure, a woman with a birthmark covering half her face who is barely able to make a living by her skills as a needlewoman. After falling hopelessly in love with Alastair Mackinnon, Isabel is confronted by thugs who destroy all her needlework in an attempt to force her to reveal the location where he is hiding. Threatened with the destruction of his letters, the only part of him she possesses for herself, Isabel reveals Mackinnon's location, and the men let her go. Subsequently, she pays a great emotional cost for having betrayed her lover. When she meets Sally to ask her for help, she says, "'I'm so sorry.... I betrayed him. I'm ashamed...'" (Pullman, *The Shadow of the North* 183). Sally's reply is "'I'm sure you didn't mean to. Someone tricked you or forced you, didn't they'?"[4] (186). Sally pities poor Isabel and she and her friends take her in, just as they once did with Adelaide, to protect her. But this act of kindness and generosity on their part is the catalyst that sets off not one, but two deaths. One of Isabel's duties in exchange for room and board is to walk Chaka, Sally's dog, every evening. Cloaked and in the dark, the man sent by Axel Bellmann to kill Sally instead attacks Isabel, who is barely wounded, while Chaka loses his life in defending Isabel, attacking the man, and killing him. Later, when their photography shop and home is burning down, Isabel stays in her room, intending to die in the fire as payment for her actions. Yet Frederick attempts to rescue her, and in so doing, loses his own life. Certainly losing her faithful companion Chaka and her lover Frederick are tremendous emotional costs to Sally and to those around her. Even Jim is said to "weep" over Frederick's death (317). This is only one of many examples across the four novels of a tremendous cost that characters must incur as a result of interceding into another person's life with an act of love and support, and every time that Pullman stays with the path of realism in not shying away from tragic consequences, he steps a bit further away from tidy resolutions.

Aside from these two tragic losses in Sally's life, we must remember that her story also begins with personal loss. *The Ruby in the Smoke* opens with the revelation that Sally's beloved father has died in a shipwreck. At first, Sally is able to control her emotions in the face of this loss, but eventually, her nightmares reveal that there is a mystery in her past connected to loss that she must overcome. When she awakes from her nightmare, she "surfaced like a swimmer, in mortal fear of drowning. She heard herself sobbing and gasping, and remembered: *There's no father. You're alone. You must do without him. You must be strong*" (Pullman, *The Ruby* 28; italics in original). Despite the feeling of suffocation that comes with the realization that she is a woman alone in a man's world, she learns to stand up for herself in the face of fear. After she is placed in her Aunt Caroline's home and she is expected to submit to a domestic role to earn her living, she finds the courage to leave without any clear plan of where she will go. Thus, the self-sufficiency her father taught her spurs her on to take care of herself, find a job, and a home, and these are all examples of growth that only come as a result of great loss. She learns to confront difficulties head on: "problems, she thought, were things you faced, not things you ran away from" (72).

Later in the novel, Sally inadvertently becomes pulled back into the nightmare when she and Frederick enter an opium den: "everything was dark again. She felt a desolating sense of loss —" (Pullman, *The Ruby* 101). Even though she re-experiences emotional devastation in going under the influence of opium, she talks herself into using the drug later under the supervision of Trembler (188), which is the only way she can find out the truth of her past. When she awakens from the experience, "she had changed, and so the world had changed" (203). It is only by confronting a terrible fear — the fear of voluntarily taking a highly addictive drug that has destroyed so many lives — that Sally is able to recall the devastating memories of her past, memories which reveal that Captain Lockhart was not her father. When Mrs. Holland confirms for Sally that Major Marchbanks, an opium addict himself, was her real father, and he sold her for the priceless Ruby of Agrapur, Sally experiences yet another tragic loss.

Five. The Sally Lockhart Quartet

Additionally, she learns that Captain Lockhart was a bachelor and thus her mother was not the strong woman she had been raised to believe in: "And that was Sally's mother gone. Wiped away at a stroke: and it was almost the worst blow of all to know that that wonderful, vital woman had never even existed" (210). So Sally faces a fear to find the truth, and the truth shatters her world. But the end result is that her newfound wisdom spurs her to mature. She will not be defeated: "Oh, there would be difficulties, hundreds of them. But she would cope" (230).

Such a belief becomes incredibly important later when Sally consummates her relationship with Frederick, only to lose him so abruptly afterward. She quite willingly takes on the role of single parent in *The Tiger in the Well*, and she refuses to be ashamed that Harriet was born out of wedlock. Learning that Mr. Parrish has designs on taking her child (and only physical link to Frederick) away from her, she does what any strong woman could be expected to do: she attempts to go through the legal system to keep custody of her child and control of her business and reputation, but finding that the legal system fails her, as it would have failed so many women of the time period, Sally leaves everything behind to go into hiding until she can solve the mystery of why she has been targeted. Again, Sally must experience great loss. She immediately finds herself without money or shelter and thrust into the life of those in poverty. These losses of the comforts to which she has become accustomed have a profound effect on her.

For one thing, Sally has always seen herself as a tried-and-true capitalist. But being faced with the impact of seeing real women and children living in filth and decay awakens in her the desire to help those less fortunate. When she is rescued from sleeping on the streets by Morris Katz, who takes her to the mission run by the East London Socialist Women's League (Pullman, *The Tiger* 185), she finds that there is a world of poverty she never knew existed. Dr. Turner fills her in on the work they do to save women and children, explaining, "Not sure about God anymore. Think he's turned his back.... There are thousands, thousands out there starving" (193). To earn her keep, she takes on the job of helping Miss Robbins, the president of the league, to investigate an area where a privy is "blocked and overflowing" (194), and she is struck with horror at the living conditions: "That anyone could stay for more than a few minutes in this noxious atmosphere, far less live in it, was incredible, yet here people were" (195). Seeing the horrific conditions of the lower classes gives Sally pause as she "was torn between her desire to fuss over Harriet and her awareness of the much worse sufferings of some of the other children" (228). When she realizes that Daniel Goldberg, a champion of the exploited, has been targeted by the Tzaddik (Ah Ling), she concludes that she can protect both her daughter and others by risking her life (259). She becomes a servant in Ah Ling's home, where she is threatened sexually by his manservant Michelet and comes into direct contact with the grotesque villain who aims to kidnap her daughter and enslave her.

Later, when she is face-to-face with her nemesis, Ah Ling, she delivers a passionate speech about evil in which she blames him and those in power for exploiting the lower classes for their own personal gain, yet she also shoulders a significant amount of culpability for herself when she cries, "'And you know what's at the heart of it all? ... The gnawing poison cancer destroying and eating and laying waste at the heart of it all? It's not only you, you poor pitiful man; it's me, too. Me and ten thousand others'" (Pullman, *The Tiger* 350). It is her early adherence to capitalism and her eventual disregard for the companies in which she holds shares that pay low wages or deny work, or landlords that refuse to make repairs, that become part of the entire chain of evil of which she is a link. She explains that it is only as a result of the mission and Daniel Goldberg and her exposure to the poor that she is finally able to see clearly the way that everything is "connected" (350), and that undeniably, evil means seeing the connections and looking the other way (351). It is obvious that the personal losses she has incurred have given her a wakeup call, and the result is an overflowing of compassion and empathy so strong that she attempts valiantly to save Ah Ling's life, despite his deeds. The awakening of compassion for one who has wronged her is proof that betrayal has caused Sally to gain wisdom and mature.

Through Sally's interactions with the poor, she becomes conscious that even though she has been dealt a tremendous blow, she still has tremendous advantages: her education, her unusual skill set, and her staunch supporters, who may be in Africa during most of this story, but who rally to her aid upon their return. Furthermore, she has her business contacts, people who are willing to work with her or invest in her even after everything that has been done to destroy her reputation. It becomes obvious to her that despite the traumatic period in her life in which she is presently mired, that there is a definite end to some of her suffering, when others may never experience changes in their circumstances. Therefore, she realizes that she has advantages others do not, which is why she includes herself as part of society's problems. Shouldering some of the blame for society's ills is the mark of a wise and empathetic person. It is clear that if Sally had not lost almost everything, she might never have come to this growth in character and achieved an understanding and sympathy for those less fortunate. By the end of *The Tiger in the Well*, having escaped a certain death, Sally is ready to become an agent of social change: "There were movements to join, things to learn, groups to organize, speeches to make.... She'd seen at last the work she was born to do. She felt absurdly lucky. To have real, important work to do, and to know it!" (Pullman, *The Tiger* 406).

Once Sally comes to this life-changing epiphany, there is little "story" left to see its effects. She marries Daniel Goldberg, a champion for human rights and social activist, so it can be assumed that she embraces a more socialist agenda. However, the fourth narrative, *The Tin Princess*, removes Sally and Dan from the picture almost entirely, and so it is difficult to discern how her work changes to encompass her new world view. In the beginning of *The Tin Princess*, Pullman reveals that Sally and her husband are off to America so that Daniel can "study labor relations in Chicago" and she can "look at the stock market in New York" (Pullman, *The Tin* 25). Aside from an occasional mention by the other characters and the serendipitous knitted sweater that assists an imprisoned Jim Taylor, Sally is absent from the narrative.

Nicholas Tucker takes issue with the final novel of the series for this reason. Tucker believes that the last novel lacks the depth of the others and is not as believable with its focus on another nation entirely and a monarchial struggle for the throne, falling under the category of "almost pure romance" with very little exploration of social problems (46). I would argue that this novel reads quite like the first novel in the series, though, in that the first novel is about establishing Sally Lockhart as a character, teaching the reader her background, revealing the losses that have defined her, and beginning her quest to find the truth of her past. Sally's quest is a self-centered one initially. This is understandable, as we must know and help ourselves before we can become effective agents of change in others' lives. For this reason, I would suggest that *The Ruby in the Smoke* is also much more of a romance than the very socially conscious third novel. Similarly, Adelaide becomes Sally's natural symbolic descendent in *The Tin Princess*, where the text is primarily centered on who Adelaide is, how she came to be in the position of princess, how her past trauma affects her search for identity and self, and how she claims that sense of self in taking power of Razkavia upon her husband's tragic death. Likely the reason *The Tin Princess* isn't as "successful" (Tucker 46) comes from the fact that it sets the stage for a larger story to come.

Carol Jean Pingel praises the novel for its detail, indicating that "the reader can smell the beer and hear the sausage sizzle" (43), but like Tucker, she claims the end of *The Tin Princess* is "a bit less satisfying" than Pullman's other works (43). Interestingly, Pullman said soon after its publication, "I think it's the best thing I've written, but then I always think that about my most recent book" ("I have a feeling" 29). True, as a stand-alone novel, it does end on a rather climactic and strange note with Adelaide nearly killed by Carmen Ruiz but found sleeping on the floor, with Carmen's dead body lying on top of her (Pullman, *The Tin* 290). However, the ending is obviously a springboard to a continued story. Tucker states that Pullman has indicated a desire to write more stories about this set of characters (50). I asked Pullman about his intentions for and whether he had deliberately ended *The Tin Princess* with a cliffhanger and used the novel as an exposition of sorts, by finishing the story of Sally and Daniel by sending them to America and by positioning Adelaide and Jim to the be next major protagonists in the series, and he replied, "You're absolutely right. I see Jim and Adelaide rather as the Nick and Nora Charles of the 1880s and 90s — a couple on the fringe of the glamorous worlds of the stage and the aristocracy, solving mysteries together, being tremendously sexy and cool. I'd love to do a few stories of that sort."[5]

Therefore, since Pullman sets the stage for a second narrative series depicting the world of Adelaide and Jim, readers could probably expect the same trajectory for Adelaide as that given to Sally. Clearly Adelaide has the drive and desire to take what she has learned and help others, and a budding relationship between her and Jim is potentially destined to mirror Sally's relationship with Frederick Garland in terms of their mutual respect and equality. Pullman has obviously left the door open to continue the maturation process of these beloved characters.

Conclusion

In Pullman's remarks on the genesis of *The Ruby in the Smoke*, first called *The Curse of the Indian Rubies*, a play for a school-aged audience, he indicates that the series began from some postcards he purchased in an antique shop many years before he felt inspired to write Sally's tale. He described one postcard as depicting a little girl sitting on the knee of a man dressed in working-class clothing meant to symbolize a sentimental poem named "Daddy." Another postcard showed the little girl's mother dressed in angelic garb, peering down with love upon her from Heaven. After a time, Pullman began to consider what the story of the girl and her parents might be, but he also wondered about the person the viewer could not see, the one behind the camera (Watkins 28). As the idea for a story formed in his mind, Pullman added one element that was not reflected in the postcards: a 16-year-old girl who was facing imminent danger on her way to the photographer's studio (28). Pullman immortalizes this purchased postcard on the page in *The Ruby in the Smoke* when he describes a stereoscopic photograph that is taken of Adelaide sitting on Trembler's knee (Pullman, *The Ruby* 132). Later, in *The Tin Princess*, Becky notices the stereoscope and photo in Adelaide's room and remembers to tell Jim and Sally; Sally's copy of the photograph, shown to Becky, identifies Adelaide as the now grown up little girl she and Jim and Frederick once rescued (Pullman, *The Tin* 4; 20). It is interesting to consider, would there be a Sally Lockhart if Pullman had never purchased those postcards one day? Would Pullman have taken what he learned in writing the playful penny dreadful/detective stories of Chapter Four and recast those elements in a more sophisticated light to include an awareness of 20th century sensibilities in a new style of Victorian historical thriller? And for that matter, would there be a Lyra if there had not first been a Sally?

Six

I Was a Rat! and *How to Be Cool*
The Intersection of Fantasy and Realism Through Social Satire

> "But *inclusiveness* is the whole point: the fantasy and the realism must connect."
> — Philip Pullman, "The Republic of Heaven"[1]

Can a fairy tale written in the midst of *His Dark Materials* and an adolescent satire inspired by real students once taught by Philip Pullman have any connection to one another? At first glance, it would seem unlikely. Pullman's fairy tale *I Was a Rat!* features a small boy who appears on the doorstep of an elderly couple, claiming that he was a rat, and he has little to no memory of what transpired before the moment he realized he was a boy. The story that follows reads at times like a fantasy in which Roger (as Bob and Joan name him) innocently interacts with different people only to be mistreated, ridiculed, or exploited, while the tabloid media, the most obvious nod to a historical time period and a definite gesture to realism, exacerbates his plight. In the end, he is rescued by Bob and Joan who keep the dark world at bay outside their door. By contrast, *How to Be Cool* is a story about a group of teenagers who are obsessed with the latest fashions and on a quest to be the cool kids. Unexpectedly, one of the teens stumbles on the offices of an organization sanctioned by the government called the National Cool Board; offended that he and his friends are not responsible for creating trends, Jacob (a.k.a. Gaf) and his friends seek to infiltrate the organization and define coolness for themselves. The novel ends with an unsteady resolution as the head of the institution that has lost power offers to join forces with the young people, only to be rejected by them.

It would seem that there are no strong links between these texts, and yet the connections are there. Both narratives depend on some level of fantasy to facilitate the plots, yet the fantasy is merely a vehicle to tell stories grounded in realism. Pullman has never been comfortable with being labeled a fantasy writer. In answer to the question "Did you write *His Dark Materials* as fantasy?" Pullman explains, "I don't like fantasy. The only thing about fantasy that interested me when I was writing this was the freedom to invent imagery ... but that was only interesting because I could use it to say something truthful and realistic about human nature" ("Q & A"). Arguably, Pullman had the same goal in mind when he wrote *I Was a Rat!* and *How to Be Cool*. Behind the imaginative elements in each are truthful assertions about the insidious control that people and institutions can hold over the innocent. Whether the innocent are youngsters, such as Roger, or teens, such as Jacob and his friends, it seems that the media, the educational system, corporations, and the government all form an oppressive body that has the potential to demean, ridicule, or exploit those who lack power.

How do these two novels illustrate the path from innocence to experience? Both depict innocent protagonists who are duped by deceptively well-meaning authority figures, yet the heroes learn through trial and error that often they must be very careful of those in whom they place their faith, and in the case of *How To Be Cool*, the youths may even come to the realization that no one is to be trusted but themselves. Both texts conclude with a superficial resolution, for there is an undercurrent of realistic cynicism that points to a potentially difficult future for the characters, for certain elements of the societal structures that condition their worlds are not about to change for the better any time soon.

I Was a Rat! *and Fairy Tale Intertexts*

Pullman's fairy tale *I Was a Rat!* was written in 1999 during the time that he was writing *His Dark Materials*. As Chapter One discussed, Pullman had already worked with the Cinderella tale type in 1998 with *Mossycoat*, but as Smith defines it, that text was a "re-vision" (10). *I Was a Rat!*, by contrast, embraces a combination of postmodern intertexts. From Smith's list of possibilities, Pullman's book utilizes "Writerly: Implicit reference to a fairytale in title" (Smith 10) through the protagonist's humorous declaration that he was a rat, for Roger was turned from a rat into a page, a staple of the Cinderella story, but he missed the opportunity to be disenchanted and returned to his animal form. The story also fits the intertext "Allusion: implicit reference to a fairytale within the text" (10), because Roger makes reference to knowing the true identity of the princess and even says that the kitchen folk all know who she is. This references the hidden identity of the Cinderella or Mossycoat character who may be known as one person to some but who remains a mystery to others. The tale is also a "Fabulation: crafting an original fairytale," because Pullman's tale picks up where Cinderella might have left off, taking a minor character and positioning him as the new fairy tale's protagonist, and shaping an entire world of innovative characters and events around him. As Tucker explains, the story is so original that it merely has its genesis in the Cinderella story, and readers may not even see those minor connections until the final chapters (73).[2] Pullman also uses the intertext "Metafictional: discussion of fairytales" (Smith 10) in the chapter-separating tabloid discussions that illustrate the impending marriage of the princess to Prince Richard, which is "like something out of a fairy tale" (Pullman, *I Was a Rat!* 1). Lastly, Pullman features the "Architextual/Chronotopic" intertext, which utilizes a "'Fairytale' setting/environment" (Smith 10). From the presence of an elderly couple who are respectively a cobbler and a washerwoman, two standard fairy tale character occupations, to the addition of symbolic slippers, to being saved from certain death by the intervention of a helper, and to the quest-like nature of Roger's journey to find acceptance, nurturing love, and a home, the story is steeped in what Kate Bernheimer calls "*a fairy-tale feel*" (3).

Vanessa Joosen's "Philip Pullman's *I Was a Rat!* and the Fairy-Tale Retelling as Instrument of Social Criticism" explores the dual nature of a story that intermingles two types of narratives. Joosen asserts that Pullman's work "negotiates between the fairy tale's traditional generic features on the one hand and a late-twentieth-century setting and thematics on the other hand. Whereas in some aspects it produces a confrontation between the two frames of reference, in several others it smoothes out the tensions" (197). Joosen points out that the tale in some ways reflects an "unspecified time and location" (197), for which traditional fairy tales are known, but the text is made more complex with its obvious nods to the late 20th century through its inclusion of *The Daily Scourge*, which is "strongly reminiscent of British tabloids" (199) and performs the function of widening the narration beyond third person omniscience to polyphonic with the paper itself becoming a "voice," even if a disreputable one at that.

Six. I Was a Rat! *and* How to Be Cool

Furthermore, Shelley King's "Democratic Reading: Ideology and Genre in Pullman's *I Was a Rat!*" explains that the tabloid works better as a device than the broadsheet newspaper because it "appeal[s] to a longing for the marvelous," and tabloids are known for "reporting marvels as truth" (165–66). King's essay further mentions the "real-world" connection between Pullman's princess and a real princess, Princess Diana, asserting that this link is "no doubt jarring to some readers as recent political history meets cultural classic" (181). King points out that on his website, Pullman discusses his inspiration for the story as deriving from a scene he pictured of a boy who suddenly appears and claims he was a rat. Linking rats to princesses was a natural association for Pullman, who says he thought of "two in particular, a real one and one from a story" (qtd. in King 184). Pullman admits he relishes hearing of the moment when adults reading the book to children have an epiphany and realize "the other story it's connected to" but then he stops just short of filling in that blank for the reader (qtd. in King 184). King makes a very strong case for the "other story" being the rise and tragic demise of Diana Spencer, Princess of Wales (184). Additionally, Vanessa Joosen makes the claim that Pullman's story alludes to the famous torture and death of Jamie Bulger (200–06). There is yet another potential reading of the text, however, which reconciles the fantasy and the realism in a way that has not been considered in depth to this point and takes into account the child as orphan and barbarian with a real-world link to a famous feral child.

I Was a Rat! *and the Feral Child*

Laura Peters' essay "Revisiting the Colonial: Victorian Orphans and Postcolonial Perspectives" focuses on the way that Pullman's *His Dark Materials* highlights the plight of orphans in Lyra's "neo–Victorian world" (94). Lyra and Will, Peters argues, are not orphans in a strict sense, but they must become orphans to position themselves to be the saviors of other displaced children (95–97). Peters describes the historical background of orphans in the Victorian age, which is informative in establishing a framework for the gross mistreatment of Roger, a child who is not only an orphan but an orphan with animal-like behavior. Peters states that in the mid-1800s, "orphan children were emigrated out to empire in increasing numbers, initially by Boards of Guardians responsible for their care and eventually through an increasing number of schemes" (99–100). Two women, Macpherson and Rye, targeted what they referred to as "'street arabs,'" "'waifs and strays,'" and "'gutter children'" (qtd. in Peters 100). Understanding that there were "thousands" of orphaned children in the cities, and that as much as 60 percent of the reformatories held orphaned children, emigration was offered as a panacea (100). As Peters indicates, "orphan children living on the street were most likely to be criminalized both by need and by association ... generat[ing] a sense of social failure within Victorian culture" (100). This social reality led to "racial and colonial overtones" in the way orphan figures were viewed; subsequently, the orphan was often misaligned with the savage or barbarian, lacking proper civilization (100).

Such societal demonization of a class of children would of course have devastating effects on the perception of orphans themselves as human beings, and clearly we have seen in prior chapters many examples of the ramifications of exploitation of parent-less children. But what might be an even stronger strike against a child in need of nurturing care would be if he literally imbued the animalistic behavioral traits that his fellow orphans were only assumed to carry. In other words, what could be worse than being a child who has no parents and must survive on the streets, but a child who is half-animal and barbaric, in other words, a feral child?

Contrary to popular belief, feral children have not necessarily been raised by wolves. While feral refers to children "who have spent much of their formative years in the wild, without any contact with other humans for a significant period of their lives" (BBC), it also means "reverted to an untamed state ... of or characteristic of a wild animal; savage" (*American Heritage Dictionary*). Pullman's iconic heroine Lyra Belacqua is described in this light; a "barbarian" (*The Golden Compass* 34), "a coarse and greedy little savage" and "a half-wild cat" (36), Lyra is street-smart, unkempt, and a force to be reckoned with when she leads her peers in "deadly warfare" (35) with rival gangs of children. It is Lyra's more feral qualities that make her unlike other children, belligerent and opinionated, strong and fiercely independent. Her traits prepare her for her journey to the north to save her friend Roger and the other children, and they also make her naturally suspicious of duplicitous adults. Her half-wild wariness serves her, for instance, when she is able to see that Mrs. Coulter is not to be trusted despite her affectionate pretense, and the ability to be able to read the threatening actions of Mrs. Coulter's dæmon and her attempts at self-control lead Lyra to escape from her clutches. In fact, it appears that no one but Lyra is able to notice Mrs. Coulter's strange odor that she emits when angry: "Mrs. Coulter seemed to be charged with some kind of anbaric force. She even smelled different: a hot smell, like heated metal, came off her body. Lyra had felt something of it earlier, but now she was seeing it directed at someone else, and poor Adèle Starminster had no force to resist" (91). Thus Lyra's animalistic characteristics tend to aid her during the course of her journey and position her to save countless numbers of children, and later, all of those in a state of limbo.

By contrast, the young boy in *I Was a Rat!*, given the same name as Lyra's best friend Roger, is arguably a fully feral child whose actions strongly resemble animal behavior and whose language and thought processes are much more simplistic. As a result, his journey is more specifically focused on the path to attaining freedom and acceptance. While Pullman's story of Roger may initially appear to be a playful, imaginative fantasy, Roger's barbaric behavior and the subsequent exploitation by adults bent on his "civilization" process reflects the harsh realities for poor, displaced, and feral children. Secondly, Pullman's feral child illustrates the path from innocence to experience, for Roger emerges as the true innocent when he finds that he is surrounded by adults who are at best indifferent and at worst malicious betrayers. His early helpers, Bob and Joan, also become experienced when they learn that the people and institutions set up to protect children fail Roger, requiring the two of them to intervene to become his saviors. A sense of hope lies in the fact that there are redeemers for such children, but the reality is that they are rare.

When Bob and Joan, an elderly childless couple, open their door one night to find a small boy who has no memory before three days ago when he used to be a rat, they do their best to care for him, but so many seek to exploit him that it becomes increasingly difficult to keep him safe. What is remarkable about Roger is the resemblance his story bears to the real-life case of Kaspar Hauser, a young teen who emerged from the woods in the early 1800s, who was both gawked at and studied, until his most tragic death a few years later. The first to make this connection was Jack Zipes, in *Breaking the Magic Spell*, who links Pullman's *His Dark Materials* with Hauser's story based on Pullman's portrayal of wild children and society's wish to see them civilized (220). Zipes contends, "his trilogy and fairy-tale parody, taken together, reflect Pullman's hopeful vision of transforming darkness" (220). Zipes has even coined a phrase for this, the "Caspar

Hauser problem" (220) which he says runs through most of Pullman's work. However, other than this brief mention, Zipes does not explain the uncanny similarities between the real-life Kaspar and the fictional Roger, and arguably, there are many. Furthermore, in a correspondence with Pullman via email, in response to my mention of the Zipes quote to him and my own reflection that the Kaspar Hauser story seemed to be strongly reflected in Roger's narrative, Pullman stated, "Kaspar Hauser, absolutely yes.... The Kaspar Hauser narrative is practically Roger's."[3] Just as he has done so many times before, Pullman takes his inspiration from another story to craft something of his own, but unlike the characters in the literary works which have often inspired him, Kaspar Hauser was a real person with a story that in many ways, resembled a fairy tale.

According to Douglas Candland, there are around 300 or so cases of feral children, children raised by animals, or children raised in neglect (qtd. in Shattuck introduction). Probably the most famous documented feral child was Victor, the Wild Boy of Aveyron, whose story was chronicled in Roger Shattuck's *The Forbidden Experiment*. Yet a less familiar feral child appeared the year Victor died, and his name was Kaspar Hauser (196). On May 26, 1828, this young man stumbled out of the woods in Nuremberg and was discovered by a townsperson (Candland 39). His gait and mannerisms were like that of "an intoxicated person," and he carried with him a letter of introduction, asking permission to serve in the cavalry (39). Taken to the Captain, he spoke only two phrases, which roughly translated to "'I want to be a horseman as my father is' and 'Don't know' (or 'dunno')" (39). He refused all offered sustenance but for bread and water, which "he swallowed greedily and with extreme satisfaction" (40). Led to a stable, he fell into a deep sleep upon a pile of straw. He showed neither fear nor surprise, but simply a "dullness," and while his body was that of an adolescent, he had the "demeanor" of a toddler (40).

Given the name Kaspar, which means "clown," he was born in 1812 and placed with a family at 6 months, with whom he stayed until he staggered out of the woods (Candland 41). Hauser was kept first in a prison cell, where people came to gawk, stare, and bring him gifts until he was placed with guardians (45). Eventually he was forced to attend German high school, where he "suffered as it were [a] second imprisonment" (48–49). He learned to speak, yet he lived in a half-wild state; eventually, he related memories of his confinement. He claimed to have been imprisoned in a "cell/hole/cage clothed in a shirt and breeches" (44). Sitting down in the dark, he knew no sounds, nor the passage of time. He was given bread and water and cared for by a man whom he could barely see, who eventually presented some passing interaction with him when he helped him learn to stand, to walk, and to write his name (44). Once freed from confinement, Kaspar amazed those who studied him with his over-acute senses of night vision, hearing, and smell (Newton 141). However, much notoriety surrounded Hauser's case, and after two attempts on his life, by a man who was never caught, he died three days after the second attack (Candland 50–51).

Why was Hauser murdered? Theories suggested he was a prince in line to the throne of Baden who was kidnapped and replaced with a dying or dead infant (Newton 170). Legend said he was the legitimate son of Stephanie de Beauharnais (the niece of Napoleon's wife Josephine) and Karl the Duke of Baden (170). In fact, *The London Dispatch* ran a story in April 1838 asserting this as truth (171). However, the story was seen as both fact and fiction in the time it ran, with noted Scottish folklorist Andrew Lang claiming it was merely a fanciful story (167). While some still dispute Hauser's lineage, Michael Newton in *Savage Girls and Wild Boys* asserts that in the 1990s scientists exhumed his body and proved there was no DNA evidence to link him to the royalty of Baden (178). Newton poses the question, "Might Hauser have been stabbed not for what he actually was, but for what everyone thought he was, a prince in exile, the exceptional embodiment of an old myth" (178). Newton continues, "Hauser, like Victor before him, seemed to the people of the time the embodied fulfillment of fantastic narratives they were telling about themselves" (128–29). Similarly, Pullman's fictional character, like Hauser before him, demonstrates, just as Newton suggests, "just how greatly the need for a Hauser figure remains" (178).

Pullman's narrative of Roger, then, alludes in many ways to Hauser's. First, when the boy who was a rat comes to Bob and Joan's door, he appeals for assistance from Bob, a cobbler by trade (Pullman, *I Was* 3). The first two men Kaspar Hauser met when he came from the woods were shoemakers (Newton 129). They remarked that Kaspar was "dressed like a stable boy" (129) with a letter of intent to enter the service; similarly, Pullman's child is dressed in a page's uniform, and Bob remarks that he must be "in service [...] [going] along with the master or mistress in a coach" (*I Was* 5). Similar to Hauser, who greedily ate his bread and water, Roger attacks his bread and milk with gusto and "put his face right down into the bowl and began to guzzle it up directly, his dirty little hands gripping the edge of the table" (5). Pullman's child has no sense of time or place; he only knows that he is "three weeks old" (7), has siblings all the same age, and his parents are somewhere "under the ground" (8). Even more intriguing, when Bob insists they must call him a name, the first name Joan suggests, which she later abandons, is "Kaspar" (9). Also, the rat-boy christened "Roger" often repeats the word "dunno" (5), linking his speech to Hauser's first spoken word. Furthermore, Bob makes direct reference to the strange boy's feral state as he sleeps: "He might be a wild boy. He might have been abandoned as a baby and brung up by wolves. Or rats. I read about a boy like that only last week in the newspaper" (10).

The allusions to Hauser continue when Roger eats his breakfast the next morning and tells Bob and Joan that he only ever ate in the dark before that day (Pullman, *I Was* 13). Later, they take him to city hall, an orphanage, the police station, and the hospital, all in an effort to get some help for this unfortunate displaced youngster (15–28). When their efforts are stymied, they take him home, care for him themselves, and send him to school. Having no proper training in how a child should behave in public, Roger, like Hauser, finds himself in trouble and caned for being disruptive (30–37). In turn, he escapes this second form of confinement to run away to the marketplace, where he knocks a stand over and is taken to the police station (38–41). After being rescued by Bob and Joan, the "Philosopher Royal" hears of his case and decides he must investigate, but only to serve himself: "There'd been children brought up by wolves before, but no one had ever studied a child brought up by rats. It would make him famous!" (47).

Taken to the palace, Roger becomes the subject of various experiments. His answers to psychological questions provoke a response from the Philosopher Royal, who writes, "Cannot distinguish truth from fantasy" (Pullman, *I Was* 49). He soon learns Roger has some connection with royalty, for he knows the names of the king, queen, prince, and princess. The Philosopher Royal thus makes the note: "Fantasy-identification with figures of glamour. Common among lower classes. Indicates humble origin for boy" (51–52).

Meanwhile, another adult plots to benefit from the rat-boy. Mr. Tapscrew, a proprietor in a fair's traveling show, plans to trap the boy and create "a whole freak show of rat-humans" (Pullman, *I Was* 56). Finding Roger by a dustbin, Mr. Tapscrew imprisons him in a small cage. Tapscrew's wife outfits him with a large rat costume complete with hand-sewn scabs and pustules, and they place him in a pit filled with rotten food and dirt. Told to eat what visitors throw at him and grunt instead of talk, Roger puts on a convincing show as the "world's only genuine living rat-boy" (74) until he says "thank-you" when someone throws him a potato (76). Although he had learned to say thank you from Bob and Joan, he is now beaten for his act; ironically, he reverts to a completely animal-like state in order to survive. This act of reversion, incidentally, has been shown with the well-publicized case of the girl known as Genie, a child confined to a room in her home in California for 13 years, who, among other atrocities, was beaten by her father if she spoke. Some time after she was rescued in 1970, she learned to speak some words and phrases, although when placed in foster care, she was beaten again for vomiting and subsequently reverted to the state in which she was found (NOVA).

The indecencies committed on Roger continue by those who pretend to be well-meaning, when one day, a gang of hooligans offers him an escape from Tapscrew's show, but Roger complies only to be treated like an animal once again. Billy and his gang of robbers decide they need a "wriggler," someone who can fit into small spaces and unlock doors for them. Roger, happy to be included, obeys. Caught by the police again after one of the gang's escapades, Roger finds himself the subject of study by the Quarantine Department, where he is caged and sitting on straw, being peered at by the Government Chief Scientist (Pullman, *I Was* 118). At this point in the story the media interferes and exaggerates Roger's actions, leading the press to call for Roger's "extermination" to keep the streets safe "for our children" (122). A tribunal is held, at which all characters testify, and things look desperate for Roger, until Bob and Joan remember the princess, about whom Roger spoke: she was the only person he could remember from his past. They appeal to the princess for aid, taking her a pair of handmade scarlet slippers. When they explain what has happened, the princess cries, "I know who he is! ...But you mustn't ask me any more about it! Please! It's a deadly secret" (151).

Unlike the legend of Kaspar Hauser which connected him to royalty by birth, Roger is not the illegitimate child of the Princess Aurelia, but he is part of a secret: in the past, she knew him as a rat and called him Ratty; she used to be known as Mary Jane, until the fairy tale transformation took place. The Princess was once a humble girl herself, and Roger really was a rat until he was transformed, along with his siblings, as one of the princess's page boys. At a pivotal point in the text, they meet and wish for the lady who transformed them to come back; with their request unfulfilled, the princess uses the power of the press to get what she wants: his freedom. The next day's edition of *The Daily Scourge* reports: "It took the clear-sighted vision of a fairy-tale Princess to penetrate to the heart of the matter and see the astounding truth. THE MONSTER WAS ONLY A LITTLE BOY" (Pullman, *I Was* 161). In the end, as Roger is reunited with Bob and Joan, he claims that being a rat and being a human are both quite difficult in their way, so he will "stick to cobbling" (165).

Even though Roger's benefactors are all real people and not fantastic creations, the construction of the story itself provides a connection between fantasy and reality, for it was fantasy in the first place that got Roger turned into a boy from a rat, yet with no fairy godmother to reverse the spell, he had to live with the consequences. The fairy princess teaches him this, for she is not happy with her choice to become the wife of a philandering prince, but she promises to be the best princess she can be. For that reason, it is fitting that the story begun in fantasy grounds itself in reality in its conclusion, where Roger promises to learn the trade of cobbling and live securely with his new family, for "the world outside was a difficult place, but toasted cheese and love and craftsmanship would do to keep them safe" (Pullman, *I Was* 165). Thus, the story itself has both fantastic and realistic elements, and to subvert the fairy tale, which often begins in some version of reality and ends in fantasy, Pullman begins this story in fantasy and ends it in reality. Additionally, he shows the path from innocence to experience as learned by his protagonist, Roger, parts of whose life seem to mirror that of Kaspar Hauser's and perhaps other documented feral children.

I Was a Rat! *and the Failure of Institutions*

Despite the "feel-good" conclusion of the story, in which Roger is safe and secure from the outside world, enjoying a meal with his adoptive parents, there is an underlying current of cynicism that may reflect Pullman's own strong opinions about the failures of multiple agencies to address the needs of children, including various government and educational bureaucracies, private individuals with public power, and the media. Granted, the story of Roger may be just that: a story, in which the gross mishandling and mistreatment of a cute but uncivilized child, caught up in the aftermath of a fairy tale gone wrong, is nothing more than an exciting series of escapades meant to create tension and conflict, the hallmarks of a page-turning narrative. Pullman himself often remarks that he is not in the business of delivering messages to readers. I asked Pullman about the theme of innocence and experience in his body of work, and his response was "If there isn't some theme of that sort, the work will be frivolous, or superficial, or empty. But I can't start with a theme; I have to discover what it is part way [sic] through. I know some writers can, but I have to start from some vivid little apprehension of character or setting or some curious little event. The theme will emerge later."[4]

Something that complicates the business of "theme" in Pullman's work, especially the works which lend themselves to criticism of elements in contemporary society, is that Pullman is quite ready to make his opinions public regarding the failures of many institutions to address the needs of children and adolescents. In her introductory essay to *Critical Perspectives on Philip Pullman's* His Dark Materials, Katharine Cox discusses Pullman as social critic, noting that in 2009, his official website was modified to provide links to numerous articles he has written on many subjects (2), including education, religion, and politics. Therefore, it becomes difficult to separate what may be a simple child's story from an allegorical condemnation of exploitative institutions, and to be sure, this is part of the inherent complexity in a book like *I Was a Rat!*

The first public institution which fails to support Roger's needs is the City Hall, for the government bureaucracy is set up in such an illogical fashion that the office of "lost children" turns out to be incapable of helping Roger, because he is not lost, but "found" (Pullman, *I Was* 15). The worker filling out the form intended to help Roger comments that "our records are very thorough. There are no lost children in the city, boys or girls.... There's nothing we can do about found children. We only deal with lost ones" (16). By setting up an agency that claims to help the type of child who, according to their records, does not exist, while deliberately turning a blind eye to those in need of care, the government fails in its duty to protect the innocent while claiming otherwise. To add insult to injury, Roger eats a pencil at this office and Bob is charged a significant amount of money to replace it (17), and eventually, the worker claims that it is not her job to assist them (18). On one level, this interaction reads like a satirical trip to the Department of Motor Vehicles, but the rudeness exhibited by the City Hall worker points to a more ominous feeling that the institutions on which people often depend to aid those in need are often cold, unfeeling mazes of bureaucracy that do more harm than good. In fact, the very next stop on their quest to find help for Roger is the orphanage, and Bob and Joan stand outside, look and listen, "[shake] their heads" (20), and walk away.

The Police are no more help to Roger, for the sergeant immediately searches for ways to pass Roger's problem on to someone else. First, he accuses them of wasting his time (Pullman, *I Was* 22), then he says they should take Roger to the hospital (23), calling him a potentially "escaped lunatic" (24). Tying together Roger's charming but odd behavior and lack of memory with lunacy, the sergeant portends that Roger will likely end up a criminal anyway (24). Later, when Roger finds himself in trouble after his escape from caning at school, the sergeant looks at Bob "triumphantly" (39) as if to say "I told you so." After a short visit to the hospital, where he is told to simply stop being who he was (a rat) and be who he is (a boy), he is dismissed and told to attend school (28).

The school authorities also treat Roger poorly, for they have already decided Roger's fate. Because he is an orphan, and because he is strange and unusual, with rat-like behavior, he *will* be a troublemaker. There is no sense of benefit of the doubt or attempt to nurture him, only intense scrutiny as the administrators wait for him to make a mistake. At school he is put into what seems to be the most difficult teacher's class and then immediately told to stand in the corner after he laughs out loud (Pullman, *I Was* 32). When the students start to mildly bully him by hitting him with rubber bands and he cries out, Mrs. Cribbins raises her hand at him and in defense, he does the only thing he knows and bites her. The wound is superficial, and Mrs. Cribbins "had to squeeze quite hard to force a drop of blood out" (34), but it is almost as if she invited his attack. It is as if she had in mind from the moment he entered her classroom that she would find a way for him to leave it, and this is precisely what occurs with his caning by the Head of the school (36–37). By the end of this scene, then, Roger has come up against several authority figures, all of whom have assumed the worst of him, and he is worse off than he was before he showed up on Bob and Joan's doorstep, for now he is traumatized.

When the Philosopher Royal enters the picture, the reader may wonder if now, finally, Roger will receive a true psychological examination and actually be helped. However, he is only exploited, because the Philosopher

Royal is keen on profiting from a book he would write on Roger, for "no one had ever studied a child brought up by rats. It would make him famous!" (Pullman, *I Was* 47). Tucker reflects, "there are moments [in this story] that have much in common with sections of *His Dark Materials*. The image of an orphaned child up against a heartless organization is reminiscent of Lyra's plight ... recall[ing] a similarly pitiless cruelty shown by scientists and their masters towards the children" (75). The Philosopher Royal is no different in his desire to exploit Roger than Mr. Tapscrew, who creates a sideshow act around Roger (Pullman, *I Was* 74) who must publicly beg for scraps and frighten audiences into paying for the privilege to see him. Even the gang of children who ask him to be their "wriggler" (82) only wish to exploit his size for their personal gain in their robberies. Between the neglect, indifference, and negative assumptions of the first group of adults who traumatize him and the exploitation of the second group of adults and children, Roger is left without any advocates and in a terrible position.

Just when it seems no other entity can make Roger's plight worse, one does. Perhaps the most horrifying display of anger and hate comes to Roger from the media. The most strongly cynical side of Pullman's story focuses on the machinations of an overzealous media bent on exaggerating the truth to create interest and sell papers. Roger is not a dangerous child by any stretch, but as Watkins asserts, *I Was a Rat!* "is a story about stories, spinning off from the story of *Cinderella* and satirizing the media's sensationalist storytelling" (43). The fact that in a mere 165 pages,[5] Roger goes from being a child desperately in need of a home and care to a child facing execution simply because the media took hold of his story and demonized him, is chilling. Of *The Daily Scourge*, Tucker says the back and forth of the paper's attitude towards Roger is a "brilliant exercise in mimicry [that] also makes a more serious point about the dangers of gutter journalism" (75). The abrupt shift between discussing frivolous topics such as a "palace make-over" (Pullman, *I Was* 29) versus calling for continued caning in schools (43) reflects the contemporary tendency of the tabloid to involve itself in controversy without actually engaging in debate, for in both articles, *The Daily Scourge* unabashedly takes a position: use tax money to fund an unnecessary and wasteful palace redecoration, and "keep on whacking" children (43). In its article on crime, it would seem at first that *The Daily Scourge* attempts to provide a more well-thought-out argument in trying to discern who is to blame for crime. However, the article moves from blaming teachers, to parents, to the Church, to the Government, and firmly ends on blaming the kids themselves, making the most vulnerable members of society the scapegoat for all society's ills (107).

The most egregious offense of the media in Pullman's story is, of course, its call for the extermination of the "monster," with the article clearly positioned to garner more support as it is credited to the tabloid's "star reporter Kevin Bilge" (Pullman, *I Was* 115) as opposed to the anonymous editorials that have peppered the text earlier. The language of the report is deliberately sensationalized, with claims of the "wound[ing]" of workers and the use of the logical fallacy "experts believe" (with only one unnamed scientist credited). While the report does end with a brief mention of a few nameless politicians opposing the extermination, it is clear that the push for extermination itself will encourage sales of the paper. In a very brief succeeding chapter titled "The Freedom of the Press" (116), the story of the monster has so engrossed the people that all other stories have ceased to be important, and the tabloid subsequently seizes the opportunity to sell an extra 250,000 copies of a "special weekend supplement" (116). Playing again with the notion of a paper which has already decided for the public the way they should land on the issue of the day, the supplement contains even more loaded language, calling poor Roger a "hideous mutation," "evil and bloodthirsty," and printing a tear-out coupon asking readers to check a box indicating whether or not the "evil monster" should be killed, with the box for "yes" significantly larger than the box for "no" (117). Furthermore, when there appears to be a defense mounting to save Roger, the paper denigrates the other side, using the phrase "so-called scientists," putting the word "defense" in quotes, calling its claim "absurd," and continuing its use of strongly connotative words to portray Roger as evil, "the monster demon from hell" compared to the "helpless children" and "kiddies" who are the offspring of those calling for Roger's death (126). The tabloid even incites disobedience and potential riot by quoting a man who suggests that people keep their children home from school if Roger is not killed and somehow turns that into "there will be bloodshed" three paragraphs later (126).

Interestingly, the tabloid only changes its tune when the princess becomes connected to the case in revealing Roger's identity. Understanding that stories about royalty, especially the new princess, will sell papers, *The Daily Scourge* acts very quickly to become supportive of Roger as a boy and not a monster once Princess Aurelia is linked to him. The language is abruptly altered to reflect Roger's sweet innocence, calling him "a normal little fellow" and "mischievous," then instantly condemning those who lacked "compassion" for Roger in the past and ending the article by wondering how many other "innocent children" are at risk of mistreatment by the justice system (Pullman, *I Was* 161). As the reader might expect, the paper never prints any admission of having stoked the fires of outrage, nor does it print any retraction of its earlier condemnations of this innocent boy. It is as if the tabloid is oblivious to its own printed words.

Thus, there is much at stake in this deceptively simple tale about one of Cinderella's pages who missed his chance to be turned back into a rat. Despite its sense of humor, jocularity, adorable illustrations, and fast-moving plot written in language that its stated age range can understand, Pullman works with some very dark themes here. The narrative similarities between the real-life Kaspar Hauser and the fictional Roger set the stage for a deeper look at the way a real child had been mistreated and exploited in history. But the darkness does not end there, for Pullman shows that the majority of people who are in positions to help someone in need tend to shirk their social responsibilities and cultivate self-serving behavior. The path from innocence to experience, then, is walked here by Roger and the elderly couple who become his saviors, for they, too, appeared to have faith in these various systems, but their faith is gone by the conclusion of the story. Recognizing that only they are suitable and loving guardians, Bob and Joan open their home and their hearts to this small, vulnerable boy. Interestingly, Roger recognizes that being a rat is "easier" (Pullman, *I Was* 164) than being a boy, but he still chooses the tougher path, being a person. Recognizing that "the world outside was a difficult place" (164), Roger sticks close to his adoptive family, and in a move that shows camaraderie with the real Kaspar Hauser, he follows in the footsteps of his adoptive father by taking on his trade (164).

How to Be Cool and *Youth in Revolt*

How to Be Cool, published by Heinemann in 1987, is a bit of an anomaly for Pullman, for unlike most of his other fiction, he writes from a contemporary perspective.[6] As Nicholas Tucker states, "this pleasant-enough story never quite achieves take-off" (76), and yet there are many intriguing elements in this story about displaced youth fighting corrupt adults in a fast-paced and exciting narrative. *How to Be Cool* is a satirical story about a group of intellectually lazy but culturally inspired juveniles who spend their time following trends and coming off as the cool kids in their school. Through dumb luck, Jacob, also known as Gaf, stumbles upon a door in a wall that leads to the offices of the National Cool Board, an organization that has apparently been creating and setting the trends that he and his friends have followed for years. Incensed at feeling controlled by a corporate entity whose sole purpose is the exploitation of youth, Jacob and his friends decide to beat the Cool Board at their own game by creating an alternative organization that they control, which they call "How to Be Cool." A struggle for supremacy ensues as the National Cool Board tries to take Jacob's organization down, and in the novel's conclusion, the National Cool Board offers to join forces with Jacob's group, which Jacob firmly rejects. The novel thus ends nearly as it begins, with Jacob vowing that they'll just "'do ... what we always do ... stay cool'" (Pullman 184), while the future of the National Cool Board is ambiguous and Jacob noncommittal about the future of his group.

Pullman explains that he was inspired by many different sources when he conceived of this novel. For one, he says "telly" was a catalyst. Secondly, he points to his years as a middle school teacher, stating, "I was teaching in a school where the three boys at the centre of the story were in my class. With their permission I used their own names. The picture I tried to draw of them was as lifelike as I could make it. I was just tickled by these 13-year-old boys being so into designer clothes, designer shoes, designer everything."[7] Pullman confirms that the three boys "were delighted" at his characterization of them.[8] Pullman also explains that the Head Teacher was intended to represent a stereotypical administrative figure. Finally, Pullman states that the time period became a source of inspiration for his satire, for it was "during the reign of the great evil Queen of Darkness, Mrs. Thatcher — when organisations that had been set up ... by the post-war Labour government, during the founding of the welfare state, were being taken apart and sold off piecemeal to private investors.... There was an organisation called the National Coal Board, which obviously became the National Cool Board, and the fantasy just grew from there."[9]

Additionally, an interview with Robert Butler called "The Art of Darkness" may offer some insight into the behavior Pullman observed among adolescents he encountered when teaching middle school that he later recalled in this work. Butler states that Pullman worked as a teacher for 12 years at three different schools in Oxford teaching students in the 12 to 13-year-old age range. One school was working class, one middle class, and the other a hybrid. Despite the socio-economic differences, he noted that the same behavior prevailed. "There were certain roles that always had to be filled: the clown, the smelly one who no one wanted to sit next to, and the king and queen," Pullman explains (qtd. in Butler). In regards to the behavior of girls in particular, Pullman says that they would either fall into the group of "little Paris Hiltons" or be less mature and innocent, often giving him gifts. Whatever group the girls moved into, and he notes that often adolescents would change the group to which they belonged, students immediately adapted by demonstrating the characteristics of those in the new group. Pullman exemplifies the power of the "cool" queen through Dierdre in his novel when he says that, "she had all the girls in the class right under her control" (*How to* 22). After Dierdre offers the name for their proposed group and a suggestion for what should be written on the poster, Jacob is initially hesitant to take her advice, "but then he thought of all the followers she had" (22), and he decides she can be part of their group, knowing she will bring legions of kids with her without even trying. Certainly this exposure to adolescent behavior informed Pullman's depiction of the youths in *How to Be Cool*, for the book focuses on the efforts that those in control make to become the kings and queens, leading others to copy the trends, no matter how ridiculous they are, in a desperate attempt to fit in with the "cool" crowd.

Despite the evident reasons behind the genesis of the book, Pullman believes that the book is the product of such a small slice of history and culture that it lacks relevance today, stating that it might have had appeal for about "a three-month window,"[10] and the short-lived television series did not widen its popularity.[11] On occasion, Pullman can be dismissive of his own work, as his remarks on *How to Be Cool* and *The Haunted Storm*, which he rarely acknowledges, demonstrate. Interestingly, Pullman's Sally Lockhart novels also represent a single era in history, and yet they do not suffer from being bound by their cultural background to be well-regarded among both fans and critics. Perhaps this is because Pullman seems more "at home" in writing about the Victorian era, as he does so adeptly in a significant number of his novels. Even *His Dark Materials* has a Victorian era "feel" in certain elements of physical setting and the relationship between men and women. As he says in an interview with Catherine M. Andronik, "I don't do realistic fiction well" (43). Rather, he prefers to use the apparatus of fantasy or alternative historical or fairy tale settings in which he can make observations on "what it's like to be human ... [and] what it's like to grow up" (43).

How to Be Cool has been virtually ignored by critics, lacking substantial reviews or analysis and garnering only the occasional sarcastic comment such as the following from a blog entry for the *School Library Journal* written by Elizabeth Bird, a librarian, who explains, "Let this reassure all the authors of children's books out there. You can be the greatest writer in the world and still produce middling fare in your early years. Today's example is *How to Be Cool*." Granted, the novel is not a masterpiece, but it also has some merit and should be given a proper analysis, for it functions as a step in the career of an evolving writer. Regardless of the novel's narrow time period and setting, there are satirical elements worth elucidating in the larger context of one of Pullman's recurring themes: the juxtaposition of youths in revolt against inept, corrupt, or exploitative adult-centric hierarchies.

Firmly set in the 1980s, Pullman's satire is about a set of characters initially estranged not by chance, like Roger in *I Was a Rat!*, but by choice, from their parents, teachers, and other authority figures. In this way they are somewhat similar to their younger counterparts in the New Cut Gang books. Their ages are not discussed, but Jacob says that he hopes he will not turn out like his sister Louise when he reaches 15 (*How to* 2). This remark places him at under 15, but likely he is fairly close due to his and his friends' autonomy and activities. Each character who interacts with a parent, teacher, or other authority figure does so as little as possible, at meals, or after school only briefly, or when called in to the Head's office. Unlike *The New Cut Gang* books, where most of the children simply do not show up for school, these adolescents do attend, but they do as little as possible. There are many ways they have perfected to make it appear they are working in class when they are doing nothing at all (18–19), and the students have no respect for their teachers. They view school more as a place to interact with one another socially and show off their newest trendy outfits. They are essentially juvenile delinquents similar to the New Cut Gang members, but they do not involve themselves in solving crimes or playing harmless pranks on the inhabitants of their neighborhood; rather, they are seen as somewhat threatening by the adults who cannot seem to command their respect.

Another similarity to the New Cut Gang books is the characters' penchant for trying to make a quick buck through various schemes. For instance, they decide to do a photo shoot with their friend Gobbo, who is able to set off the coolometer to its highest setting, and then put the photos in the *New Modes* magazine, claiming that they work for the National Cool Board, as a way to circumvent the cool board's trend-making process and put out trends of their own first (Pullman, *How to* 56–58). The scene where they dress Gobbo and a crowd assembles is somewhat reminiscent of the New Cut Gang's preparation of Dippy Hitchcock as a store mannequin. Of course Jacob's cool kids find a way to make money with this scheme by offering to let those in the crowd stand before the coolometer for a fee (60). This can be compared to the New Cut Gang's rejected offer to test out camping equipment for Mr. Rummage in front of a crowd in exchange for a fee (*Thunderbolt's Waxwork* 5). Later, when Jacob's sister Louise is revealed to be the most "cool" of everyone in the world, she spits out her gum onto the street, and David retrieves the gum and cuts it into 26 pieces to sell at 50p each (*How to* 182). With this similarity between characters always looking for ways to earn money, Pullman's teenagers are quite similar, even though the time period in which they live is separated by a century.

Another similarity between texts is the depiction of corrupt adults set on exploiting young people. *Spring-Heeled Jack* presented the villain Mack the Knife and the superintendent Mr. Killjoy and his assistant Miss Gasket; the New Cut Gang had to prove that Mr. Rummage and Mr. Horspath were the true criminals; and Jacob's group learns fairly early on that Mr. Cashman, aptly named, is out to exploit trends to ensure a steady flow of cash from unsuspecting youth. Jacob's view into the world of the National Cool Board workers reveals a group of what could best be termed social outcasts, "the biggest bunch of creeps Jacob had ever seen ... they all had spots and greasy hair" (Pullman, *How to* 10), those who lack any sense of cool in behavior or appearance. These are the very type typically excluded from Jacob and his friends' competing group "How to Be Cool," and they spend hours doing so-called "research," creating new trends and "detrendifying" if anyone creates an unsanctioned trend. The goal of the Detrendifying Squad is to shut down any following that young people create for themselves, ostensibly because the Cool Board cannot justify its existence if youth come up with their own ideas. As Alex, the head of the quad says to his minions, "You know the rules.... Two is a tendency. Three is a trend" (46). Tucker states that "Pullman clearly detests the modern

Part II: Stories of Experience

consumer world ... and goes out of his way to say so. He also insists on a teenager's right to come to his or her own conclusions" (77). Thus, when Mr. Cashman is defeated and offers to make Jacob and his friend Gobbo wealthy if they will allow him to buy their allegiance, Jacob lacks the trust in him as an authority figure to acquiesce, and he makes his own decision in spite of the promise of a quick buck.

Even though *I Was a Rat!* was written about 12 years after *How to Be Cool*, there is an interesting link between them in terms of *The Daily Scourge*'s attack on who is to "blame" for crime. The tabloid paper first accuses teachers of creating "anarchy in the classroom" (Pullman, *I Was* 107), claiming that there is no longer order and too many bullies are permitted to take over when adults should be responsible for enforcing discipline. The teacher's spokesperson in the article blames the parents, which leads the tabloid to admit that "family values have crumbled away" and morality is a thing of the past (107). This leads to parents blaming "the Church" for the problem, while the Church then blames "the Government," which in turn blames "the kids" (107). While Pullman does not delve into the issue of religion in *How to Be Cool*, all the other objects of blame are satirized in his book, none with more biting sarcasm than the educational system, and no part is left untouched, from the lackadaisical students, to the worn-out, disgruntled, or absent-minded teachers, to the utterly inept Head who is more concerned with promoting himself and his school as a fun place than an institution of serious learning. In fact, Pullman might even be suggesting that if there was any real interest in teaching and learning going on in the school, perhaps the students would not be so wrapped up in meaningless fashions, trends, and competition.

It could be argued that Pullman reverses the structure of the tabloid blame piece in *How to Be Cool*, for he begins by criticizing the kids. From the first introduction of Jacob (Gaf), David, Gobbo, and Nings in school, readers find that they spend their entire day pretending to work. In fact, they seem to have it down to a science, pretending to take surveys, leaving a gluey mess about when they cut pictures from magazines to put in their books, or creating "drama" of various sorts to put the teacher on edge (18–19). Sometimes they take bets on a teacher's behavior, such as David's scheme to earn money by taking bets on when the Maths teacher's pants will fall down (84). Their entire scheme to run the "How to Be Cool" organization is cooked up during school hours, during which they decide on the name of their organization, make a poster, and hold a type of audition of students to join their group (22–23). It seems that the classes only run well if one of them becomes distracted, such as the day that Jacob hears he is a wanted man and "peace reigned in the classroom.... The class did more work that afternoon than in the whole of the previous month" (34).

Yet it is apparent as one reads further into the text that the students have achieved this measure of control over the classroom because those in authority have been affected by the strict rules about education put in place with a series of government changes that restricted the power of teachers and changed the face of education for decades to come. For example, Jacob, Nings, and David end up in advertising for a third year in a row, because they did advertising in both English and Humanities the prior two years. Knowing that all they must produce is something they've done before, a poster about the topic, "they were safe for six weeks" (Pullman, *How to* 19). The presence of a standard curriculum with repetitive elements or benchmarks that students must pass repeatedly is a natural outgrowth of the assessment-driven National Curriculum, which Derek Gillard, in "Education in England: A Brief History," explains came about with the era of Margaret Thatcher: "Thus the twin aims of Margaret Thatcher's education policies in the 1980s were to convert the nation's schools system from a public service into a market, and to transfer power from local authorities to central government." Pullman has written extensively on the failures that have accompanied the National Curriculum, and as the articles on education posted on his author website and elsewhere reveal, his work as a teacher for over a decade gave him unique insight into the problems that come with limitations imposed by a strongly regimented delivery of knowledge. In "Let's Write It in Red: The Patrick Hardy Lecture," for instance, Pullman notes that he was "lucky" to have been permitted to learn the facets of storytelling while he was employed as a teacher, "before the National Curriculum sifted in the land like the Red Death in the Edgar Allan Poe story. No Key Stage or Component or Unit prevented me from telling my class the stories I wanted to tell" (60). He adds that teachers are so overburdened with minutiae that the next iteration of authors will unlikely spring from their fold, because "they have too many other stupid things to do to have time or energy left at the end of the day to sit down and write" (60). Pullman's ascerbic observations on the National Curriculum elsewhere may even be symbolized in the figure of Mr. Cashman who seems to embody all that is "wrong" in the state of education.

Unlike Pullman's other texts, in which villains are isolated and as a result more easily defeated, Mr. Cashman represents an entire organization that has been sanctioned by the government for 40 years, not only permitted to but encouraged to exist, and yet the government also has indicated that it would like to "de-nationalize" the board and let it be taken over by private interests, which might have consequences for banks, London, and the national economy (*How to* 29). In fact, once the coolometer is invented, natural laws of gravity and physics are altered and the universe has the potential to "unravel" (151). Thus Pullman presents a world based in reality with a few fantastic elements to comment on the larger issue about how youth interests are exploited in a way that creates income for large corporations and the government, leading to a form of mind control, and he implies that when people become aware and try to retaliate, the world as they know it is threatened in more ways than they could have anticipated. Mr. Cashman also represents the betrayer of youth culture and therefore leads the novel's characters down the path of becoming experienced when they realize that he is only interested in manipulating them for his own personal gain. In this way, Pullman's novel is linked to his other novels that deal with what one might call "weightier" concerns of large-scale manipulation, control, and exploitation of people in many different age groups, circumstances, or time periods.

Conclusion

Wendy Parsons and Catriona Nicholson once asked Pullman about his "conception of childhood and the bleak attitude the books display about adult irresponsibility" as well as "the predatory aspects of relationships between adults and children" (130). While they were referring to *His Dark Materials*, they pose an intriguing query that can shed light on the satirical pieces Pullman has written. Pullman responded, "I think children have a fairly bleak view of each other and themselves. It's only sentimental adults who think kids are sweet and angelic" (130). Certainly this remark applies to his re-imagined fairy tale *I Was a Rat!*, for most of the children are destined to follow in the footsteps of the unfeeling and uncaring authority figures who serve as role models. Additionally, the cast of characters in

Six. I Was a Rat! *and* How to Be Cool

How to Be Cool begin their tale with a somewhat jaded view of adults in positions of authority and are only more distrustful by the story's conclusion. Both books reflect the "predatory aspects" of adult behavior towards the innocent, which brings the stories out of the realm of pure fantasy, crashing into the real world.

Maria Nikolajeva, in *Power, Voice and Subjectivity in Literature for Young Readers*, notes that "the removal of parents is the premise of children's literature. The absence of parental authority allows the space that the fictive child needs for development and maturity, in order to test (and taste) his independence and to discover the world without adult supervision" (16). Roger is orphaned; Jacob and his friends are not, but their self-imposed isolation and limited interaction with teachers and parents leads them to the position of virtual orphans, who must negotiate a tough world with only their wits as self-protection. Due to Roger's age, it is a given that he will need to find protectors, but Jacob and his friends are more likely to be able to take care of themselves. In either case, as Tucker says, there is hope in the existence of the rare adult who is more interested in love and support than in power and wealth (74).

Despite the fact that Pullman believes his book *How to Be Cool* suffers from a short-lived relevance, his satirical vision of the marketing of "cool" in 1987 may have been prophetic. On 27 February 2001, a *FRONTLINE* program aired called "The Merchants of Cool." Narrated by correspondent Douglas Rushkoff, the program "talks with top marketers, media executives and cultural/media critics, and explores the symbiotic relationship between the media and today's teens, as each looks to the other for their identity" ("Synopsis"). Rushkoff explores the very lucrative business of so-called "cool hunters," marketing firms that study youths and their trends in an effort to discover innovations and find a clever way to sell the trends back to the masses. This creates "one enclosed feedback loop," asserts Rushkoff, which generates enormous revenue streams for those companies seeking to exploit the financial powerhouse of teenage spending. Pullman's vision of the marketing of cool begins with the National Cool Board creating the trends they want youth to follow and taking steps to "detrendify" anything they see youths generating themselves. As Jacob thinks to himself, "He was dead smart at picking up all the cool that came from outside.... But he'd never actually made anything up" (Pullman, *How to* 48).

Yet through the course of Jacob's journey, he and his friends reject having cool dictated to them and retaliate by creating cool for themselves, which brings down the National Cool Board. Realizing that youths themselves can be counted on to create the trends, the conclusion of Pullman's novel indicates that the head "cool hunter," Mr. Cashman, sees an opportunity in joining forces with youth. Much like Rushkoff describes in the *FRONTLINE* documentary, there is no need to create the trends if the marketing firm simply observes the trends and then exploits them. It may sound promising, then, that Jacob rejects Cashman's offer to work together. But as Rushkoff shows, the corporate hierarchy does not need compliance from young people to take their trends and sell them back to them. They only need the power of observation, focus groups, and feigned interest in youth culture to get the youth to speak. In other words, Jacob and his friends may have won the battle for cool supremacy, but in the face of the corporation, they have probably not won the war. Perhaps Pullman's novel should be read again, for what reads as over-the-top satire holds many disturbing elements of truth.

Seven

The Broken Bridge and *The White Mercedes*
The Impact of the Sins of the Father (and Mother) in Young Adult Contemporary Novels

> "Your life begins when you are born, but your life story begins at that moment when you discover that you are in the wrong family."
> — Philip Pullman, Interview with Robert Butler[1]

Philip Pullman's *The Broken Bridge* (1994) and *The White Mercedes* (1992) feature a female and male protagonist, respectively, and contrary to most of his works, both novels are contemporary, representative of the era in which each was published. *The Broken Bridge*, set in Wales, portrays Ginny, a somewhat shy, introspective, artistically talented 16-year-old girl, while *The White Mercedes*, later published as *The Butterfly Tattoo*,[2] is stationed in Oxford and depicts Chris, a quiet, thoughtful, and innocent 17-year-old boy. While the two novels share many facets, the outcome of Chris's story may be darker and less hopeful than Ginny's. Commonalities include the protagonists' search for identity, complicated by their parents' prior marital problems, including infidelity and divorce or abuse. Each protagonist is also deeply affected by the initial euphoria and subsequent pitfalls that accompany opening up to the vulnerability of first love. Both characters also face traumas through which they lose their innocence and gain wisdom, but only after paying a price: Ginny loses her mother a second time when she realizes she was abandoned by choice in the past and present, and Chris loses his first love Jenny when circumstances collide to make him an accomplice to her murder.

The difference in the two novels lies in their endings. Chris seems hesitant to trust anyone in the future, and yet he also draws an incorrect but innocent conclusion about Jenny's final word "Dad" scrawled on the wall in her own blood. The reader is cognizant of Chris's ability to console himself post-tragedy based on his assumption that Jenny's relationship with her father was positive, which the third person omniscient narrator reveals to be undeniably false. Ginny, on the other hand, having learned the truth about her mother, reconciles her connection to the famed artist by accepting that her talent for producing art is the only legacy worth honoring as she moves forward. The conclusion of Ginny's story is more uplifting and hopeful because Ginny does not move forward based on a false assumption as Chris does; however, Pullman reveals that a belief in a fallacy can generate both positive and negative outcomes.

While we have seen significant evidence in prior chapters that exposes Pullman's ability to faithfully elucidate the snares set for orphaned or neglected youth, he addresses here another set of concerns for the teenager who possesses a fully intact or single parent family, but who has been forced to face one or more of the following problems: child abuse, parental separation, infidelity, divorce, foster parenting, and even kidnapping. Lest readers jump to the conclusion that life is automatically easier should a child grow up with one or both parents, Pullman sets the record straight: often the sins of the father (or mother) have a profound and lasting effect on their sons and daughters, particularly when it comes to their ability to form loving relationships with others and to achieve a sense of identity.

Fear, Love, Approval, and Abandonment in The Broken Bridge

Having exhausted all means of independent inquiry into the unknown portions of her childhood, and having been twice rejected by the mother she never knew, Ginny Howard confronts her father Tony at the conclusion of *The Broken Bridge*. In a stunning series of revelations, Tony admits to Ginny, "Fear is why it happened, fear is why I haven't talked about it. That's the reason for everything" (Pullman 196). Ginny's father was raised by an abusive mother who instilled in him the polarizing emotions of fear and love — fear that she would do something horrific to punish a simple

Seven. The Broken Bridge *and* The White Mercedes

childhood transgression, but love because she was his mother and he desperately sought her affection and approval. Tony relates two harrowing incidents to Ginny that formed the core of his personality: in one case, he and a cousin were caught by his mother while they were "comparing [them]selves with each other in the most innocent way" (197). Her response was an immediate "explosion" as she grabbed him forcefully and shoved him into the tub, running scalding water over him, berating him with the words "filthy," "dirty scum," and "unwholesome," all while he frantically clung to her, proclaiming his love (197). The second incident involved his being caught for stealing and eating chocolate. His mother, enraged, seized his beloved teddy bear and chopped it to bits with an ax, claiming that Teddy would have to be "killed" because Tony was too old for him (199). Tony's father simply sat idly by, seemingly afraid of his wife, encouraging Tony's obedience.

As Tony explains to his daughter, these terrifying incidents in his past led him to seek his parents' approval. Thus, he married Janet to appease them, for they wished him to marry their closest friend's daughter to cement the two families' personal lives and business relationships. Evidently, the fact that Tony did not marry for love led him to stray from his marriage upon meeting Ginny's mother, Anielle Baptiste, an enticing artistic woman his parents, particularly his mother, would never have approved of based on her ethnicity. This affair led to Ginny's birth and the demise of his marriage when Janet refused to adopt Ginny, resulting in Tony leaving Janet, their son Robert, and his past behind.

Tony Howard may be a minor character, but his approach to life, motivated by fear and love, profoundly affects Ginny. After Anielle abandoned Ginny and left her with nuns, Tony attempted to gain custody, but his efforts were stymied by reports that he was an unsuitable father. He later found that his mother was responsible for the lies, and he kidnapped Ginny and travelled the country with her, hiding until his money was spent and the authorities caught up with him. Several years later, he obtained custody, and to save Ginny from further trauma, he invented a story about her mother, telling her that Anielle died soon after she was born. The belief in the fantasy of a gifted artist who met her tragic end all too early leads Ginny to develop an interest in art and painting that carries her through her teenage years, giving her a mission to follow, to become a great artist to honor the memory of her deceased mother.

This grand narrative affects Ginny both positively and negatively.

Part II: Stories of Experience

Carrying the genes of a talented artist, Ginny has a natural affinity for creating art, and she views her geographical landscape with a painter's sensitivity: "Unlike memories of people, memories of things came easily to her; she had only to think of an object or a place to find it before her, correctly textured, three-dimensional, casting shadows" (Pullman, *The Broken* 17). In his lecture "Reminiscences of Ardudwy," Pullman is uncharacteristically open about the years in which he lived in north Wales and gained "the education of [his] sensibility, of [his] feelings"; he hones in on the profound effect of the landscape on his emerging interest in the visual arts. He recalls Llandanwg, the place that inspired "'Ginny's realm,'" described in detail in *The Broken Bridge*, with an eye toward the subtleties of color, shape, and texture with which he, and later his protagonist Ginny, fell in love (Pullman, "Reminiscences"). Comingling his newfound ardor for producing and learning about art with the awakening of his feelings of romantic love, inspired by the way the sunlight once "caught the hair of a girl from the other class called Carol Powell" (4), Pullman's nostalgic reminiscences are mirrored in Ginny's aesthetic appreciation. In no other work by Pullman is a character so inspired by and in love with the facets of her landscape. Ginny has a sense of ownership over her "kingdom" because she knows it, draws it, and loves it (*The Broken* 11), this "space of magic and beauty, Ginny's realm, her kingdom, her queendom" (11).

Ginny's aesthetic appreciation is buttressed by her connection to her deceased mother. When she is visiting with Stuart, she tells him she intends to be a painter, not simply because she is skilled, but also because "'my mother was a painter. Was going to be a painter. So I'm carrying on for her'" (Pullman, *The Broken* 9). Ginny sees her chosen vocation as a manifestation that will honor the memory of the mother she never knew, to claim a genetic heritage that utilizes her innate gifts. In fact, in talking to Wendy, the social worker, Ginny claims that painting is the single most crucial force driving her life, because in creating art, she is "kind of doing it for her, doing the things she couldn't do" (98). Interestingly, when the story that has inspired Ginny begins to unravel, she tells Wendy defiantly that she will feel "cheated" if she learns her mother was not an artist (98). What Ginny does not know at that time, of course, is that she has been cheated by her biological mother in a much more devastating manner than she ever imagined.

Thus the story that Ginny believes about her mother creates a strong desire in her to become a successful artist, an admirable goal. However,

Seven. The Broken Bridge *and* The White Mercedes

it also sets her up for betrayal, because the truth eventually emerges when she finds out that her mother abandoned her as a child and furthermore, denies her connection to her in the present. After Stuart gives Ginny the art magazine with proof of her mother's paintings, she travels to L'Ouverture Gallery to see the exhibit which features Anielle Baptiste's work (Pullman, *The Broken* 173). The experience is bittersweet, for Ginny is able to see her mother's extraordinary and inspiring talent, but she also faces rejection head-on when she produces a photograph of her mother and her mother replies, "'You're making a mistake' ... 'It has nothing to do with me....' 'I'm a painter. I'm not a mother'" (184). Evidently her mother has no interest in resurrecting any relationship with Ginny, and thus Ginny faces parental abandonment immediately after she realizes her mother is still alive. Were the story she was told about her mother accurate in the past, she would not have to face such a devastating rejection as a teenager when she truly needs a female role model.

Perhaps a caveat, then, is that on her journey to find out about her past, Ginny forms the beginnings of beneficial relationships with two older women. One is Helen. Seeking answers, Ginny travels to meet Helen, her best friend Rhiannon's elder sister, and she eventually finds herself pouring out her anxieties about her father to this woman who may actually be having an affair with him. The particulars of Helen's and Tony's relationship are never revealed, but Helen is not happy in her marriage and sees Tony, who is now single, somewhat regularly. Even though Rhiannon has no relationship with her sister (in fact until Ginny meets her, Rhiannon knows little of her), Ginny enlists Helen's aid in trying to find out more about Chicago Joe and the possible link between her and Pont Doderig, "the broken bridge" (Pullman, *The Broken* 58). While Ginny's suspicions about Joe are incorrect, her need for the guidance of an older woman is apparent in the way she confides all her suspicions and fears to Helen, and of course, Helen is the one person who suggests her mother may in fact be alive (128).

Another older confidante is Wendy Stevens, the social worker. Just as Ginny's exchanges with Helen are tentative at first, and more open later, she is quiet and wary of Wendy initially only to eventually find herself opening up about her relationship with her father. In "The Impact of Parental Divorce on the Intimate Relationships of Adult Offspring: A Review of the Literature," Amber J. Ottaway describes research findings that show a correlation between women who are children of divorce and emotional insecurity, stating that such women "fear abandonment as well" and therefore "seek out intimate relationships" (6). I would suggest that Ginny's failure at forming an intimate relationship with Andy, which will be addressed shortly, increases her level of emotional insecurity about young men, an insecurity already in place due to her sudden mistrust of the man to whom she has always been the closest, which in turn encourages her to seek a different type of intimacy in the new connections she makes to Helen and Wendy. In Margaret and Michael Rustin's "A New Kind of Friendship — An Essay on Philip Pullman's *The Subtle Knife*," the authors discuss *His Dark Materials* and the fact that some authors who write about children facing abandonment present the view that heroic children have no need for parents, while Pullman instead takes the view that children need some form of guardian, for his characters' "identities are formed through their inner identifications with their parent-figures, and through their struggles to find their own way ... to differentiate themselves as separate persons needing to live their own lives" (240–41). Such links to older women who both show much more care and compassion for her than her negligent mother are positive outcomes in the midst of the betrayals that Ginny uncovers.

Of course the closeness between Ginny and her father — they were "almost like brother and sister, like equals" (Pullman, *The Broken* 8), means that Ginny must navigate the waters of her father's sexual life. Her father at 37 years old has never remarried, but he has many girlfriends, whom Ginny refers to as "the breakfast ladies" (9). When one of the women stays for several months, it is Ginny who urges her father to be "respectable" (9) and marry her, and soon after, Holly never returns. Ottaway asserts that "researchers have found that young adults from divorced families typically portray an accelerated courtship pattern and experience more interest in relationships ... seek[ing] intimacy and committed relationship with the hope that such relationships will fulfill their needs for affection" (38). Granted, Ginny is not the typical child of divorce, for she believes her father to have been married to her mother who then died. But the conflicts she faces in having to deal with a parent who is sexually active and pursuing relationships outside the context of marriage are quite similar to the difficulties adolescent children of divorce face when one or both parents decide to "move on." Ginny does not question her father's sexual relationships with the "breakfast ladies" when they are only present for breakfast, but when Holly becomes a more permanent resident, Ginny pushes her

Seven. The Broken Bridge *and* The White Mercedes

father to legitimize their union. Ironically, Ginny later finds out that she was the product of her father's affair, making her a child born out of wedlock and infidelity. Yet Ginny resists the notion of extended affairs and seems more intent on the apparent intactness of the marital institution. After all, she reflects early on that she liked "being at the Calverts' [Rhiannon's family] because among other things they were a family, they were complete" (Pullman, *The Broken* 18).

When it comes to her own foray into a romantic relationship, Ginny hesitates to make her feelings known but so strongly idealizes the perfect union that eventually she makes the first move, only to face humiliation. She harbors a great affection for Andy, the only other black teenager in their area, who is "much darker" than Ginny, "mysterious, glamorous with a kind of evasive magic," and two years older (Pullman, *The Broken* 12).[3] Initially the reader assumes Ginny's fondness for Andy is platonic, but her romantic inclinations quickly emerge. She moves from being happy to see him to being "secretly delighted" when he touches her face affectionately (65). When it comes time for the barbeque, she puts significant effort into her appearance simply because Andy will be there: "It was only the beach, but it wasn't only the beach, because Andy would be there, and she wanted to look as good as she would if she felt good" (112). Ginny determines that this night will be different from the usual parties at which she hugs the sidelines, and she gives herself over completely to her infatuation with Andy, "rest[ing] her head on his shoulder and breath[ing] in the complex intoxicating smell of him ... she was obsessed, she was drunk with him, she was in love" (117). Swept away by fantasy, she kisses Andy on the cheek as she dances with him, until the beautiful moment is ruined by laughter from her friends; she assumes they are making jokes about their race, but everything comes into focus when Robert asks her about the gay man with whom she was dancing. "Stupid, naïve Ginny, the only person in the world who didn't know" (119), is devastated and now worries that her friendship with Andy will be forever altered. Thankfully Andy is mature enough to brush the incident aside, but the experience teaches Ginny something about romantic idealization.

It is interesting to note that as her relationship with her father becomes more strained, her wish for the perfect romance with Andy increases, supporting Ottaway's observations that adolescents from families with marital strife often seek "the one 'perfect' partner to be satisfied" (4). Ginny identifies Andy as the perfect partner for her because he is both black and adopted, living in a white world, "looking black" but "feeling white" (Pullman, *The Broken* 12) and tied to her by their racial and national identity. What she fails to see is Andy's sexual orientation, even though the signs were evident, and she also fails to observe that there may be a better partner suited for her in Glyn Williams, who connects with her at the novel's conclusion (213–17). She still has not overcome her shyness and self-doubt, but she is able to extend a hand in friendship to someone she does not idealize, and this time she seems more intent on taking things slowly than jumping in head-first into a grand relationship.

Thus the fear, love, and approval that plagued Ginny's father's upbringing creates a deep impact on Ginny's life. It creates a bond between father and daughter that works for them only until Ginny is able to understand her father's connections with other women and until Ginny investigates her past, at which point she and her father become distant, their relationship strained. In this space, Ginny gravitates towards others, attempting to fill the void left by the distance with her father. The relationships with Helen, Wendy, and Andy are all natural manifestations of Ginny's desire to fill her life with intimate relationships, whether romantic or platonic, to help her feel more emotionally secure. It is clear from her father's open confession and explanation of childhood abuse, coupled with Ginny's own observation of her paternal grandmother's wrath and unlocked memories, that she believes her father, empathizes with him, and forgives anything he may have kept from her to protect her. After she meets with her estranged mother and faces rejection and abandonment a second time, she realizes the goodness in her father and reconnects with him.

Between her passion for art and her awakening sense of compassion for others, Ginny moves from innocence to experience. Pullman creates a positive character arc for Ginny. She was indirectly affected by abuse, but her father seems intent on breaking the negative patterns he learned. The most difficult thing Ginny must overcome is her idealization of relationships, but there is every indication that she has learned to temper her romanticism by the end of the story when she appears open and willing to explore a friendship with a boy who has been under her nose the entire time. As Karen Sands O'Connor states in "High Winds and Broken Bridges," "Ginny finds out the truth about her past, but can never be whole or innocent again" (125). But the loss of innocence carries with it an immense amount of growth. Like the typical Pullman heroine, Ginny is stronger and wiser as a result of the difficulties she has faced.

Seven. The Broken Bridge *and* The White Mercedes

Divorce in The White Mercedes

At a NeMLA[4] conference in 2001, I observed a panel discussion on gender in contemporary young adult literature. The panel considered the presence of optimism versus pessimism in relation to gender in stories about adolescents. The consensus reflected a preponderance of optimistic stories related to girl protagonists and a corresponding pessimism tied to tales about boy protagonists. While there are many exceptions to these stereotypes, the panel participants saw a trend emerging, especially in the contemporary adolescent problem novel. I asked Philip Pullman for his thoughts on this tendency. His response follows:

> If I were preparing a paper on the subject I'd probably say that this is still a world in which many male privileges remain undiminished, but that in one area men/boys are now considerably disadvantaged compared to women/girls, and that's in popular representation. It's become commonplace and unquestioned in TV commercials, for instance, to depict men as stupid and women as clever, or boys as primitive and thuggish and girls as cool and successful. If I were young and unsure of myself right now I'd feel pretty despicable, if that were the only representation of maleness I saw. From my own observation, girls have always been more sure of themselves, more grown up, than any boy — both when I was a boy myself and later, when I was a teacher observing both sexes try to negotiate a way of being together. It doesn't take much to destroy someone's confidence, and it seems to me these days that almost the whole media apparatus is trying to do that to boys and young men — for no other reason than to make money, of course. If much of what you see on TV represents you as a bumbling idiot who gazes in stupefaction at the slightest little difficulty which a girl then comes along and solves in a moment, and if in the real world you can't find a job because there are no jobs to be had, and your fellows sneer and scoff at anything that looks like school work, and the only little bit of power you can gain is by frightening people, it's no wonder if the world is a bleak place for you.[5]

With Pullman's penchant for writing stories that feature strong heroines, his portrayal of Chris Marshall is unusual, but it provides an answer to his observations that young men are portrayed in a stereotypically simple light. Chris is a strong, sensitive, multi-faceted protagonist whose story contains both optimism and pessimism, making it more reflective of an authentic teenage male's life experience than the stock characterization of young men Pullman sees in the media. Pullman addressed the male protagonist quite some time ago with his first books *The Haunted Storm* (1972) and *Galatea* (1979),[6] but the most complex, nuanced male character he has conceived of is surely Chris Marshall.

Like Ginny, his contemporary counterpart, Chris is affected by the circumstances surrounding the divorce of his parents and their foray into subsequent relationships, which also encourages his idealization of love and romance. Chris does not necessarily begin the novel by wrestling with existential questions (though these do come up later), but he is facing down the aftermath of his parents' divorce which has a tremendous effect on his desire to romanticize a love relationship.

Pullman spends a fair amount of time in the novel discussing Chris's parents' lives post-divorce as seen through Chris's eyes, a state of affairs that troubles and confuses him. His mother, for instance, "cried bitterly and locked herself in the bedroom ... and when she came out she'd be brittle-cheerful and drink more wine than she used to" (Pullman, *The White* 16). In response, Chris's dynamic with his mother alters drastically as he moves from being a typical teen with all sorts of restrictions to the role of "a sort of sympathetic brother ... someone who could talk about sex and lovers and mistresses without getting confused and embarrassed" (16). As Wallerstein, Lewis, and Blakeslee assert, children of divorce are often rushed into adulthood: "The child becomes the backstage prop manager making sure the show goes on" (361). Chris's mother expects him to detach from his father and accept immediately that they are not together, then to embrace the man with whom she begins a sexual relationship. Mike Fairfax, her new lover, seems to be the only one able to bring his mother out of her depression. Such changes lead Chris to feel uncomfortable in his own home, resulting in his spending more time working for Barry Miller and less time interacting with his mother (Pullman, *The White* 16–17).

At the same time Chris's dynamic with his mother changes, so, too, does his comfort level around his father. His father moves in with Diane, his former secretary, who is attractive and much closer in age to Chris than to his father, "and to know that she was sleeping with his father and having sex with him made it confusing to look at her. And to look at his father" (Pullman, *The White* 16). In fact, Chris often blushes in embarrassment around Diane, because he almost feels "as if she liked him" (45) and he is obviously attracted to her. When he stands near Diane, Chris even notices her scent and thinks she looks younger than Jenny, the object of his affection, and the two who are "closer in age, personality, and manner to each other than either was to ... the father, the lover," are in obvious discomfort when in the others' presence (51).

Since Chris's primary reaction to the divorce is coming to terms with

Seven. The Broken Bridge *and* The White Mercedes

his own feelings versus those of his parents' feelings — he "hated it" while they are "calm" and "matter-of-fact" (Pullman, *The White* 15) — he initially escapes into his job, but later, he unsurprisingly and unconsciously adopts their behavior by falling head-over-heels for Jenny. Going back to Ottaway's research on adolescent children of divorce, those who witness their parents openly explore their sexuality post-divorce "portray an accelerated courtship pattern ... [and] are more likely to be involved in some form of intimate relationship, whether it is casual or serious" (38). Furthermore, they "may convey their insecurity about being in a relationship by initiating physical intimacy with another person" (39). Readers are not told about Chris's parents' backgrounds, but both of his parents become sexually intimate quickly post-divorce (in fact, the text implies that Chris's father had an affair with Diane, suggesting that his father explored physical intimacy with a younger woman while married). The quickness of their rebound relationships post-divorce and the fact that both appear to be "over" the betrayals and the trauma so efficiently may even model for Chris the suggestion it is easier to smooth over rough patches in life if one becomes sexually intimate with a new partner.

Chris does not immediately seek a sexual relationship with Jenny, probably because he is a virgin. However, he is very easily caught up in romantic idealism, reflected by the way he falls deeply in love at the first glimpse of Jenny: "The line of her throat in the faint light from across the lake was enough, on its own, to make him fall in love.... He was lost" (Pullman, *The White* 8). After his brief exchange with her, he pledges to remember her always, whether he ever sees her again or not (14), and he thinks and dreams of nothing but Jenny for days until he sees her by accident (17–18). When he watches her cry at the end of the *Romeo and Juliet* performance, his romantic yearning for her intensifies, and he tells her he loves her and invites her to stay with him while he house-sits for his father (55–56). When she does not arrive on Friday night as promised, he becomes distraught with longing for her: "He felt an invisible cord joining the two of them, stretching tightly through the night from his heart to hers" (58). Devastated, he begins to imagine that he invented their earlier encounter and feels utterly embarrassed over his overblown feelings (57).

The next day when Jenny arrives, it is not surprising that they end up in his bedroom very quickly; engaging in physical intimacy, Chris tells Jenny he bought condoms, but Jenny has also come prepared and takes charge of the use of birth control (Pullman, *The White* 67). Interestingly, Chris "felt sorrowful" at her practiced hand, for "she'd done this before;

she wasn't altogether new to it as he was" (67). Evidently Chris intended a more innocent beginning to their weekend; after all, he invited her to "play house," with the table set for two on a Friday evening and music playing softly in the background (57). When she never shows, he becomes distraught at the thought that he has lost her, which likely spurs him on to the physical encounter and loss of his virginity so soon after she arrives the next day. Just as Ottaway describes, the swift movement to an intimate relationship seems to cement his love for her and connection to her. If he sees his parents reflecting a sense of peace and happiness upon engaging in sex with a new partner, it may be that Chris is simply modeling their behavior in an effort to feel a deep connection to another human being now that his link to his parents is so tenuous.

Opposite Ginny Howard, whose disconnect with and mistrust of her father fostered new relationships, Chris undergoes the opposite pattern, for after growing closer to Jenny, he becomes paranoid, possessive, and moody. Ottaway's research supports this when she states that adolescent males who experience divorce are "more likely to exhibit distancing behaviors" and have trouble with "emotional intimacy" (39). Many of Chris's feelings about Jenny are expressed only in his own mind. He is unwilling to confide in his feelings for her in anyone else, and he is even reserved in expressing his feelings to her. Having rapidly tied himself to Jenny emotionally and physically, Chris naturally becomes possessive of her. Moody and suspicious, he assumes that she is sleeping with someone else, first Piers, and later his boss Barry. It is Chris's possessive behavior which fuels his anger, his anger which fuels his revenge, and his revenge which inadvertently causes Jenny's death. It is reasonable to tie all of these events to Chris's being a child of divorce. Chris's world was upended by his own parents' breakup, and the distancing with them likely occurred due to the way they handled their divorce and subsequent relationships. Naturally, when he finds a person to whom he can give himself physically and emotionally, a person with whom he shows complete vulnerability instead of the guarded behavior that governs his interactions with most everyone else, he wants to hang on to her at any cost, and he is immediately threatened when he believes that his tie to her is put in jeopardy.

Juxtaposed with Chris's paranoia over losing Jenny after circumstances separate them following their tryst, Chris also discovers that his substitute father, Barry, is a great betrayer. Having once envisioned Barry and his wife and child as the perfect family, Chris is stunned to find that Barry has been unfaithful (Pullman, *The White* 95), with infidelity now tainting two marriages in his world. Wallerstein, Lewis, and Blakeslee argue that "divorce is a watershed that permanently alters [children's] lives. The world is newly perceived as a far less reliable, more dangerous place because the closest relationships in their lives can no longer be expected to hold firm. More than anything else, the new anxiety represents the end of childhood" (362). Pullman elucidates this view in an interview with Anita Vachharajani, who notes that Pullman's characters tend to inhabit the space between adolescence and adulthood. Pullman explains, "It is a very important time of transition for everyone — transition from one form of thinking to another.... We develop a sense of where we are intellectually, which is not always the same as where we find ourselves dwelling." Thus Chris's reaction to the news that his idol Barry is as flawed as his parents perfectly illustrates this transition from innocence to knowledge: "Chris sat silent, sick to his heart. Everyone and everything and everywhere he looked was rotten, corrupt, poisoned to the core" (Pullman, *The White* 95).

In addition, Chris learns that Barry has created several false stories about his past in order to disguise his criminal activity. Chris's anger about Barry convinces him that he must give Fletcher (aka Carson) Barry's whereabouts, knowing full well that Barry will be confronted and caught, which inadvertently puts Jenny in the wrong place at the wrong time. This makes him indirectly responsible for her death, a fact he must live with the rest of his life, knowing that his desire for vengeance played itself out and destroyed the very person he loved most.

In a nod to *Romeo and Juliet*, Chris contemplates suicide, but "his courage failed" (Pullman, *The White* 167), leaving him alive to face the ramifications of his actions. In terms of innocence and experience, it is more fitting that Chris does not kill himself over his mistake. It is a mark of a more resilient young man that he recognizes what he has done, the role he has played in this young woman's death, that he instead stays alive with this knowledge. The knowledge means that he will probably be a different person, less trusting, less idealistic, and tougher.

Sexual Abuse in The White Mercedes

While Chris unfortunately holds himself entirely to blame for Jenny's demise, Jenny may have been headed for further trauma before she even met Chris, for she may be permanently scarred from sexual and physical abuse at the hands of her father. The few narrative sections which relate Jenny's interior thoughts prove that she carries the mark of molestation with her and it has strongly affected her relationships and her life circumstances. Jenny is a risk-taker, who fluctuates between being extremely wary about the intentions of others and being completely detached from fear of dangerous situations in which she seems to deliberately put herself. This behavioral pattern suggests a known neurophysiological effect involving "depletion of catecholamines," which results in "psychological constriction and numbing" alternating with times of "hyperarousal" (Gil 18). This documented symptom of abuse may explain why Jenny fails to consider that she might be assaulted by attending a party to which she has not been invited with no escort and a group of inebriated men in her wake (constriction and numbing) while she simultaneously has a heightened sense of fear around Tommy Sanchez that is accompanied by PTSD-like flashbacks of the way she feels men like him want to hurt her (hyperarousal), an awareness that causes her to steer clear of him.

    The first time Chris meets Jenny is at the university party which she "crashes." Wearing a borrowed gown, she is running from Piers and his drunken buddies. Were Chris not to have appeared, Jenny likely would have been assaulted by the men, and as she says to Chris, "If they'd caught me, I wouldn't have had a chance. And no one would have believed me afterward" (Pullman, *The White* 23). She is aware of the way men see her: "They were usually much older than she was, old enough to be her father, and they seemed to sense some quality in her that aroused them. And then they stopped being men and became something like tigers ... intent ... on consuming her, destroying her, rending her apart" (83). She trusts innocent boys and men who do not view her as a sexual object, like Derek and Ollie, the men she squats with, but they are drug addicts and eventually arrested, and living with them is not really safer than sleeping on a friend's floor, and yet this is the life to which Jenny has become accustomed and which she sees as a safer alternative than living with her abusive father.

    When Jenny returns home after sleeping with Chris, she finds her roommates have been arrested and she cannot return to the flat. She admits to herself that she could go back to Chris's father's home and ask for help, but "she felt too uncomfortable to speak to him, in view of what she'd been doing in his house" (Pullman, *The White* 73). She further complicates matters by conflating Chris's father with her own, and since her own

Seven. The Broken Bridge *and* The White Mercedes

father's actions never leave her mind, she has a fear of confronting Chris's father and decides to continue sleeping at friends' homes. Through her behavior, Pullman suggests that once she considers herself to be "damaged" by her abusive father, she becomes a survivor in terms of escape from him, but seems to have little regard for future abuse of perhaps a lesser degree from others. She is complacent in her drifter lifestyle and when she loses her home, rather than reach out for help to improve her situation, she allows her low self-esteem to dictate her move and instead sleeps on a friend's floor rather than ask her boyfriend for help.

Jenny's low opinion of herself is revealed throughout the text. For example, when she babysits for Barry and his wife, she feels an enormous pull to express her affection for their little boy Sean. The first kiss she gives him is maternal, but the second kiss dances on the edge of propriety as it seems more like a kiss from one lover to another than motherly, so Sean backs away in "surprise" (Pullman, *The White* 99), and Jenny immediately chastises herself, declaring that she is ruined and has no business being around a small child. Jenny seems acutely aware of the cyclical, generational patterns of abuse known to professionals; in *Treating Abused Adolescents*, Eliana Gil asserts that by 1994, "the proposition that childhood victims are more likely to grow up to victimize others ... is firmly established" (Finkelhor and Dzuiba-Leatherman qtd. in Gil 16). Jenny assumes that as a sexual abuse victim she is doomed to repeat the pattern of pedophilia that cursed her childhood: "She wanted to take that little boy's face and press it to her breast. She wanted to kiss him again a hundred times. Desolate with self-hatred, she sat on the edge of the sofa ... and wondered how deep the corruption went that her father had put into her. She was no better than he was.... She shouldn't live at all" (Pullman, *The White* 99). Gil further discusses studies done by McCann and others that reveal a plethora of symptoms manifesting in victims of child abuse, which include "profoundly negative self-esteem, and feelings of guilt and shame" (17).

Jenny's approach to sex also reflects her low opinion of herself. She admits that she has slept with many men in order to try to erase the memory of her abusive father, but her father's eyes stared back at her through every man's face (Pullman, *The White* 30). This excludes Chris, with whom she feels a sense of sadness after their lovemaking instead of fear (71), with the added conflict that she wants to confide in Chris about the pain of her past but worries if she tells him the truth, he will "come to see her as she s[ees] herself: corrupt, poisonous, tainted" (84). When Barry finishes showing Jenny the work she will do for him, she allows herself the moment to fantasize: "Jenny felt a premonition of absurd happiness ... she would be working ... and by some extraordinary coincidence ... the door would open and there would be Chris. And everything would end happily" (120). Of course, at the moment of her fantasy, Chris does see her and Barry and comes to a very dark conclusion about their relationship; ironically he sees her as tainted even though in this circumstance, she is entirely innocent. Essentially Jenny is so deeply affected by the abuse in her past that for the most part, she thinks of herself as unworthy of a particular kind of life thereafter.

Interestingly Jenny's path seems to lead from experience to innocence through the course of the novel, for she grows up with a contaminated view of family relationships that, to her, may only be alleviated by delving into a secure and loving relationship with Chris. Barry is a part of this view; Barry makes no moves on Jenny and instead, treats her with respect and kindness. It is her view of his supposedly happy family and the assumptions she makes about the love between them that linger in the shed she works on in the midst of the Edenic forest: "she felt safe among the sunny trees, surrounded by the secret innocent life of birds and insects" (Pullman, *The White* 147). In this seemingly untouched, new landscape, where no memory of her past encroaches on her present and where only Barry's kind presence is known to her, she sees the world in a new light, leading her to imagine a new outcome for her future. In fact, where she earlier thought she would never go to school or follow a life like Chris had planned for himself, that night she returns to baby-sit despite her earlier hesitation and talks with Sue about taking courses and going to college: "There might be a way there after all," she reflects (149). When she has fully embraced her future and the thought that she would see Chris again, she embraces Sean as she leaves, thinking, "It was safe to be fond of anyone now" (158).

Jenny's final missive to Chris, then, reflects the end of her innocence, for in the midst of her hopes and dreams for the future, she is brutally and mistakenly murdered. By writing "dad" on the wall, it is as if Jenny is acknowledging the truth of her life as a victim of abuse, suggesting that no matter what changes in her life, no matter who she meets or what plans she makes, the specter of abuse and violence is always right around the corner. Having no idea why she has been shot, Jenny seizes her dying moment to proclaim to Chris what she could not articulate face-to-face, that her father was the one who put her on this path. She has already voiced to herself that she did not deserve to live when she kissed Sean; her brutal death is only a manifestation of what she believes she deserves. Knowing Chris's innocence, it is possible that Jenny assumes he will blame himself for her death; perhaps Jenny's final message to Chris, then, is to try to keep his innocence intact by telling him that the one responsible for everything ultimately is not him, but her father. Thus Jenny moves from experience to innocence back to experience.

Chris's trajectory is the opposite. Pullman initially describes him as having an innocent face (Pullman, *The White* 7). Through the course of the story, Chris grows in suspicion and paranoia, his mood becoming darker and more somber. After the moment that he begins to feel the world is laced with corruption, Chris's "mind divided itself against him" (123) and he starts to lose trust in everyone and think the worst of them (125). At this moment of his ultimate mental confusion, enter the serpent, Fletcher, aka Carson, who delivers a powerfully symbolic argument to Chris that convinces him to betray Barry:

> We're not innocent; we *know*.... The Garden of Eden.... The tree of knowledge of good and evil.... Before you eat the fruit you're innocent, whatever you do is innocent, because you don't understand. Then you eat it. And you're never innocent again. You *know* now. And that's painful; it's a terrible thing.... Losing that innocence is the first step on the road to real knowledge. To wisdom, if you like. You can't get wisdom till you lose that innocence.... You can't do good unless you stop being innocent. All the real good in the world is done by people who've tasted the fruit of that tree [*The White* 141–42].

Tempted by the serpent, Chris "falls" and betrays his friend, which leads to the loss of the woman he loves. Thus Chris travels on the path from innocence to experience, for in losing something precious, he gains wisdom about others and himself; yet as a caveat, Jenny's final word to him may restore some sense of his innocence, making the path he follows lie opposite hers.

Conclusion

In her essay "'Why Don't We Ever Read Anything Happy?' YA Literature and the Optimistic Ending," Susanne Nobles discusses the ease with which readers find pessimism in life and literature, noting the contrast inherent in Nilsen and Donelson's characteristics of young adult literature (referenced in a previous chapter), which includes the prominence of optimism, a natural consequence of characters' attainment of goals (2). Nobles defines the optimistic adolescent novel as one that concludes with a sense of hope, a range of possibilities, and links forged by the protagonist to other people (2–3). The "ideally optimistic novel" allows the character to prevail entirely against his or her difficulty and is often indicative of a fairy tale-like rendering, while other more realistic optimistic novels end with the character "okay," suggesting the new directions that he or she may follow next (4). Nobles defines the pessimistic young adult novel as one which "leaves the reader with no hope" (2), "leaves the main character with the appearance of no options" (3), and "a lack of connection to family and/or friends," which ostensibly forces the character to face continued trials in isolation (3).

Considering Nobles' definitions, then, we may conclude that *The Broken Bridge* is essentially an optimistic novel. Ginny faces many trials and awakens to betrayal and suffering, but her story ends with her more deeply connected to her father who has finally confided in her, a burgeoning relationship with a potential boyfriend, a better understanding of the people in her world, and a renewed vigor to prove herself as an artist, despite the rejection of her newly discovered but estranged mother. Sands-O'Connor reflects that the separation from her mother is absolutely integral to Ginny's quest of inner harmony (128). The final scene, in which "her hand itched for a pencil" (Pullman, *The Broken* 218), includes her observation of the landscape and the people around her in this world in which "anything was possible" (218), reflecting a positive outlook for Ginny despite the hell she has been through in the past few weeks. As Ebony Elizabeth Thomas concludes, "in the end, she thrives" (57).

On the other hand, *The White Mercedes* has a far different feel to its conclusion, a tone which suggests a mixture of optimism and pessimism, creating a hybrid text unlike either of the types about which Nobles describes. On the side of optimism, Chris Marshall draws his own conclusions about Jenny's mysterious message, assuming, based on her father's "cover[ing] his face in court" (Pullman, *The White* 170), that Jenny was trying to say that she had a deep love for her father and wished he had been there at the moment of her death. Based on that interpretation, Chris decides that a family should always remain connected, and he is "comfort[ed]" by the assumption that he and Jenny understood this about

Seven. The Broken Bridge and The White Mercedes

one another in her final moments (170). Certainly this is a positive outcome for Chris because it implies that after the story ends, there are options open to him. Perhaps he will be inspired to reconnect with his own family. Perhaps he will aspire to a long-term relationship that reflects a close-knit family unit, much like the one he thought he witnessed with Barry, Susan, and Sean. Essentially, Chris's interpretation of the events "balance[s] the death and destruction with windows of hope" (Nobles 2).

However, there is also a sense of pessimism inherent in this novel's ending, for the reader realizes that Chris's assessment is completely wrong. Chris is therefore moving on with his view balanced on the edge of a false belief. There is much irony in this for in the weeks following Jenny's death, Chris draws the conclusion that "he had acquired another kind of wisdom.... Knowledge like that was rare. It put a mark on you. He'd be hard to fool again" (Pullman, *The White* 169). Evidently, though, he is immediately fooled in court. There are two ways to look at such a conclusion: on one hand, Chris has been through a great trial and gained wisdom about human nature. He believes he will be more cynical and more discerning of others' motives and perhaps erect a wall of suspicion in order to keep himself from being duped again. Such an outcome leads the reader to think he may cut himself off from relationships, and unlike Ginny, there does not seem to be the sense that he wants to forge connections with others, making this conclusion more pessimistic. However, where Jenny is concerned, and where the idealization of what it means to be a family is prominent, Chris is able to lose his cynicism and give her father the benefit of the doubt. It never seems to occur to him to take a negative view on Jenny's message. Instead, he seems to search for and find the only positive interpretation of her final word, suggesting that he may be wiser, but he has not lost his sense of hope. Thus, Chris ends his story in solitude and introspection, indicating a temporary rift between him and the outside world, but Pullman allows for a ray of hope to shine a light, and even if that hope is built on a falsehood, it will lead Chris to a better chance at happiness than a full grasp of the truth might.

Does the optimism versus the hybrid of optimism and pessimism tie to the gender of the characters? It is hard to say. Perhaps it may tie to Pullman and his own experiences as a teenager and later as a storyteller. His "Reminiscences at Ardudwy" alludes to the story of Ginny Howard — the landscape, the importance of art, and the imagery of Wales to his teenage years. But embedded in his love of landscape is the idea of first love, articulated so brilliantly through the story of Chris Marshall. I asked Pullman if the choice to write about heroines more so than heroes has ever been deliberate. He answered that the primary reason for this is that he likes to write in the third person omniscient narrator's voice, and since he has not experienced life as a woman, he finds this point of view works for the detachment necessary to tell a heroine's story.[7] However, taking together the sentimental tone of his reminiscences about first love in his essay along with the story of Chris Marshall, it is clear that Pullman did something unique in his take on the story of *Romeo and Juliet*— he provided a close rendering of the male voice and the male psyche, the passion and love and lust and longing coupled with the pain and heartache of possible rejection and loss. In the end, these two contemporary texts are brilliant examples of characters moving on the path from innocence to experience or its reverse who are conditioned by the actions of their elders, but who also are independent enough to learn from the past and try to break from the patterns that affected them. Furthermore, while readers may be distressed to find that Chris intends to erect the next stages of his life on the belief in a false hope, such an act does not necessarily negate a happy future. After all, did not Ginny Howard live most of her life believing in something that was not true, and did it not inspire her to become the wonderful, giving, intelligent, and perceptive young woman who is able to navigate the harsh waters of rejection and get back on her feet?

Eight

The Good Man Jesus and the Scoundrel Christ
A New Path from Innocence to Experience

> "This is a story..."
> — Philip Pullman, from the back cover of the dust jacket[1]

    Throughout this work, we have observed characters representing a range of ages, socioeconomic backgrounds, and life circumstances face self-ordained quests, pre-destined trials, suffering, and trauma learn how to navigate the treacherous waters of their worlds and emerge stronger and wiser, realizing that life is precious because of its many opportunities for growth. Philip Pullman is a champion of the underdog, and his characters choose to learn from their mistakes or the failings of others, moving forward with their lives to become survivors. They choose to turn trauma into triumph. But what of the protagonist who takes another path? Is there a hero in Pullman's fictional world who struggles mightily then follows the alternative path to commit a further betrayal? In *The Good Man Jesus and the Scoundrel Christ*, Pullman creates Christ, a deeply conflicted, dynamic character who ultimately chooses to betray his brother Jesus in the name of faith, constructing a deception-laden foundation for the basis of Christianity. Despite the controversy surrounding this innovative reimagining of the gospels, Pullman's text undeniably reveals that when people are faced with recovering from personal difficulties, they always have the power of choice. They may rise above their circumstances and turn trauma into triumph, or they may rationalize and justify their wrongful actions, only to discover that they have set disastrous consequences into motion, making them the architects of their own tragedies.

In *His Dark Materials*, Lyra followed a path similar to Christ when she unwittingly became responsible for Roger's death. Yet she redeems herself and those who have died by holding to the truth in the land of the dead. Lyra becomes the new Eve when she brings about salvation and freedom to a Republic of Heaven. Conversely, Christ, through his well-intended but deliberate embellishments to the truth, brings about a system by which the institutional church will grow in authority and dogma to obscure the message of love for which Jesus stood. Through the characters of Lyra and Christ, Pullman illustrates two paths to experience and the ripple effects either choice may create.

The Controversy

If Philip Pullman made an enemy of many Christians when he penned *His Dark Materials*, then he opened himself to further ire when he wrote *The Good Man Jesus and the Scoundrel Christ*. The use of the adjective "scoundrel" alone raises controversy, as heard when an audience member at the Sheldonian Theatre, Oxford chastised, "Mr. Pullman, the title of the novel seems to an ordinary Christian to be offensive. To call the Son of God a 'scoundrel' is an awful thing to say." Pullman's response was an unabashed proclamation for the right to free speech and is printed here in its entirety:

> Yes, it was a shocking thing to say, and I knew it was a shocking thing to say. But no one has the right to live without being shocked. No one has the right to spend their life without being offended. Ah, nobody has to read this book. Nobody has to pick it up. Nobody has to open it. And if they open it and read it, they don't have to like it. And if you read it and dislike it, you don't have to remain silent about it. You can write to me. You can complain about it. You can write to the publisher. You can write to the papers. You can write your own book. You can do all those things, but there your rights stop. No one has the right to stop me writing this book. No one has the right to stop it being published, or sold, or bought, or read. And that's all I have to say on that subject.[2]

Pullman confirmed in an email that he had received more than 50 letters prior to the book's publication "telling me I would go to hell and so on," but a scarcity of outrage ensued after it was published. He speculates that many generate controversy over what they call personal attacks on faith because this is "the expected thing to do.... [Yet] very few people *believe* it with any fully thought-out reasoning." Pullman credits Peter Hitchens, the late Christopher Hitchens' brother, with the most "vivid reaction," for he called Pullman's book "'mean and spiteful.'"[3] Ron Charles's review argues that Pullman "takes some obnoxious liberties with the foundational story of Christian faith and relentlessly flogs the church." Pullman's own recent comments, including his declaration, "'I hope the wretched Catholic church will vanish entirely'" (Barton), add to the inflammatory rhetoric surrounding the controversial text.

However, some critics are more concerned with other facets of the book, namely, the belief that Pullman did not break that much new ground. In "Pullman Sleeper," Joseph Bottum argues that "this is, after all, pretty tired, old stuff" (61). Bottum explains that the search to classify the true Jesus has been underway for over one and a half centuries (61).[4] "The problem," Bottum says, "is that we tend not so much to discover the historical Jesus as to create a blank spot on which to project our spiritual fantasies.... The historical Jesus turns out to be whatever the questing historian wants to find: a moral teacher or revolutionary prophet or kind preacher of love" (62). JoAnn Conrad's critical review in *Marvels and Tales* asserts that Pullman's text is more derivative than many realize. She explains, "The very core premise of the two twins is not only widespread in mythological tradition, but it is also specifically anticipated in the apocryphal Gospel of Thomas, written in the third century, in which Didymos Judas Thomas is Jesus's twin and scribe" (395).[5] Conrad notes that Pullman makes one major change to the Gospel of Thomas, which does not contain narrative sections but only Jesus's proclamations. In his version, Pullman fleshes out the narrative backbone of the story by describing Christ as chronicler of events witnessed personally and by an informant, and he alters the stories with an eye toward improvement (note that this storytelling mode fits the goal of a fairy tale re-vision as described first by Jack Zipes and later Kevin Paul Smith).[6] As Conrad also notes, many of the stories in the text were folkloric, and "Pullman merely taps into that reservoir" (395).

Some critics take issue with literary motifs, such as Tim Rutten, a reviewer for the *Los Angeles Times*, who decries Pullman for "fall[ing] back on the hoariest of conceits: the evil twin," a convention Rutten calls "schtick," and for "misus[ing] the character he calls Christ, abusing him for didactic and polemical purposes." Rutten also criticizes Pullman for not living up to the standards of the Canongate Myths Series, which claims to retell the great myths in a "'contemporary and memorable way.'" As Rutten claims, Pullman "comes up decidedly short of the mark" because he has too much "ambivalence" regarding the story of Jesus, noting that he shows reverence for Jesus but anger towards his followers and the church.

Still, other critics have been more charitable to Pullman, recognizing his skill as a storyteller and praising his ability to shine light on another epic and generate conversation. Ron Charles admits that despite the anticipatory hue and cry, that the book "is — God forbid — kind of inspiring." The Archbishop of Canterbury Rowan Williams' assessment of the work is also flattering. Having once asked Pullman in a public forum why he had not yet written about the life of Jesus, Williams said the book is "a very bold and deliberately outrageous fable, then, rehearsing Pullman's familiar and passionate fury at corrupt religious systems of control — but also introducing something quite different, a voice of genuine spiritual authority" (qtd. in Vickers). Williams praises Pullman for his "pitch-perfect rendering in modern idiom" that comes across when he reimagines the words of Jesus for the contemporary reader. Additionally, Salley Vickers' review in *The Telegraph* concludes, "Myths ... evade conscription and cannot be damaged by interpretations, however controversial. I cannot imagine the ironical Jesus taking umbrage at anything in this account of His life. Pullman has done the story a service by reminding us of its extraordinary power to provoke and disturb."

In discussing the power of myth (apologies to Joseph Campbell), Vickers raises an intriguing point. Pullman's story may have been encouraged by the Archbishop of Canterbury, but it is part of the Canongate Myths Series. A note at the conclusion of the novel reads, "Myths are universal and timeless stories that reflect and shape our lives — they explore our desires, our fears, our longings and provide narratives that remind us what it means to be human. *The Myths* series brings together some of the world's finest writers, each of whom has retold a myth in a contemporary and memorable way" (n. pag.). Jeanette Winterson, A.S. Byatt, and Margaret Atwood, among many other great writers, have taken an iconic "story" and recast it. In an email, Pullman explains that he was told about the Myths series by Canongate publisher Jamie Byng before the series was created, and Byng asked Pullman to write a piece. Pullman's preface concerning his thoughts about myth was then "printed on a single sheet of paper and [given] away with the first titles." Years later, Pullman "thought about doing a Jesus myth" and after discussing it with Byng, was supported in

Eight. The Good Man Jesus and the Scoundrel Christ

moving forward. He says, "So it was always going into that series from the beginning, but that didn't govern the way I wrote it at all."[7]

It is not clear if knowing that the book began as an entry into a series on myth would temper the outrage of some who feel the comparison of Christianity with mythology damages the perception of their religion. As Ron Charles wryly observes, "If you play with 'The Odyssey,' people are mildly amused; if you fiddle with Jesus, people begin collecting dry sticks." But the stories told by writers like Margaret Atwood in *The Penelopiad* or Jeanette Winterson in *Weight* are epics with one dominant master narrative, until now. In the series, writers altered the events of the epics to create a new story, generating renewed interest in age-old myths for contemporary readers, imbuing new life into ancient tales. In fact, Pullman "hopes in fact that his book will lead people back to the Bible itself. 'Because then they will see how many contradictions and inconsistencies there are between the gospels,' he explains, 'instead of this single monolithic story'" (Barton).

The Counter-Argument and Genetic Fallacy

When Pullman suggested that anyone shocked or offended by his story of Jesus "write [his or her] own book," he anticipated Gerald O'Collins' counter-argument, published in 2010. Called *Philip Pullman's Jesus*, Collins lays out a carefully reasoned, though ultimately flawed argument against Pullman's text. Granted, O'Collins' text provides a thorough comparative study between Pullman's text and its Biblical sources, making it a good resource for those who want a catalog of chapters and verses that likely inspired Pullman. However, O'Collins' insistence that Pullman has violated the parameters of historical fiction presents a logical fallacy. I asked Pullman if he had read O'Collins' book and he said he was sent a copy by a reader but realized from the opening chapter that O'Collins misunderstood his intentions.[8]

The basis of O'Collins' argument against Pullman's text is mired in a genetic fallacy. O'Collins assumes that because Pullman's novel is a work of historical fiction, he must adhere to stringent rules. In his section titled "Historical Fiction," O'Collins writes, "Those who write novels about totally fictional characters who live in an imaginary place and at an imaginary time enjoy complete freedom in creating events, dialogue, scenery and the rest" (1–2). He cites J.R.R. Tolkien's most famous works which are set in a place he created with invented characters. O'Collins continues, "But those novelists who write about Jesus and other persons who belonged to human history and left well-documented lives write under the constraints of the available evidence" (2). He allows that they have the right to create dialogue, additional characters, and imbue the work with descriptive setting elements, but that is where the writers' freedom stops, for "readers expect authors of historical fiction to remain faithful to the known, central facts.... Writers of historical fiction may not play fast and loose with history" (2).

This is a fallacy, for O'Collins assumes Pullman's text is flawed by its origin. Joseph W. Turner's "The Kinds of Historical Fiction: An Essay in Definition and Methodology," argues that there are three categories of historical fiction required to acknowledge "that neither history nor fiction is itself a stable, universally agreed upon, concept" (333). Pullman's novel moves among all three types: "those that invent a past, those that disguise a documented past, and those that re-create a documented past" (335). Perhaps the crux of the problem between O'Collins' interpretation versus Pullman's approach is that readers and authors tend to emphasize either the "'*historical* novel'" or the "'historical *novel*'" (Turner 336). Pullman believes his work fits the latter, having emphasized in interviews that this is *his* story. Turner states that the "expectations" of readers reveal the conflict over where the line is drawn between documented history versus dramatic license, which creates a "tension" for the novelist (342). As Turner concludes, "the historian is supposed to restrict himself to historical events, while the documented historical novelist need not" (344).

In one illustration of the conflict between O'Collins's reading of the text versus Pullman's intentions, O'Collins contends that "in first-century Palestine 'Christ' or 'Messiah' was *never* a personal name" (21), prompting skeptics to inquire "What personal agenda persuaded him [Pullman] to promote an impossible idea" (21) in bestowing this name on "an alleged twin brother of Jesus" (21). Pullman's response is that he wrote "'a fable'" (21). Pullman explains, "Any originality my version possesses is to stress the difference between Jesus the man and Christ the myth. The twins idea just helped me to dramatise that. Of course I'm not saying that there really were twins ... or that the imaginary brother of Jesus really was Christ."[9] Abrams and Harpham elucidate, "Some of the greatest historical novels also use the protagonists and actions to reveal what the author regards as

Eight. The Good Man Jesus and the Scoundrel Christ

the deep forces that impel the historical process" (230), something that Pullman obviously intended in his rendition of the story of Jesus. Throughout O'Collins' criticism, he refers to "widely accepted demands" and "normally accepted requirements" (96) related to historical fiction, yet nowhere does O'Collins cite sources which properly define the wide parameters of historical fiction as Turner and others have elsewhere. Perhaps O'Collins' argument would have more weight were he to have suggested that writers of historical fiction should *attempt* to embed their work with facts, but he clearly states that historical fiction has rules to which Pullman did not adhere, thus the basis of his argument is founded on a fallacy.

O'Collins further notes that readers of historical fiction "will not be amused to find the assassination of Julius Caesar shifted from Rome to Alexandria. Nor would they look with favour on an author who took the liberty of inventing a secret marriage between Queen Elizabeth I and Philip II of Spain" (2). Again, O'Collins' argument is flawed, for readers of historical fiction often expect factual changes to occur in a retelling. Interestingly, earlier in his book, O'Collins calls Pullman a "world class master of fantasy fiction" (x). If he is a writer of fantasy, then does he not have complete freedom to fantasize? Pullman's addition of a twin brother is no different than his retelling of the story of Adam and Eve at the conclusion of *The Golden Compass*. This version of the Genesis story includes dæmons, and of course, there are no dæmons in our world or in the Bible. Pullman's clever retelling of the expulsion from the Garden of Eden is in keeping with the larger story he has chosen to tell about another world similar to ours. Pullman has often stated that what is more important than anything is the story itself. Therefore, in keeping with his intention to retell the story of the Gospels with alterations, he has captured the majority of the known facts in his retelling while altering some portions to present another view. One wonders if *The Good Man Jesus and the Scoundrel Christ* were included within the context of *His Dark Materials* inside one of the many worlds separate from our own if the controversy would be less heated, because the text were embedded inside a work of so-called "fantasy"?

In O'Collins' epilogue, he speculates that Pullman has deliberately tried to discredit all of Christianity by retelling the Gospels. O'Collins says, "What better way could there be for demolishing Christianity than by suggesting that it was founded on deliberate fraud" (95). O'Collins' question leads me to recall the moment that a student in my class read Pullman's retelling of the Genesis story and exclaimed, "He can't do that!"

When I asked her why, she suggested he was undermining all of Christianity by changing a detail of the Genesis story. My response to her then was the same as my current response to those who believe that Pullman as one man has the ability to bring down an entire religion with a retelling: one's faith must not be strong if it is so easily shaken by a reimagined *story*. One wonders if Pullman had chosen to alter less iconic portions of the story of Jesus would O'Collins object with the same fervor? In other words, is the issue for O'Collins and others who oppose this text the fact that in his retelling, Pullman altered the portions of the story that most would find objectionable as opposed to changing elements of lesser "importance"?

While it is clear that Pullman is not the first nor will he be the last to spark furor over his occasional dalliances into religious subject matter, it is troubling that the outrage seems to obscure an element in his text that sheds light on his body of work as a whole: this book, like so many of his others, is about the path from innocence to experience. In a recent article by Helen Brown in *The Telegraph*, Pullman explains that when he initially talked with his publisher David Fickling about Milton, *Paradise Lost*, and the decision to write *His Dark Materials*, he had "been brooding about the abstract theme of the books — the difference between innocence and experience — for many years.... And everything in the past 15–16 years since has been controlled by the gravitational pull of it" (2). Thus it should be no surprise to readers that *The Good Man Jesus and the Scoundrel Christ* also bears the imprint of the theme that has been the underpinning of his literary career.

Evaluating the Story on Its Own Merit

Putting aside the novel's controversy, is it possible to evaluate it in a vacuum, as a story, even a fairy tale? Certainly Pullman has immersed himself with fairy tales and fairy tale retellings and continues to work with the genre, with his *Fairy Tales from the Brothers Grimm: A New English Version* set to be released on 8 November 2012.[10] If readers distance themselves from the elements of documented history and consider the characters as fictional entities, does the story as Pullman tells it reveal anything innovative to the reader? Furthermore, does the story address the movement from innocence to experience, the free will and choices that confront so many in Pullman's world?

Eight. The Good Man Jesus and the Scoundrel Christ

A consideration of structuralist Vladimir Propp's dramatis personae in *The Morphology of the Folktale* may move readers in this direction. The three characters around which Pullman's tale spins are the hero, the false hero, and the villain (80). Propp illustrates three ways the "spheres of action" can be displayed among the characters: either the action relates to a single character, or he may shift through more than one sphere of action, taking on different roles over the course of the tale, or one sphere of action is completed by more than one character; in other words, a tale may produce more than one hero (80–81). When Pullman juxtaposes the good versus the evil twin, he utilizes the hero versus the false hero fairy tale trope. This motif is carried through countless fairy tale variants, such as *The Goose Girl*, in which the proper heir to the throne is denied her birthright and must fight to depose the corrupt imposter and attain her rightful place. In tales like this, the hero and false hero are static entities, remaining good or evil from the start of the tale to its finish. Pullman's story twists this convention through his third person omniscient narration to show Christ as a conflicted, dynamic character who moves back and forth between hero and false hero.

When Pullman's narrative begins, Jesus and Christ are presented as opposites from birth onward, for Jesus is strong, while Christ is weak. Christ is in need of constant care and attention, while Jesus is a child who thrives on his own more than his sickly brother. Because Mary must take time to lavish more attention on Christ at his birth, he is the one who is lying in the trough and first seen by the shepherds who have come to witness the birth of the messiah. He is sickly and not "meant" to rule, but he takes the place of the true ruler by default in this scene. For her part, Mary "was proud and happy that her little helpless son was receiving such tribute and praise. The other didn't need it; he was strong and quiet and calm" (Pullman, *The Good Man* 14).

When Pullman covers some of the early years of Jesus and Christ's lives, Jesus plays the role of the troublemaker, "boisterous" and "getting into mischief" with other children, while "Christ clung to his mother's skirts and spent hours in reading and prayer" (*The Good Man* 22). Jesus, described as a "bad boy" (23) by Mary, damages the dyer's cloth, and Christ "make[s] it all better" (23) and corrects Jesus's prank. Later Jesus defies the rules of the Sabbath by making mud sparrows; when he is about to be reprimanded, Christ "clap[s] his hands" to bring the sparrows to life, while Christ defends his brother and calls him "a good boy really" (24).

Christ is able to create magic while Jesus causes problems for himself, and yet "the children of the town preferred Jesus" (25). When the twins are twelve, Jesus disappears for several days, and eventually the family comes across a confrontation in which Jesus plays a part (28). Because he has been inscribing his name with clay on the temple wall, Jesus is branded a "'blasphemer'" and nearly punished until Christ intervenes and argues that Jesus "'means well'" (30). Thus Jesus is permitted to go free (30). Through these stories, Christ emerges as the more mature, knowledgeable, articulate son, the hero, and Jesus, the irreverent troublemaker, seems to be the false hero. However, as the tale progresses, the characters' roles change.

Once the twins are grown, their differences shine even brighter, for "Jesus took no notice of Christ, but ... Christ was always forbearing, and keen to display a friendly interest in his brother's work" (Pullman, *The Good Man* 31). At Jesus's baptism, Jesus refuses to baptize John at John's request. When Christ notices what appears to be an omen, a dove aloft that lands on a tree, he "wondered what it might mean, and imagine what a voice might say if it spoke from heaven and told him" (36). At this moment, Christ's desire to improve the story begins. When he tells Mary about the event, he alters it to include having been spoken to by God, and Mary agrees that it must be true and calls the event "'your special baptism'" (37). Readers should note that Christ fabricates a detail before he meets the stranger, so the desire to embellish truth lies in him innately. He further adds to the story of Jesus's baptism when he tries to convince his brother that the dove came, "hovered above your head," and a voice from heaven uttered, "'This is my beloved son'" (38). Jesus refuses to believe him (38). As Christ pushes Jesus to become a greater influence in the encounter in the wilderness, Jesus is angered and tells his brother to leave, calling him a "scoundrel" (39). Christ pleads his case, calling for Jesus to carry out miracles to entice people to follow him and to set up "the authority of one supreme director ... [with] councils of learned men to discuss and agree on the details of ritual and worship" (43). Jesus attributes this vision to "the work of Satan" (44). Unable to convince Jesus to listen to his plan, Christ returns to Nazareth and begins to observe Jesus from a distance, deciding that his message would be more effective if altered (55). Once the stranger enters the picture and gives him a little push, Christ becomes the chronicler of Jesus's actions, always conscious of improving the story.

While Christ has the initial idea to chronicle the actions of Jesus for posterity, it is his meeting with the ubiquitous stranger that spurs him to

Eight. The Good Man Jesus and the Scoundrel Christ

embellish and interpret what he hears and sees for greater effect. The stranger tempts Christ by heaping praise on him, stating that while Jesus is the focus of the people, Christ is "'the one I should speak to'" (Pullman, *The Good Man* 57). When Christ questions why he is preferred, the stranger notes that Christ was the one given gifts at his birth and he brings up the times thus far that Christ has improved history with embellishment (57). Christ is further duped when the Stranger says, "'I want to make sure that you have your rightful reward. I want the world to know your name as well as that of Jesus. In fact I want your name to shine with even greater splendour. He is a man, and only a man, but you are the word of God'" (58). The hero and the false hero are referenced in this temptation, for the Stranger convinces Christ that he is the true Messiah while Jesus is the imposter. In thinking back to tales such as *The Goose Girl*, part of the reason the false hero is able to usurp the throne is because she so believes that she deserves the honor.

Later, the stranger pushes Christ harder by coming to his aid to defend him when he is accused of being a spy. The stranger ingratiates himself and claims, "'Sometimes there is a danger that people might misinterpret the words.... The statements need to be edited, the meanings clarified, the complexities unraveled for the simple-of-understanding'" (Pullman, *The Good Man* 73–74). The stranger appeals to Christ's flaw of pride, for in his previous interactions with Jesus, Christ spoke of people being too simple-minded to understand his word and needing miracles to be fully convinced. This sets Christ apart as intelligent and perceptive, and the stranger thus lifts him up above his fellow man, igniting in him his prideful nature to tempt him further.

The stranger is Propp's classic villain. Many critics have discussed the stranger's possible identity, but readers need look no further than Christ's own words to see the plethora of possibilities. Over the course of the tale, Christ thinks he may be an "important teacher" (Pullman, *The Good Man* 59), "the priest" (73), "a member of the Sanhedrin" (75), a "Gentile, perhaps a Greek philosopher" (100), an "angel" (126), and finally a man who reminds him of "a prosperous dealer" (244). The stranger never identifies himself, though there are a few words associated with him that point to Satan. O'Collins argues that he represents Satan, claiming that he says, "'My name is legion'" (57). This is a misrepresentation of Pullman's text, for what is written is that Christ asks the stranger, "'There are others besides you, sir?'" and the stranger replies, "'A legion'" (146). The word "legion" may be significant, but O'Collins has misquoted Pullman. It is true that at the conclusion of the text Christ refers to the stranger's words as "'subtle'" (241), another word that alludes to the serpent in the garden, and Christ also recognizes that if the stranger had been intending to "tempt him into rash words, this was exactly the way he would do it: lead him by soft questions" (123). Furthermore, the stranger brings up Satan by stating that he is not him (223). For answers, readers may look to Pullman's own interpretation of his identity. In a review by Lynn Neary, Pullman says, "'I wanted the reader to wonder about it. And I hope people will talk about it and wonder who this could be.... If I had to name the stranger — which I try not to do throughout the book and whenever Christ seeks to know his name, the stranger asks him a question or evades it in some way — but if I was pinned to the spot and forced to say what he was, I would say he was the spirit of the church, really'" (1).

Whether he represents an organization or a single entity, the stranger is a static character whose function is to tempt Christ into betraying his brother. When Christ asks him if he is doing the right thing in writing down Jesus' words, the stranger says, "'I'm sure we can rely on you'" (Pullman, *The Good Man* 74). Later the stranger argues that Christ's job is to help change the outcome of the future, saying, "'*What should have been* is a better servant of the Kingdom than *what was*'" (98–99). He contends that Christ is "'letting truth into history'" (99) by subtly changing Jesus' words and actions, suggesting that Christ must be "'wiser'" than Jesus (125). Considering that Christ had always seen himself as the lesser brother, the servant of Jesus, it is evident that the stranger goes after what will affect him most: his tortured sense of self-importance. By offering him platitudes and praise, telling Christ that he is the true hero, the stranger is the sole character in the text who exalts Christ instead of his brother, building him up to the point where he sees that his actions are not only rationalized but holy. In a moment of irony, the stranger utters these words to Christ: "'human life is difficult; there are profundities and compromises and mysteries that look to the innocent eye like betrayal. Let the wise men of the church hear those burdens'" (171). Of course, the stranger preys on Christ's innocence and tricks him into betraying his own flesh and blood.

Thus the stranger affects Christ through temptation, turning Christ's conscience into a state of turmoil as he desires to become the hero but must ignore his inner voice to do so. For instance, early on, when he alters the story of Jesus and Peter, "he gathered himself and wrote down what

Eight. The Good Man Jesus and the Scoundrel Christ

the disciple had told him, up to the point where Peter spoke. Then a thought came to him, and he wrote something new" (Pullman, *The Good Man* 103). He alters the story and then "he tremble[s] ... wonder[ing] if he were being presumptuous in making Jesus express the thoughts that he himself had put to his brother in the wilderness" (103–04); then he reconsiders the words of the stranger and feels himself "uplifted" (104). Christ rationalizes his version of the story, and any time there appears to be conflict between Jesus's words or actions and Christ's feelings, he seeks the stranger's validation to support him in battling his inner conflicts (115–19).

Christ accurately describes his own dual nature when he claims that his brother acts with "passion" while he acts by "calculation" (Pullman, *The Good Man* 135). Yet he also rationalizes his attempts to control the future by saying that he alone is able to understand the "consequences" while Jesus cannot (135). Further evidence of the conflict in Christ's mind comes from the fact that he professes great love for the brother who seems to ignore him entirely. Christ claims to "feel like a ghost" or "a daydream" next to his brother (136). Does he betray his brother because of loss, because he feels lesser and desires glory for himself? Or does he betray him because he truly believes the act will exalt his brother? This conflict is exemplified in Christ's words to the stranger when he is at his most torn: "'You've caught me in a net so that I'm tangled like a gladiator and I can't fight my way out'" (174). Christ seems aware that the wheel he set into motion is spinning out of control, but he is unable to change the course of history (or truth). When he agrees to fake the resurrection, he says to the stranger that he has "a bitter conscience and a heavy heart" (228). At this point, Christ already knows that he has made a tremendous mistake and is struggling in the depths of his soul.

This betrayal, this great lie on which Christianity is then founded, turns Christ into the hero of the story as long as he is perceived to be Jesus himself. But in his own conscience and in Pullman's characterization, he is again the false hero, because his recasting of the story of Jesus has set things into motion which will bring about destruction. It is clear from the way Pullman's tale ends that Christ is sickened by his own actions and indecisive about the future. He seems to be aware that he has been the victim of temptation and unsure if he has set some grand plan into motion which will cause a great tragedy to occur for ages to come. Tucker states, "Christ finally agrees to soften the absolute message of his brother to make it more acceptable. But he is also in agony over this last act of betrayal, and rather than pulling any authorial strings at this point in the argument, Pullman leaves final judgment to his readers" ("The Good Man"). As the novel concludes, Christ asks his wife Martha what he should do, and she tells him to eat and drink, but the bread and wine are gone. Consumed by the stranger, it appears that symbolically, Jesus is gone from the tale and history is forever altered by Christ's version of truth. Pullman says of him, "Christ is this complicated character, and I call him a 'scoundrel' in the title but we soon come to see he [is] not so much of a scoundrel as a confused man. Christ is like a figure in a novel," Pullman says. "He's the only figure in the story who is like a figure in a novel, because he is the only one who is made up" (Neary). Clearly Christ is much more than a static figure, but a round protagonist who shifts between false hero, hero, and false hero again over the course of this grand narrative.

A Brief Connection to His Dark Materials

It is evident from the conclusion of Pullman's tale that he moves beyond a discussion of the hero versus the false hero, beyond the mythic or fairy tale aspects of this great story, and comments on the nature of storytelling. To go back to *His Dark Materials*, in which storytelling plays a key role, Lyra enters the land of the dead and is unable to pass by "No-Name" the harpy who suggests Will, Lyra, and the Gallivespians might pass through the door to find the ghosts if Lyra tells a story (Pullman, *The Amber Spyglass* 292). Believing that "she'd just been dealt the ace of trumps," Lyra launches into a tale she constructed previously, "shaping and cutting and improving and adding ... settling into her storytelling frame of mind," crafting a fantasy for the attentive harpy (292). No-Name viciously attacks Lyra, repeatedly screaming, "'Liar!'" (293) so frequently that the word "liar" and the name "Lyra" become one in the same (293). Will uses the knife to cut through the door to escape to the "realm of the ghosts" (293) temporarily, but it is clear that by telling lies, something Lyra has relied on much for her journey, she has angered the harpy and in effect entrapped herself and the others in the land of the dead.

After reuniting with Roger and the other ghosts, Lyra and Will wonder how they can free themselves. Pullman's epigraph for Chapter 23, titled "No Way Out," lights the path. From St. John, it reads, "And ye shall know the truth, and the truth shall make you free" (qtd. in *The Amber*

Eight. The Good Man Jesus and the Scoundrel Christ

Spyglass 306). With the ghosts in a panic trapped in the underworld, Will suggests that Lyra "tell them the truth" while he and the others keep the harpies at bay (313). Surrounded by the dead, "Lyra beg[ins] to talk about the world she kn[ows]" (314). She depicts anecdotes about her escapades with Roger at Jordan College, and Roger's ghost, nearby, agrees that these events really happened. She offers details of everything that made Jordan College and Oxford real to her, the sights, the sounds, the smells, the activity, the fights and allegiances (314–15). "Exhausted" (315), Lyra finishes her tale, to notice that the harpies have come to listen as well. Stunned and scared, she asks why they are no longer attacking her, and she is told that the harpies have only had "the worst" to feed on all this time because the only power the Authority prescribed was this ability, and so they have fed on sickness and death (316). What Lyra has just offered them is goodness and light, and they have become entranced.

The harpies state that they must attack Lyra when she tells "'Lies and fantasies'" (Pullman, *The Amber Spyglass* 317) but they do not feel compelled to violence when her story is "'true'" (317), for truth and goodness is "nourishing" (317). Tialys offers a bargain: in exchange for hearing true stories from those who pass through this realm, the harpies will agree to lead them out (317). The harpies will have the right to refuse passage if they are not told the truth (318). Thus a treaty is reached, and the truth sets them all free into what becomes the Republic of Heaven. Thus Lyra, the "new Eve," learns in her experience that only truth can save mankind.

Conversely, in Pullman's reimagined gospels, Christ lies to humanity in an effort to save them. The stranger insists that the world Jesus conceived of is too perfect, too unattainable, and says, "'Isn't it better to compromise a little, to come inside and improve something, than to stay on the outside and offer nothing but criticism?'" (Pullman 45). He convinces Christ who carries out his plan, basing Christianity on what turns out to be a fabrication: a faked resurrection, coupled with embellished stories of miracles. Thus Christ lies to save humanity, but the implication at the end of Pullman's story of Jesus is that they will not be saved. Rather, great wars will be fought in the name of this faith, and there will be rules and dogma and a misuse of the words of Jesus in the name of institutionalized religion. In effect, the world will go the way it is described through much of *His Dark Materials*.

Both Lyra and Christ become betrayers. Lyra must betray Roger, her dearest friend, though she does so without knowing it will happen. She unwittingly brings him to his death. Christ might be said to do the same, for he believes that something will happen to save Jesus at the last minute, exclaiming to the stranger, "'You let me believe that something would happen to prevent the worst. And nothing happened, and the worst came'" (Pullman, *The Good Man* 224). He is devastated, just like Lyra, to find that he has played the pivotal role in bringing about the death of the one he loved most. The difference, though, lies in the fact that through her words of truth, Lyra is able to save Roger's spirit and let him go free. Christ, on the other hand, brings about actions that imprison the real message of Jesus.

In working with her intuition and telling the truth, Lyra brings about a positive change, while in telling lies and doing nothing to prevent the way "the story [was] changing little by little" (Pullman, *The Good Man* 236), Christ brings about tragedy. Thus Lyra as the new Eve brings the Republic of Heaven to the world and truth to the afterlife. Christ is given the opposite treatment; he struggles with what is moral and correct and errs on the side of temptation. Controlled by the stranger and his darker impulses, he eventually realizes that his actions, though initially well-intended, were calculated and will usher forth tragic consequences. Christ balks against his intuition and rationalizes his acts, which results in his epiphany. The path he followed may have been the wrong one. The ending of the story suggests only strife for Christ as he must bear witness to the tragedies that will occur as the words and actions of the brother he so loved are lost over the course of history as zealotry lays poised to take over.

Final Thoughts

In the final analysis, *His Dark Materials* and *The Good Man Jesus and the Scoundrel Christ* reveal that one may begin his or her journey as an innocent and be affected by loss and trauma, and he or she may emerge stronger or weaker as a result, for loss has profoundly different effects on different people. Pullman shows that Lyra turns her trauma and loss into truth, wisdom, and grace, while Christ turns his conflict and suffering into half-truths that reach far and wide into the future. Therefore, both Lyra and Christ move from innocence to experience, but the path each takes is very different. Pullman shows readers that heroes are human, flawed, and do not always choose wisely. Pullman writes so often of

Eight. The Good Man Jesus and the Scoundrel Christ

redemption, and so perhaps another newly created story awaits Pullman's Christ: a story in which he rises from his past mistakes and emerges to tell a new tale.

But then again, perhaps Christ stays on his path and continues to embellish the truth. He is already mentally calculating ways he can continue to improve the story of Jesus's life, death, and resurrection when Pullman's story ends: "There were a hundred details that could add verisimilitude. He knew, with a pang that blended with guilt and pleasure, that he had already made some of them up" (Pullman, *The Good Man* 243). In "'Let's Write It in Red': The Patrick Hardy Lecture," Pullman describes an experience he had riding a train with a family with two young girls in the midst of writing a story (44). As the girls discussed what they were "'allowed'" to do in the tale, one girl suggested that when they come to a thrilling bit of the story, they should "'write it in red'" (45). Pullman muses about the rules he believes are part and parcel of writing stories, but also the caution that writers not become so self-conscious that it shackles them creatively (58). He claims that writers must always move forward, not attempting to go backwards into the realm of the innocent to try to lose self-consciousness, but to move in new directions and develop new interests in their subject matter, for knowledge and experience usher growth (58–59). At the conclusion of this essay, Pullman admits that he will "come clean and tell the law-court truth" and become a "reliable" narrator, for the truth of the matter is that one of the little girls on the train said, "'Let's write it in blue'" (62). And thus the literary magpie decided to take something from a true story and recast it to his own liking, noting that "Blue makes the point, but red makes it better" (62). It is as if Pullman is suggesting one should never let the truth get in the way of a good story, a mantra he has followed throughout his literary career. As Elizabeth Rose Gruner states in "Wrestling with Religion: Pullman, Pratchett, and the Uses of Story," "truth and lies are simply two different ways of getting at the same thing" (284).

Therefore, is it only a terrible tragedy that Christ chooses to embellish his tale? Does choosing the path of destruction always signal an end? Or can it signal transformation, the death of the old, and rebirth? What Christ sets into motion will cause tragedy, but in a world with no strife, no betrayal, and no loss, people would not have to fight back to survive. For it is in confronting pain and heartache and sadness that people are tested, and it is through rising up after tragedy that people grow. As Pullman has said in one form or another through so many of his literary works, one must lose to gain, and any fall is an important catalyst for change. Therefore, if Christ himself "writes it in red," he may inadvertently aid humanity who will be forced to overcome trauma to move from innocence to experience. In the words of American Buddhist nun Pema Chödrön, "Only to the extent that we expose ourselves over and over to annihilation can that which is indestructible be found in us" (10). Perhaps what permeates Philip Pullman's fiction, then, is that which is indestructible: the seeds of wisdom, grace, love, and most of all, hope. Hope for survival after a great fall; hope for a brighter tomorrow; and hope that the art of storytelling will continue to possess the power that it has for centuries — the power to make us whole again.

Chapter Notes

Introduction

1. See Bridge 118.

2. A disclaimer about Pullman's influences and allusions: Pullman and I engaged in a lengthy correspondence during my work on this book, during which he answered all my questions with candor and wit. Because these essays are my arguments, my claims about allusions in his work are my own and do not reflect anything that Pullman has indicated unless otherwise noted in comments I cite from him. As he says in the interview with Marie Bridge, "I suppose when you're describing characters in action, when you're writing a story, you must be basing it on people you've observed, things you've seen, or things you've read about in other fiction, but not always consciously. One of the traps you fall into ... is of writing a scene which is terrific and wonderful, and then you go and read it in somebody else's book, which you then remember you read last year. So a lot of what happens when you're making up a character in action ... comes directly out of your own experience" (106).

Part I

1. See Pullman, *The Golden Compass* 32.

Chapter One

1. See Pullman, "Carnegie Medal Acceptance Speech."

2. The omission of *I Was a Rat!*, which some critics have called a fairy tale re-vision, is intentional. In Kevin Paul Smith's *The Postmodern Fairytale: Folkloric Intertexts in Contemporary Fiction*, he defines re-vision as "putting a new spin on an old tale" (10); since *I Was a Rat!* begins after the Cinderella story ends, it is arguably not a re-vision but an original fairy tale that incorporates allusions to the Cinderella tale type.

3. A list for readers is here: "1. Authorised: Explicit reference to a fairytale in the title 2. Writerly: Implicit reference to a fairytale in title 3. Incorporation: Explicit reference to a fairytale within the text 4. Allusion: Implied reference to a fairytale within the text 5. Re-vision: putting a new spin on an old tale 6. Fabulation: crafting an original fairytale 7. Metafictional: discussion of fairytales 8. Architextual/Chronotopic: 'Fairytale' setting/environment" (10).

4. In an email dated 11/16/11, Pullman explains that "*Mossycoat* came about because my publisher David Fickling wanted to do a series of little books, each to cost one pound, containing well-known folk tales retold by modern writers. I chose to do that one because I think it's a great tale. Fourteen or so of those tales have just been published in one volume under the title *Magic Beans*."

5. Pullman, Message to the author, 16 Nov. 2011, e-mail.

6. In an email dated 11/16/11, Pullman explains that the Aladdin revision "was another David Fickling commission."

7. Pullman, Message to the author, 16 Nov. 2011, e-mail.

Chapter Two

1. See Carter 183.
2. See Birmingham Stage Company. According to the website, the novelized form of *The Firework-Maker's Daughter* is now performed again as a stage play adapted by Stephen Russell in 2003.
3. Pullman, Message to the author, 4 Dec. 2011, e-mail. The ellipsis marks are mine.
4. See Bobby "What Makes a Classic?" Countless interviews reflect the prevalence of this question and Pullman's two responses, but I have referenced two different sources of the response in my essay.

Chapter Three

1. See Pullman, "I have a feeling this all belongs to me" 27.
2. The primary exception is the second book of the Sally Lockhart quartet. *The Shadow in the North* was originally published as *The Shadow in the Plate* in 1986; when republished, it was reorganized with selected portions rewritten and a few plot points altered. Full discussion of the changes appears in an endnote in Chapter 5. Other than this variation on his own work, there are no narrative changes to be seen in other works other than reissues with shorter novels compiled together in longer editions.
3. I will be using a translated version of this opera for this essay, and as such, all portions quoted will be in English. See Weber.
4. See Miller for a brilliant analytical essay on the Faustian allusions in Pullman's *Clockwork, or All Wound Up.*
5. Pullman cleverly alludes to his own work through the ads on page 111: The ads for the Beefo Animal Stimulant and the St. Elmo Electric Undergarments are references to *The New Cut Gang: Thunderbolt's Waxwork* (1994) in which the character Dippy Hitchcock is given a stimulant meant for horses to keep his courage up, and Thunderbolt Dobney's father is found to be making undergarments with an electric current to help women with back pain.
6. Pullman's "three pages a day" method of writing is referenced in countless interviews, but readers should see Mountford for more information about his paper and pen choice and other interesting tidbits.
7. Since the two editions are virtually the same but for pagination due to the changes in font, I will be using the more recent 1998 edition for all page references. While I have had access to a copy of the Chatto and Windus edition, it is very rare and difficult to find, making the newer edition more appropriate here should readers wish to confirm any of the citations.

Chapter Four

1. See Fried.
2. I asked Pullman why he focuses so often on the plight of exploited children and adolescents and whether this interest came from something in his childhood or background as a teacher, and he responded, "There's nothing mysterious or psychological about it. The biggest problem in writing a story about children is how to get rid of the parents. Every writer who's tried knows that. Maybe I'm trying to avoid a revealing answer here, but maybe I'm right and it is as simple as that. If you want a child to have adventures, get rid of the people who are going to make it their first business to stop him or her falling into danger" (Message to the author, 4 Dec. 2011, e-mail). This answer does not support Diane M. Duncan's argument, but in general Pullman does "avoid [the] revealing answer" and very rarely links his childhood to his fiction. Typically he reserves openness about his

Chapter Notes

childhood experiences to pieces written in the style of essay or personal memoir.

3. I will be using the 2002 Knopf USA edition of this text in my analysis because the text and illustrations of the 1989 edition are intact.

4. Note that Pullman opens his novel with a one-page prelude titled "The Legend of Spring-Heeled Jack" in which he explains that Jack was a Victorian-era superhero much like Batman, who "dressed like the devil" and was quite "mysterious," bringing "a very unpleasant end" to anyone committing a wrongdoing (3).

5. Several critics have speculated that Pullman's own background and the loss of his father surfaces occasionally in his work; Pullman's account of his father's demise in "I have a feeling this all belongs to me" is therefore informative for one reading *Spring-Heeled Jack*; in his essay, Pullman describes his father as someone he didn't know very well, a person surrounded by "glamour" (qtd. in Beahm 13), and when he died after his plane was shot down, Pullman described his sense of detachment from the situation, stating he may have cried but does not remember feeling emotionally affected (13). Pullman admits that only much later in life did he find out the truth about his father: "So all my life I've had the idea that my father was a hero cut down in his prime, a warrior, a man of shining glamour, and none of it was true. Sometimes I think he's really still alive somewhere, in hiding, with a different name. I'd love to meet him" (15). It is possible that his own experience affected the storyline of *Spring-Heeled Jack*, for the children "lose" their father in a very unusual, exotic way, yet seem detached from him and more attached to their mother, only to later be reunited with him after they have gone through a period of maturity. Perhaps, then, the conclusion of this novel represents some small bit of wish fulfillment for Pullman.

6. Note that in *Count Karlstein* the same phenomenon occurs: when Lucy and Charlotte are orphaned, their replacement parents are Count Karlstein and his wife. Because they are unfit parents, Hildi Kelmar becomes a surrogate parent, and at the story's conclusion, Max and Eliza, who marry, become the new Count Karlstein and his wife due to a formerly unknown blood relation. However, it is clear that even if they were not related by blood (Max) and marriage (Eliza) that the two would become the new parents to Lucy and Charlotte. Pullman seems to suggest, then, that in stories with happy endings, orphaned or displaced children eventually forge lasting relationships with their real parents or adults who act as surrogate parents.

7. There is a subtle parallel between the scene in which the children decide to leave Spangle and the scene in *The Amber Spyglass* in which Lyra realizes she must leave Pantalaimon behind to go to the land of the dead, particularly because Pan becomes a whimpering puppy, a form he has never taken prior in the trilogy. Though the two scenes are different in tone, the connection lies in the fact that Pullman sees "grownup decisions" such as the ability to make an act that hurts oneself for the benefit of the greater good as character-building and a necessity for personal growth.

8. This plot point is somewhat reminiscent of the contest described in *Count Karlstein* in terms of its focus on a character (Mack the Knife) who makes a deal with the devil (Spring-Heeled Jack), yet the devil is revealed to be Mack himself at the end.

9. See Bobby, "What Makes a Classic?" in which I wrote about the various interpretations of what a dæmon may represent, and the concept of a guardian angel or a conscience are two possibilities.

10. At the time of this writing, a New Cut Gang book is available in new form. Titled *Two Crafty Criminals!: and How They Were Captured by the Daring Detectives of the New Cut Gang*, it is a compila-

tion of the earlier two volumes. Pullman says, "I simply haven't had time to do any new New Cut Gang stories, much as I like the kids." (Message to the author, 16 Nov. 2011, e-mail).

11. A talk Pullman gave when being honored as a Fellow of the Welsh Academy mentions that he had a friend named Derek Dobney who used to take part in pranks with him, such as lighting fireworks and throwing them onto the roof of a public lavatory to scare occupants and deliberately seeking out amorous couples near the oceanfront to "stand in front and watch them till they chased us away." Pullman, Philip. "Reminiscences at Ardudwy" (Message to the author, 12 Dec. 2011, e-mail).

12. Springhall contends that the term "penny dreadful" lacks "historical precision," for there are as many as six distinct meanings of the term, which he describes (226–27). As Pullman himself has referred to his New Cut Gang books as "penny dreadfuls," it is clear that he is using the term for general purpose of explanation, and a discussion of the six various meanings of the term is therefore tangential to the analysis here of Pullman's works.

13. Pullman wrote the play script *Sherlock Holmes and the Limehouse Horror*, published by Nelson Thornes in July 2001. He also has served as the editor of *Whodunit? Detective Stories Chosen by Philip Pullman*, published by Kingfisher in 2007, and he wrote the introductory essay for this collection as well as an introductory note for each selection.

Part II

1. See Pullman, *The Amber Spyglass* 285.

Chapter Five

1. See www.philip-pullman.com.
2. Originally published as *The Shadow in the Plate* by Oxford University Press in 1986, Pullman's first version of this story contains a few differences from *The Shadow of the North*, either due to rearranged chapters or changes to the plot. *The Shadow in the Plate* opens with the scene in Mackinnon's dressing room during which readers hear the conversation that Jim interrupts; the vision Nellie Budd sees during the séance is altered to incorporate a horse Lord Wytham owns. Later, Axel Bellmann pays a man to temporarily weaken the horse so that it loses the race, which puts Wytham into further debt, setting up the primary reason Bellmann is able to secure Lady Mary's hand in marriage. Sally uses her feminine wiles in this version to catch Lord Wytham's eye, which leads to her being manhandled by him during one of Mackinnon's performances. Additionally, Nellie Budd is murdered. While Mackinnon's prior marriage to Lady Mary is a feature of both versions, there is more discussion devoted to it here; Sally talks with Lady Mary about the possibility of her divorcing Mackinnon and breaking the engagement to Axel Bellmann. Frederick steals an emerald-encrusted choker from Windlesham when he comes to see him and Sally, and later, Jim pawns it to pay off Sally's client who lost her investment. The most significant difference relates to the conclusion, for Axel Bellman is not murdered by his own steam gun, but by Lord Wytham, who confronts him in anger and shoots him right after Bellmann says he should be marrying Sally. Sally, known to Wytham only as Dolly Marchbanks, makes it appear as if Bellmann committed suicide. The steam regulator is destroyed, but by an accident stemming from a worker leaving a valve open.

3. Pullman has surprisingly escaped scrutiny in writing so openly about a young child assisting a drug addict by providing him with more opium and lighting his pipe. Terry Gilliam's film *Tideland*, which was released later in 2005, caused a flurry of negative press because in it

Gilliam shows a young girl assisting her drug addict father with his heroin, a facet of the book on which Gilliam based his film. In fact, Gilliam included a brief disclaimer on the dvd by appearing before the film to tell the audience that some might dislike or even hate the film for some of the scenes, but that in the end, he was just trying to make some observations about what it was like to be the little girl in the story. Interestingly, in the television production of *The Ruby in the Smoke*, the violence from Mrs. Holland towards Adelaide is shown, but the specifics of her assisting Matthew Bedwell with his pipe are not.

4. The TV production of *The Shadow in the North* modifies Sally's quote a bit, and in light of the focus of this study, their revision is intriguing. Sally tries to comfort Isabel by saying, "If you betrayed him at all it was from love. To have done it from stubborn pride or selfishness would have been infinitely worse." The heart of Sally's message is consistent with the subtle distinction about the nature of betrayal that I elucidated in the introductory essay.

5. Pullman, Message to the author, 18 Nov. 2011, e-mail.

Chapter Six

1. See Pullman, "The Republic of Heaven" 661.

2. An alternative title of the story is *The Scarlet Slippers*, which obviously ties it to Cinderella. The tv series which aired on the BBC in 2001 also was known by the title "Cinderella and Me," which also reveals the fairy tale that inspired the story. In "A Profile: Philip Pullman: His Wonderful Materials" by Catherine M. Andronik, Pullman asserts that he "'hope[s] they [tv producers] reconsider [the title]. Because that title gives away the whole story, the realization as you go along that, hey, this is Cinderella!'" (45).

3. Pullman, Message to the author, 3 Dec. 2011, e-mail.

4. Pullman, Message to the author, 16 Nov. 2011, e-mail.

5. I have used the Dell Yearling paperback edition of this book illustrated by Kevin Hawkes with text copyright of 1999 and illustration copyright of 2000, and the page number count reflects this printing.

6. Note that both *The Broken Bridge* and *The White Mercedes*, aka *The Butterfly Tattoo*, are also contemporary adolescent novels by Pullman, but they are significantly different in tone and style, and as such, will be explored in another chapter.

7. Pullman, Message to the author, 18 Nov. 2011, e-mail.

8. Pullman, Message to the author, 19 Nov. 2011, e-mail.

9. Pullman, Message to the author, 18 Nov. 2011, e-mail.

10. Pullman, Message to the author, 19 Nov. 2011, e-mail.

11. In 1988, there was a television series titled *How to Be Cool* based on the book, produced by Granada Television. See www.imdb.com.

Chapter Seven

1. See Butler.

2. Pullman revealed in an email dated 12 Dec. 2011 that the title of the book was changed by the publisher. Pullman said, "I prefer that title, but when it was reissued the editor felt that it would put off potential girl readers because they're not interested in cars. What do I know?" The copy I have used for citation references in this chapter is titled *The White Mercedes*, so my references in text to the title will utilize the original title.

3. While the concerns of this essay do not include the impact of racial identity on Ginny, see Thomas's essay "'Everything She Knew'" for a discussion of "the question of blended racial and cultural identity" (52) in this contemporary novel. In addition, Karen Sands-O'Connor's "High Winds and Broken Bridges" examines the

"heavily Gothicized" facets of "race, sexuality, and the absent mother" (125) with a particular emphasis on the ways that the past haunts the present in postcolonial literature. Both of these pieces also address the presence of voodoo in the text.

4. Northeast Modern Language Association.

5. Pullman, Message to the author, 18 Dec. 2011, e-mail.

6. Readers intrigued by Pullman's depiction of adult male protagonists may be interested *The Haunted Storm* and *Galatea*, both of which are rare and out of print, but occasionally available in libraries or on rare and used book sites for purchase. Pullman considers both books flawed, particularly *The Haunted Storm*, which he calls "a terrible piece of rubbish" (182) in an interview published in *Talking Books*, ed. James Carter. While both are very complex texts, they lack the precision and pacing of his other work. However, they do provide a window into Pullman's ideas and offer readers insight into his later works. Some passages are quite lyrical in terms of lush physical description as well, showcasing Pullman's early work in illustrating very vividly physical settings and tying the perception of such settings to a character's emotional state.

7. Pullman, Message to the author, Feb. 2012, e-mail.

Chapter Eight

1. See *The Good Man Jesus and the Scoundrel Christ*.

2. See the exchange between an audience member and Philip Pullman: "Philip Pullman on Freedom of Speech," Sheldonian Theatre, Canongate Books, 29 Mar. 2010, http://www.youtube.com/watch?v=HQ3VcbAfd4w.

3. Pullman, Message to the author, 4 Dec. 2011, e-mail.

4. Albert Schweitzer wrote the first definitive text in 1906, titled *The Quest of the Historical Jesus: A Critical Study of its Progress from Reimarus to Wrede*.

5. According to Robert J. Miller, editor of *The Complete Gospels: Annotated Scholars Version*, the first line of the Gospel of Thomas is "These are the secret sayings that the living Jesus spoke and Didymos Judas Thomas recorded" (305). Miller explains that Didymos Judas Thomas held status as "a popular legendary figure" and the gospel itself was "assembled before Matthew, Mark, Luke, and John had attained the ascendency that the later church codified in the form of a 'canon'" (302–03). Furthermore, Miller states in his footnotes that "Didymos and Thomas are the Greek and Semitic words for *Twin*" (305).

6. See chapter one for the brief discussion of fairy tale re-visions.

7. Pullman, Message to the author, 3 Dec. 2011, e-mail.

8. Pullman, Message to the author, 18 Dec. 2011, e-mail.

9. Pullman, Message to the author, 4 Dec. 2011, e-mail.

10. The most current release date as of this writing is shown on www.amazon.com.

Bibliography

Abrams, M. H., and Geoffrey Galt Harpham. *A Glossary of Literary Terms*, 9th ed. Boston: Wadsworth, 2009. Print.

Andronik, Catherine M. "A Profile: Philip Pullman: His Wonderful Materials." *The Book Report* Nov./Dec. 2001: 40–45. Print.

Anglo, Michael. *Penny Dreadfuls and Other Victorian Horrors*. London: Jupiter, 1977. Print.

Baker, Dierdre F. "Philip Pullman *The Scarecrow and His Servant*." *The Horn Book Magazine* 81.5 (2005): 586–87. Print.

Barton, Laura. "'I hope the wretched Catholic church will vanish entirely.'" *The Guardian* 18 Apr. 2010. Web. 15 May 2012.

Basile, Giambattista. "Cagiluso." 1634. *The Great Fairy Tale Tradtion: From Straparola and Basile to the Brothers Grimm*. Ed. Jack Zipes. New York: Norton, 2001. 394–97. Print.

BBC. "Feral Children—A269840." H2g2 researchers. 7 Mar. 2000. Web. 15 May 2012.

Beckett, Sandra. *Crossover Fiction: Global and Historical Perspectives*. New York: Routledge, 2009. Print.

Bernheimer, Kate. "The Affect of Fairy Tales." Foreword. *Fairy Tales Reimagined: Essays on New Retellings*. Ed. Susan Redington Bobby. Jefferson, NC: McFarland, 2009. 1–4. Print.

Bettelheim, Bruno. *The Uses of Enchantment: The Meaning and Importance of Fairy Tales*. New York: Vintage, 1989. Print.

Bird, Elizabeth. "The Secret Past of Philip Pullman." A Fuse #8 Production. *School Library Journal* 4 Aug. 2011. Web. 15 May 2012.

Birmingham Stage Company. *Webpages for The Firework-Maker's Daughter*. 2003. Web. 12 July 2011.

Bobby, Susan R. "What Makes a Classic? Dæmons and Dual Audience in Philip Pullman's *His Dark Materials*." *The Looking Glass: New Perspectives on Children's Literature* 8.1 (2004): n. pag. Web. 15 May 2012.

Boswell, Taimi. "Mossycoat." 1915. *Selected Tales from Oral Traditions in English or English Translations*. Web. 15 May 2012.

Botting, Fred. *Gothic: The New Critical Idiom*. London: Routledge, 1996. Print.

Bottum, Joseph. "Pullman Sleeper." *First Things: A Monthly Journal of Religion and Public Life* Aug./Sept. 2010: 61–62. Print.

Bridge, Marie, ed. "Philip Pullman in Conversation with Marie Bridge." 24 Jan. 2003. *On the Way Home: Conversations Between Writers and Psychoanalysts*. London: Karnac, 2007. 98–136. Print.

Brown, Helen. "Page in the Life: Philip Pullman." *The Telegraph* 17 Oct. 2011. Web. 15 May 2012.

Brown, T. "Interview with Philip Pullman." *Lexicon Convention*. Aug. 2000. Web. 11 Sept. 2003.

Butler, Robert. "An Interview with Philip Pullman: The Art of Darkness." *More Intelligent Life*. 3 Dec. 2007. Web. 15 May 2012.

Campbell, Joseph. *The Hero with a Thousand Faces*, 2d ed. Princeton: Princeton University Press, 1968. Print.

_____. *The Power of Myth*. New York: Doubleday, 1988. Print.

Candland, Douglas Keith. *Feral Children and Clever Animals: Reflections on Human Nature*. New York: Oxford University Press, 1993. Print.

Canepa, Nancy L. *From Court to Forest: Giambattista Basile's Lo cunto de li cunti and the Birth of the Literary Fairy Tale*. Detroit: Wayne State University Press, 1999. Print.

Carter, James, ed. "An Introduction to ... Philip Pullman." *Talking Books: Children's Authors Talk About the Craft, Creativity and Process of Writing*. Florence, KY: Routledge, 1999. 178- 95. Print.

Cervantes Saavedra, Miguel de. *The Ingenious Hidalgo Don Quixote de la Mancha*. 1604–5 and 1615. Trans. John Rutherford. New York: Penguin, 2000. Print.

Charles, Ron. "'The Good Man Jesus and the Scoundrel Christ,' reviewed by Ron Charles." *Washington Post* 5 May 2010. Web. 15 May 2012.

Chesterton, G.K. "A Defence of Penny Dreadfuls." The Defendant, pub. in *The Wayfarer's Library*. London: J.M. Dent, 1901. Web. 21 Sept. 2011.

Chödrön, Pema. *When Things Fall Apart: Heart Advice for Difficult Times*. Boston: Shambhala, 2002. Print.

Conrad, JoAnn. "*The Good Man Jesus and the Scoundrel Christ*." Review. *Marvels and Tales: Journal of Fairy-tale Studies* 25.2 (2011): 94–96. Print.

Court, Ayesha. "Writing is Child's Play for Pullman." *USA Today* 25 June 2002. Web. 28 Oct. 2010.

Cross, Julie. "Frightening and Funny: Humor in Children's Gothic Fiction." *The Gothic in Children's Literature: Haunting the Borders*. Ed. Anna Jackson, Karen Coats, and Roderick McGillis. New York: Routledge, 2008. 57–76. Print.

Dentith, Simon. *Parody*. London: Routledge, 2000. Print.

Dolish, Patricia. "Philip Pullman *Count Karlstein*." Review. *School Library Journal* Sept. 1998: 208. Print.

Dunae, Patrick A. "Penny Dreadfuls: Late Nineteenth-Century Boys' Literature and Crime." *Victorian Studies* 22.2 (1979): 133–50. Print.

Duncan, Diane M. "Love, Loss and Magic: Connecting Author and Story." *Changing English* 14.3 (2007): 271–84. Print.

Fried, Kerry. "Darkness Visible: An Interview with Philip Pullman." 10 Oct. 2003. Web. 15 May 2012.

Gil, Eliana. *Treating Abused Adolescents*. New York: Guilford, 1996. Print.

Gillard, Derek. "Education in England: A Brief History." *The History of Education in England*. Jan. 2000. Web. 15 May 2012.

Gray, William. "Pullman, Lewis, MacDonald and the Anxiety of Influence." *Mythlore* 97/98 (2007): 117–32. Print.

Gruner, Elizabeth Rose. "Wrestling with Religion: Pullman, Pratchett, and the Uses of Story. *Children's Literature Association Quarterly* 36.3 (2011): 276–95. Print.

Heydt, Bruce. "A Well-Heeled Villain." *British Heritage* Mar. 2004: 4. Print.

Hutcheon, Linda. "Harry Potter and the Novice's Confession." *The Lion and the Unicorn* 32.2 (2008): 169–79. Print.

Jackson, Anna, Karen Coats, and Roderick McGillis, ed. Introduction. *The Gothic in Children's Literature: Haunting the Borders*. New York: Routledge, 2008. 1–14. Print.

Joosen, Vanessa. "Philip Pullman's *I Was a Rat!* and the Fairy-Tale Retelling as Instrument of Social Criticism." *Fairy Tales Reimagined: Essays on New Retellings*. Ed. Susan Redington Bobby. Jefferson, NC: McFarland, 2009. 196–209. Print.

Kimball, Melanie A. "From Folktales to

Fiction: Orphan Characters in Children's Literature." *Library Trends* 47.3 (1999): 558–78. Print.

King, Shelley. "Democratic Reading: Ideology and Genre in Pullman's I Was a Rat!" *Children's Literature* 37.1 (2009): 165–93. Print.

Lang, Andrew. "Aladdin and the Wonderful Lamp." *Andrew Lang's Fairy Books*. 1889. Web. 15 May 2012.

"The Merchants of Cool." *FRONTLINE*. Writ. Rachel Dretzin. Dir. Barak Goodman. PBS, 2001. VHS.

Miller, Lisa M. "Elaborately Wound: Philip Pullman's Marlowean Muse." *The Looking Glass: New Perspectives on Children's Literature* 10.2 (2006): n. pag. Web. 16 May 2011.

Miller, Robert J., ed. *The Complete Gospels: Annotated Scholars Version*. San Francisco: HarperCollins, 1992. Print.

Milton, John. *Paradise Lost*. Introduction by Philip Pullman. Oxford: Oxford University Press, 2005. Print.

Mountford, Charlotte. "Philip Pullman on Writing." *Teatime Magazine* 18 Nov. 2011. Web. 15 May 2012.

Neary, Lynn. "Jesus' Twin: Philip Pullman Takes on the Gospel." *NPR Books*. 4 May 2010. Web. 15 May 2012.

Newton, Michael. *Savage Girls and Wild Boys: A History of Feral Children*. New York: St. Martin's, 2002. Print.

Nikolajeva, Maria. *Children's Literature Comes of Age: Toward a New Aesthetic*. New York: Garland, 1996. Print.

———. "Philip Pullman." *The Greenwood Encyclopedia of Folktales and Fairy Tales*, Vol. 2. Westport, CT: Greenwood, 2007. 784–86. Print.

———. *Power, Voice and Subjectivity in Literature for Young Readers*. New York: Routledge, 2010. Print.

Nilsen, Alleen Pace, and Kenneth L. Donelson. *Literature for Today's Young Adults*. 6th ed. New York: Longman, 2001. Print.

Nobles, Susanne. "'Why Don't We Ever Read Anything Happy?' YA Literature and the Optimistic Ending." *The ALAN Review* 26.1 (1998): n. pag. Web. 27 Feb. 2012.

O'Collins, Gerald. *Philip Pullman's Jesus*. New York: Paulist Press, 2010. Print.

Ottaway, Amber. "The Impact of Parental Divorce on the Intimate Relationships of Adult Offspring: A Review of the Literature." *Graduate Journal of Counseling Psychology* 2.1 (2010): 34–49. Print.

Parsons, Wendy, and Catriona Nicholson. "Talking to Philip Pullman: An Interview." *The Lion and the Unicorn* 23.1 (1999): 116–34. Print.

Perrault, Charles. "The Master Cat; or, Puss in Boots." 1697. *The Great Fairy Tale Tradition: From Straparola and Basile to the Brothers Grimm*. Ed. Jack Zipes. New York: Norton, 2001. 397–401. Print.

Peter, Laura. "Revisiting the Colonial: Victorian Orphans and Postcolonial Perspectives." *Critical Perspectives on Philip Pullman's* His Dark Materials: *Essays on the Novels, The Film and the Stage Productions*. Ed. Steven Barfield and Katharine Cox. Jefferson, NC: McFarland, 2011. 93–110. Print.

Peters, John. *Spring-Heeled Jack*. Review. *School Library Journal* Dec. 1991: 117–18. Print.

"Philip Pullman on Freedom of Speech." Sheldonian Theatre. Canongate Books. 29 Mar. 2010. http://www.youtube.com/watch?v=HQ3VcbAfd4w,. Web. 15 May 2012.

Pingel, Carol Jean. *The Tin Princess*. Review. *Book Report* 13.2 (1994): 43. Print.

Propp, Vladimir. *Morphology of the Folktale*. 1968. Austin: University of Texas Press, 1977. Print.

Pullman, Philip. *Aladdin and the Enchanted Lamp*. London: Arthur A. Levine, 2005. Print.

———. *The Amber Spyglass*. New York: Knopf, 2000. Print.

———. *The Broken Bridge*. 1990. New York: Dell Laurel-Leaf, 2001. Print.

———. "Carnegie Medal Acceptance Speech." *Philip Pullman*: His Dark Materials. Random House. 1995–2011. Web. 15 May 2012.

———. *Count Karlstein, or the Ride of the Demon Huntsman*. London: Chatto and Windus, 1982. Print.

———. *Count Karlstein*. London: Doubleday, 1991. Print.

———. *Count Karlstein*. New York: Dell Yearling, 1998. Print.

———. "Dawkins, Fairy Tales, and Evidence." *Philip Pullman*. 2008. Web. 15 May 2012.

———. "The Elementary Particles of Narrative." *The Lion and the Unicorn* 32.2 (2008): 127–47. Print.

———. *The Firework-Maker's Daughter*. New York: Scholastic, 1995. Print.

———. *The Golden Compass*. New York: Knopf, 1995. Print.

———. *The Good Man Jesus and the Scoundrel Christ*. Edinburgh: Canongate, 2010. Print.

———. *How to Be Cool*. London: Pan, 1998. Print.

———. "I have a feeling this all belongs to me." *Discovering the Golden Compass: A Guide to Philip Pullman's* His Dark Materials. Ed. George Beahm. Charlottesville, VA: Hampton Roads, 2007. 9–33. Print.

———. *I Was a Rat!* New York: Dell Yearling, 1999. Print.

———. "Let's Write It in Red: The Patrick Hardy Lecture." *Signal: Approaches to Children's Books* 85 (1998): 44–62. Print.

———. Message to the author. 16 Nov. 2011–19 Feb. 2012. E-mail.

———. *Mossycoat*. London: Scholastic, 1998. Print.

———. *The New Cut Gang: The Gas-Fitters' Ball*. London: Puffin, 1998. Print.

———. *The New Cut Gang: Thunderbolt's Waxwork*. London: Puffin, 1996. Print.

———. *Puss in Boots: The Adventures of That Most Enterprising Feline*. New York: Knopf, 2000. Print.

———. "Rags to Riches in Fairytales." *The Observer* 11 Oct. 2009. Web. 9 May 2011.

———. "The Republic of Heaven." *Horn Book Magazine* Nov./Dec. 2001: 655–67. Print.

———. *The Ruby in the Smoke*. New York: Knopf, 1985. Print.

———. *The Scarecrow and His Servant*. New York: Knopf, 2004. Print.

———. *The Shadow in the North*. 1986. New York: Dell Laurel-Leaf, 1988. Print.

———. *The Shadow in the Plate*. Oxford: Oxford University Press, 1986. Print.

———. *Spring-Heeled Jack*. New York: Knopf, 2002. Print.

———. *The Tiger in the Well*. New York: Dell Laurel-Leaf, 1990. Print.

———. *The Tin Princess*. New York: Dell Laurel-Leaf, 1994. Print.

———. *The White Mercedes*. 1992. New York: Dell Laurel-Leaf, 2002. Print.

"Pullman's Fairy Tales." *BridgeToTheStars.net*. 25 Mar. 2011. Web. 1 July 2011.

"Q & A." *Philip Pullman*: His Dark Materials. Random House 1995–2011. Web. 6 Dec. 2011.

Rahn, Suzanne. "Carl Maria Freidrich Ernst von Weber." *The Oxford Companion to Fairy Tales*. Ed. Jack Zipes. Oxford: Oxford University Press, 2000. 546. Print.

Rosen, Michael. "Find me a leg." *The Guardian* 27 Nov. 2004. Web. 7 July 2011.

The Ruby in the Smoke. Masterpiece Mystery. Dir. Brian Percival. BBC 4 Feb. 2007. DVD.

Rustin, Margaret, and Michael Rustin. "A New Kind of Friendship—An Essay on Philip Pullman's *The Subtle Knife*." *Journal of Child Psychotherapy* 29.2 (2003): 227–41. Print.

Sands-O'Connor, Karen. "High Winds and Broken Bridges: The Gothic and the West Indies in Twentieth-Century British Children's Literature." *The Gothic in Children's Literature: Haunting the*

Borders. Ed. Anna Jackson, Karen Coats, and Roderick McGillis. New York: Routledge, 2008. 117–30. Print.

Schweitzer, Albert. *The Quest of the Historical Jesus: A Critical Study of its Progress from Reimarus to Wrede*. New York: Macmillan, 1957. Print.

"Secret of the Wild Child." *NOVA*. PBS. 4 Mar. 1997. Web. 2 Dec. 2003.

The Shadow in the North. Masterpiece Mystery. Dir. John Alexander. BBC 15 Sept. 2007. DVD.

Shattuck, Roger. *The Forbidden Experiment: The Story of the Wild Boy of Aveyron*. New York: Kodansha, 1980. Print.

Smith, Kevin Paul. *The Postmodern Fairytale: Folkloric Intertexts in Contemporary Fiction*. New York: Palgrave, 2007. Print.

Springhall, John. "'A Life Story for the People'? Edwin J. Brett and the London 'Low-Life' Penny Dreadfuls of the 1860s." *Victorian Studies* 33.2 (1990): 223–46. Print.

Squires, Claire. *Philip Pullman's* His Dark Materials *Trilogy: A Reader's Guide*. New York: Continuum, 2003. Print.

Straparola, Giovan Francesco. "Constantino Fortunato." *The Great Fairy Tale Tradtion: From Straparola and Basile to the Brothers Grimm*. Ed. Jack Zipes. New York: Norton, 2001. 390–93. Print.

Tatar, Maria. Introduction. *The Classic Fairy Tales*. New York: Norton, 1999. ix-xviii. Print.

____, ed. *The Classic Fairy Tales*. New York: Norton, 1999. Print.

Taylor, Laurie N. "Making Nightmares into New Fairytales: Goth Comics as Children's Literature." *The Gothic in Children's Literature: Haunting the Borders*. Ed. Anna Jackson, Karen Coats, and Roderick McGillis. New York: Routledge, 2008. 195–208. Print.

Thomas, Ebony Elizabeth. "'Everything She Knew': Race, Nation, Language, and Identity in Philip Pullman's *The Broken Bridge*." *Sankofa* 7 (2008): 50–57. Print.

Trites, Roberta Seelinger. *Waking Sleeping Beauty: Feminist Voices in Children's Novels*. Iowa City: University of Iowa Press, 1997. Print.

Tucker, Nicholas. "*The Good Man Jesus and the Scoundrel Christ*." *The Independent* 18 Apr. 2010. Web. 15 May 2012.

____. *Inside the World of Philip Pullman: Darkness Visible*. New York: Simon & Schuster, 2003. Print.

Turner, E.S. *Boys Will Be Boys: The Story of Sweeney Todd, Deadwood Dick, Sexton Blake, Dick Barton et al*. 1948. Suffolk: Penguin, 1976. Print.

Turner, Joseph W. "The Kinds of Historical Fiction: An Essay in Definition and Methodology." *Genre* 12 (1979): 333–55. Print.

Uther, Hans-Jörg. *The Types of International Folktales: A Classification and Bibliography*. Part 1: Animal Tales, Tales of Magic, Religious Tales, and Realistic Tales. Helsinki: Academia Scientiarium Fennica, 2004. Print.

Vachharajani, Anita. "Interview with Philip Pullman." 8 May 2010. Web. 15 May 2012.

Vickers, Salley. "*The Good Man Jesus and the Scoundrel Christ* by Philip Pullman: review." *The Telegraph* 2 Apr. 2010. Web. 15 May 2012.

Wallerstein, Judith, Julia Lewis, and Sandra Blakeslee. "Growing Up Is Harder." *Taking Sides: Clashing Views in Abnormal Psychology*, 4th ed. Ed. Richard P. Halgin. Dubuque: McGraw-Hill, 2007. 361–71. Print.

Watkins, Tony. *Dark Matter: Shedding Light on Philip Pullman's Trilogy* His Dark Materials. Downers Grove, IL: IVP, 2004. Print.

Weber, Carl Maria Friedrich Ernst von. *Der Freischütz*. Opera Guide. 2011. Web. 15 Aug. 2011.

Williams, Rowan. "*The Good Man Jesus and the Scoundrel Christ* by Philip Pullman." *The Guardian* 2 Apr. 2010. Web. 15 May 2012.

Zipes, Jack. *Breaking the Magic Spell: Radical Theories of Folk and Fairy Tales.* 1979. Lexington: University Press of Kentucky, 2002.

———. *Fairy Tale as Myth: Myth as Fairy Tale.* Lexington: University Press of Kentucky, 1994. Print.

———. *The Great Fairy Tale Tradition: From Straparola and Basile to the Brothers Grimm.* Ed. Jack Zipes. New York: Norton, 2001. Print.

Index

Adam and Eve 169
adolescent literature, characteristics 72–73
The Adventures of Jack Harkaway 98
Aggs, Patrice 50
Ahlberg, Allan, *The Jolly Postman* 75
Ahlberg, Janet, *The Jolly Postman* 75
Aladdin and the Enchanted Lamp 4, 9, 21–28, 48
"Aladdin and the Wonderful Lamp" 23–28
The Amber Spyglass 40, 51, 75, 93, 176–177, 183*ch.4n7*, 184*Part IIn1*
American dime novel 84
Andronik, Catherine M. 76, 135, 185*ch.6n2*
Anglo, Michael 89, 97
animal helper 15–21, 81–82, 92, 95
The Anxiety of Influence 51–52
Arbuthnot Lecture 5
ATU 510A "Mossycoat" 10–12, 14–15, 119, 181*ch.1n4*
ATU 510B "The Dress of Gold, of Silver, and of Stars" 11, 13
ATU 545 "The Cat as Helper" 15
ATU 545A "The Cat Castle" 15
ATU 545B "Puss in Boots" 15
Atwood, Margaret, *The Penelopiad* 166–167
Auden, W.H. 9
Austen, Jane 66, 72

Bailey, Peter 13
Baker, Dierdre F. 41
Barton, Laura 165, 167
Basile, Giambattista 9, 28; "Cagiluso" 15
Batman 76, 183*ch.4n4*
BBC 122
Beckett, Sandra 40, 96–97
Bernheimer, Kate 120
Bernstein, Leonard 39
betrayal 1–3, 5, 7, 93, 100, 110–114, 147–148, 153, 154, 160, 163–180
Bettelheim, Bruno 14–15
Bible 9, 75, 167
Bird, Elizabeth 136
Birmingham Stage Company 31, 182*ch.2n2*
Blake, Sexton 91

Blake, William 75; *Songs of Innocence and Experience* 1, 3, 4
Blakeslee, Sandra 152, 155
Bloom, Harold 51
Bobby, Susan R. 182*ch.2n4*, 183*ch.4n9*
Boswell, Taimi 1–13
Botting, Fred 64, 66
Bottum, Joseph 165
Boys of England 98
Bridge, Marie 1, 181*Intro.n1*; 181*Intro.n2*
The Broken Bridge 5, 143–150, 160–162
Brothers Grimm 9–10, 28
Brown, Helen 170
Brown, William 85
Bryan, Diana 50
Bulger, Jamie 121
Bullying 77
Burton, Sir Richard, *Favorite Tales from the Arabian Night's Entertainments* 22
Butler, Robert 5, 134–135, 143, 185*ch.7n1*
Byatt, A.S. 166
Byng, Jamie 166
Byron, Lord 64, 87

"Cagiluso" 15
Calvino, Italo 10
Campbell, Joseph 32–49, 166
Campbellian quest 30–49; *see also* hero's journey
Candide 39
Candland, Douglas Keith 124
Canepa, Nancy L. 15
Canongate Myths Series 165–167
"Carnegie Medal Acceptance Speech" 9, 181*ch.1n1*
Carter, James 51, 62, 75, 182*ch.2n1*, 186*ch.7n6*
Cervantes Saavedra, Miguel de, *The Ingenious Hidalgo Don Quixote de la Mancha* 4, 30, 39–49
character doubling 39–49, 58–60, 65–66
Charles, Nick 116
Charles, Nora 116
Charles, Ron 165–166, 167

Index

Chatto and Windus 50, 62–63, 182*ch.3n7*
Chesterton, G.K. 87
child abuse 143–145, 150
chivalry 41–48
Chödrön, Pema 180
Christianity 1–2, 163–180
Cinderella story 119–120, 131
class oppression 67, 80, 114
Clockwork, or All Wound Up 55, 182*ch.3n4*
Coats, Karen 100
Coleridge, Samuel Taylor 75
Collins, Wilkie 96
comic books 76, 88, 92
Conrad, JoAnn 165
conscience 85–86
"Constantino Fortunato" 15
contemporary novels for adolescents 143–162
Count Karlstein, or the Ride of the Demon Huntsman 4, 50–71, 75
Court, Ayesha 74
Cox, Katharine 129
crime 76, 84, 88–91
Crompton, Richmal 85
Cross, Julie 60–61, 69

dæmon 48, 83, 93, 122
Dawkins, Richard 88
"Dawkins, Fairy Tales, and Evidence" 88
Dell Yearling 50, 62, 185*ch.6n5*
Dentith, Simon 40–41
Diab, Hanna 22
Diab, Youhenna 22
Dickens, Charles 96; *Sketches by Boz* 75
Dickinson, Emily 75
Dickinson, Peter 73
Didymos Judas Thomas 165, 186*ch.8n5*
disobedience 1–2
displaced children 72–92; *see also* dispossessed children; orphaned children
dispossessed children 72–92; *see also* displaced children; orphaned children
divorce 143–144, 147–148, 151–155
Dolish, Patricia 62–63
Donelson, Kenneth L. 72–73, 160
Doubleday 50, 62
dramatis personae 171–176
dual protagonists 30–49
Dumas, Alexandre, *The Three Musketeers* 75
Dunae, Patrick A. 84
Duncan, Diane M. 73, 182*ch.4n2*

"The Elementary Particles of Narrative" 93
The Elephant of Siam, or the Fire-Fiend 31
Eve 1–2, 6, 164, 178
exploitation of adolescents 133–142
exploitation of children 78–81, 84, 92, 118–133

fairy tales 30–31, 88, 170; intertexts 10, 119; re-visions 9–29, 118–121; tropes 9, 37
The Fall 2–3, 9
Faustian plot 55, 182*ch.3n4*
Favorite Tales from the Arabian Night's Entertainments 22
feminist heroine 104–110
feral children 122–133
Fickling, David 170, 181*ch.1n4*, 181*ch.1n6*
The Firework-Maker's Daughter 4, 30–39, 48–49
folktales 6, 73, 82; re-visions 9–29
Der Freischütz 4, 51–56, 58–59, 71, 182 ch. 3 n3
Freud, Sigmund 14
Freudian symbol 34
Fried, Kerry 72, 73, 182*ch.4n1*

Galatea 151, 186*ch.7n6*
Galland, Antoine 22
Garfield, Leon 96
Gassett, Ortega y 45
gender oppression 67, 104–110
genetic fallacy 167–170
Genie (feral child) 127
German romanticism 50–61
Gil, Eliana 156–157
Gillard, Derek 139
Gilliam, Terry, *Tideland* 184–185*ch.5n3*
The Golden Compass 7, 36, 75, 122, 169, 181*Part In1*
The Good Man Jesus and the Scoundrel Christ 5, 163–180, 186*ch.8n1*
good versus evil 52–71
The Goose Girl 171, 173
Gospels 4, 165, 169
gothic 4, 50, 59–59, 71, 96–100, 104
gothic villains 100–104
graphic novel 50, 55–62, 74–75
Gray, William 51–52
Greek myths 22
Gruner, Elizabeth Rose 179

The Haunted Storm 135, 151, 186*ch.7n6*
Hauser, Kaspar 123–133
Hawkes, Kevin 185*ch.6n5*
Heinemann 133
hero's journey 30–49; *see also* Campbellian quest
Heydt, Bruce 76
Hilton, Paris 135
His Dark Materials ix, 1, 3, 5, 9, 22, 30, 31, 32, 33, 35, 36, 38, 48, 73, 75, 83, 93, 95, 96, 97, 118, 119, 123, 135, 140, 148, 164, 169, 170, 176–177
historical fiction 167–170
historical Jesus 165–170

194

Index

historical thriller 95–117
Hitchens, Christopher 165
Hitchens, Peter 165
Holmes, Sherlock 91
home 81–82
Homer 30; *The Iliad* 22; *The Odyssey* 22, 167
How to Be Cool (TV series) 4, 118–119, 133–142, 185*ch.6n11*
Hutcheon, Linda 3, 40

"I have a feeling this all belongs to me" 22, 50, 76, 77, 116, 182*ch.3n1*, 183*ch.4n5*
I Was a Rat! 4, 118–133, 104–141
identity 143–162
The Iliad 22
infidelity 143–144, 148–149, 153, 155
The Ingenious Hidalgo Don Quixote de la Mancha 4, 30, 39–49
institutional failures 128–133
intimacy 147–150, 152–154

Jack the Ripper 76
Jackson, Anna 100
Jacobs, Joseph 12
James, Henry 90
The Jolly Postman 75
Joosen, Vanessa 120–121
Julius Caesar 169
juvenile delinquency 133–140

Karl, the Duke of Baden 125
Keats, John 75
Kimball, Melanie A. 73–74, 78–79, 81–82
King, Shelley 121
Knopf 75, 183*ch.4n3*

Lang, Andrew 125; "Aladdin and the Wonderful Lamp" 23–28
"Let's Write It in Red: The Patrick Hardy Lecture" 6, 139, 179
Lewis, C.S. 27, 32, 51
Lewis, Julia 152, 155
Lloyd, Edward 97
Lyceum Theatre 98

MacDonald, George 51–52
Mack the Knife 79–83, 137, 183*ch.4n8*
"The Master Cat; or, Puss in Boots" 16–21
McGillis, Roderick 100
"The Merchants of Cool" 141–142
Meredeth, Hal 91
Miller, Lisa M. 182*ch.3n4*
Miller, Robert J. 186*ch.8n5*
Milton, John 75; *Paradise Lost* 1, 170
Moncrieff, William, *The Elephant of Siam, or the Fire-Fiend* 31

monomyth 30–49
Morpurgo, Michael 73
Mossycoat 4, 9–15, 17
Mountford, Charlotte 61, 182*ch.3n6*
The Mysteries of Udolpho 64

National Curriculum 139
Neary, Lynn 174, 176
NeMLA (Northeast Modern Language Association) 151, 186*ch.7n4*
The New Cut Gang: The Gas-Fitters' Ball 4, 72–74, 83–92, 136–137
The New Cut Gang: Thunderbolt's Waxwork 4, 72–74, 83–92, 136–137
New York City 76
Newton, Michael 125
Nicholson, Catriona 2, 140
Nikolajeva, Maria 17, 19, 41, 141
Nilsen, Alleen Pace 72–73, 160
Nobles, Susanne 159–161
NOVA 127
Nuremberg 124

O'Collins, Gerald 167–170, 173–174
The Odyssey 22, 167
"On the Marionette Theater" 1–2
orphaned children 72–92, 95, 121–133; *see also* displaced children; dispossessed children
Ottaway, Amber 147–149, 154
ownership 47–48

Paradise Lost 1, 170
parody 40–41, 60–61
Parsons, Wendy 2, 140
pedophilia 13–14, 157, 159
The Penelopiad 166–167
penny blood 74–92, 95–117; *see also* penny dreadful; schilling shocker; Victorian pulp fiction
penny dreadful 4, 74–92, 95–117; *see also* penny blood; schilling shocker; Victorian pulp fiction
Perrault, Charles 9–10, 15–16, 28; "The Master Cat; or, Puss in Boots" 16–21
Peter and the Wolf 75
Peters, Laura 121–122
Philip II of Spain 169
picaresque 39–49
Pingel, Carol Jean 116
Pinocchio 39
Poe, Edgar Allan 139
Polka Children's Theatre 17
polyphonic narration 19–21, 50, 55, 63, 71, 120
Prokofiev, Sergei, *Peter and the Wolf* 75
Propp, Vladimir 171–176

Index

PTSD (post-traumatic stress disorder) 156
Pullman, Philip: *Aladdin and the Enchanted Lamp* 4, 9, 21–28, 48; *The Amber Spyglass* 40, 51, 75, 93, 176–177, 183*ch.4n7*, 184*Part IInl*; Arbuthnot Lecture 5; *The Broken Bridge* 5, 143–150, 160–162; "Carnegie Medal Acceptance Speech" 9, 181 ch.1 n 1; *Clockwork, or All Wound Up* 55, 182*ch.3n4*; *Count Karlstein, or the Ride of the Demon Huntsman* 4, 50–71, 75; "Dawkins, Fairy Tales, and Evidence" 88; "The Elementary Particles of Narrative" 93; *The Firework-Maker's Daughter* 4, 30–39, 48–49; *Galatea* 151, 186*ch.7n6*; *The Golden Compass* 7, 36, 75, 122, 169, 181 *PartInl*; *The Good Man Jesus and the Scoundrel Christ* 5, 163–180, 186*ch.8n1*; *The Haunted Storm* 135, 151, 186*ch.7n6*; *His Dark Materials* ix, 1, 3, 5, 9, 22, 30, 31, 32, 33, 35, 36, 38, 48, 73, 75, 83, 93, 95, 96, 97, 118, 119, 123, 135, 140, 148, 164, 169, 170, 176–177; *How to Be Cool* 4, 118–119, 133–142; "I have a feeling this all belongs to me" 22, 50, 76, 77, 116, 182*ch.3n1*, 183*ch.4n5*; *I Was a Rat!* 4, 118–133, 104–141; "Let's Write It in Red: The Patrick Hardy Lecture" 6, 139, 179; *Mossycoat* 4, 9–15, 17; *The New Cut Gang: The Gas-Fitters' Ball* 4, 72–74, 83–92, 136–137; *The New Cut Gang: Thunderbolt's Waxwork* 4, 72–74, 83–92, 136–137; *Puss in Boots: The Adventures of That Most Enterprising Feline* 4, 9, 15–21, 60; "Rags to Riches in Fairytales" 12, 14–15; "Reminiscences at Ardudwy" 146, 161; "The Republic of Heaven" 118, 185*ch.6n1*; *The Ruby in the Smoke* 4, 95–117; *The Scarecrow and His Servant* 4, 30, 39–49; *The Shadow in the North* 4, 95–117; *The Shadow in the Plate* 4, 182*ch.3n2*; 184*ch.5n2*; *Sherlock Holmes and the Limehouse Horror* 184*ch.4n13*; *Spring-Heeled Jack* 4, 62, 72–82, 92, 137; *The Subtle Knife* 75; *The Tiger in the Well* 4, 95–117; *The Tin Princess* 4, 95–117; *The White Mercedes* (aka *The Butterfly Tattoo*) 5, 143–144, 151–162
Puss in Boots: The Adventures of That Most Enterprising Feline 4, 9, 15–21, 60

"Q & A" 119
Queen Elizabeth I 169

Radcliffe, Ann 63–65; *The Mysteries of Udolpho* 64
Ragan, Kathleen 6
"Rags to Riches in Fairytales" 12, 14–15
Rahn, Suzanne 52

realism 118–142
"Reminiscences at Ardudwy" 146, 161
"The Republic of Heaven" 118, 185*ch.6n1*
role-playing 88
Romeo and Juliet 153, 155, 162
Rosen, Michael 39
The Ruby in the Smoke 4, 95–117
Rushkoff, Douglas 141–142
Rustin, Margaret 148
Rustin, Michael 148
Rutten, Tim 165–166

St. John 176
Sands-O'Connor, Karen 150, 185–186*ch.7n3*
satire 118–142
The Scarecrow and His Servant 4, 30, 39–49
Scheherazade 6
schilling shocker 74–92, 95–117; *see also* penny blood; penny dreadful; Victorian pulp fiction
Scholastic Division of Children's Books 25
School Library Journal 136
Schweitzer, Albert 186*ch.8n4*
Scott, Sir Walter 87
self-referential narration 27, 48, 61–62, 71, 182*ch.3n5*
sexual abuse 155–159
The Shadow in the North 4, 95–117
The Shadow in the North Masterpiece Mystery 185*ch.5n4*
The Shadow in the Plate 4, 182*ch.3n2*; 184*ch.5n2*
Shattuck, Roger 124
Sheldonian Theatre, Oxford 164, 186*ch.8n2*
Shelley, Percy Bysshe 64
Sherlock Holmes and the Limehouse Horror 184*ch.4n13*
The Skeleton Crew 98
Sketches by Boz 75
slapstick 69–70
Smith, Kevin Paul 10, 119–120, 165, 181*ch.1n2*, 181*ch.1n3*
social criticism 69, 95–117
Songs of Innocence and Experience 1, 3, 4
Spencer, Diana, Princess of Wales 121
Spring-Heeled Jack 4, 62, 72–82, 92, 98, 137, 183*ch.4n4*
Springhall, John 84–85, 91, 110, 184*ch.4n12*
Squires, Claire 96
Stephanie de Beauharnais 125
Stevenson, Robert Louis 87
Stine, R.L. 63
Stirring Tales for British Lads 98
Stoker, Bram 98
Straparola, Giovan Francesco, "Constantino Fortunato" 15

Index

The Subtle Knife 75
Superman 76
Sweeney Todd 84, 98

tabloids 120–121, 132–133, 137
Tatar, Maria 9–10
Taylor, Laurie N. 66
Temptation 163–180
Thatcher, Margaret 134, 139
Thomas, Ebony Elizabeth 185*ch.7n3*
The Thousand and One Nights 22
The Three Musketeers 75
Tideland 184–185*ch.5n3*
The Tiger in the Well 4, 95–117
The Tin Princess 4, 95–117
Tolkien, J.R.R. 168
Trites, Roberta Seelinger 109
Tucker, Nicholas 19, 31, 35, 67–68, 70, 83, 85, 87, 111, 115–16, 120, 131, 133, 137, 175
Turner, E.S. 91, 97, 99
Turner, Joseph W. 168–169

urban legend 76–78, 92

Vachharajani, Anita 24, 155
Varney the Vampire 84
Vickers, Salley 166
Victor, the Wild Boy of Aveyron 124–25
Victorian East End (Victorian Lambeth) 78, 87, 90
Victorian era 74–92, 95–117, 121–122, 135, 183*ch.4n4*
Victorian pulp fiction 74–92, 95–117; *see also* penny blood; penny dreadful; schilling shocker
Virgin Mary 2
von Kleist, Heinrich, "On the Marionette Theater" 1–2

Wales 143, 161
Wallerstein, Judith 152, 155
Walpole, Horace 64
Watkins, Tony 31, 78, 117, 131
Watson, Dr. 91
Weber, Carl Maria Freidrich Ernst von, *Der Freischütz* 4, 51–56, 58–59, 71, 182*ch.3n3*
Weight 166–167
Westminster College, Oxford 78
Whitbread Book of the Year 40
The White Mercedes (aka The Butterfly Tattoo) 5, 143–144, 151–162
Whodunit? Detective Stories Chosen by Philip Pullman 184*ch.4n13*
Wildfire Ned 98
Williams, Anne 66
Williams, Rowan, the Archbishop of Canterbury 166
Williams, Sophy 26–27
Winterson, Jeanette, *Weight* 166–167
The Wizard of Oz 39, 47
Wordsworth, William 87

Zipes, Jack 6, 10, 123–124, 165

www.ingramcontent.com/pod-product-compliance
Ingram Content Group UK Ltd.
Pitfield, Milton Keynes, MK11 3LW, UK
UKHW041647200825
462065UK00009B/68